Mentor For Mission

A Handbook on Leadership Principles
Exemplified by Jesus Christ

Günter Krallmann

PO Box 1047
129 Mobilization Dr.
Waynesboro, GA 30830, U.S.A.
Tel: (706) 554-1594
E-mail: gabriel@omlit.om.org
www.gabriel-resources.com

Unless indicated otherwise, Scripture quotations are from the New International Version of the Bible:
"Scripture taken from the HOLY BIBLE, NEW INTERNATIONAL VERSION. Copyright © 1973, 1978, 1984 International Bible Society. Used by permission of Zondervan Bible Publishers."

Further translations occasionally referred to:

The Holy Bible. King James Version 1611, A Reference Edition, Based on the 1962 edition of the American Bible Society, © References and appendix - American Bible Society 1962, Second South African edition 1982, Seventh impression 1990, Published by the Bible Society of South Africa, Cape Town. (abbr. AV)

The Holy Bible. The New King James Version, Compact Reference Edition, Copyright © 1985 by Thomas Nelson, Inc., Nashville. (abbr. NKJV)

The New Testament. A New Translation by James Moffatt, New Edition, Revised, Hodder and Stoughton Ltd., London. (abbr. M)

Copyright © 2002 by Günter Krallmann

Second Edition

ISBN: 1-884543-12-X

All rights reserved. No part of this publication may be reproduced without permission in writing from the publisher, except in the case of brief quotations embodied in critical articles or reviews.

Cover design: Paul Lewis

Impreso en Colombia
Printed in Columbia

This book
is affectionately dedicated to

my son Michael

and
Ntate Mosoang, Joseph Mpakanyane
Edwin Fillies, Joseph Banda
Peter Ozodo, John Kisamwa
Kishor Rana, Mohan Tamang
Jayanta Maity, Santi Tabilla

Acknowledgements

For the completion of this manuscript I feel heartily obliged to the kind assistance of a number of institutions and personalities.

It is my desire to express my appreciation for the access I was granted to various resources at the Theology Library and the J.S. Gericke-Library of the University of Stellenbosch, at the Bible Institute of South Africa in Kalk Bay, the Jacob Gitlin Library Cape Town and the Salvation Army Cape Western Divisional Headquarters in Mowbray.

My special gratitude, however, I extend to:
- Tom Hallas and Alan Lim for their stimulating counsel at the initial stage of the project
- Mr David J. Rogers, BEd(UBC), MA(Wales), FTCL, DMS for his accommodating and proficient academic supervision of the research paper which formed the basis for this publication
- Rev John Broom from whose skilled editorial guidance I could benefit for polishing my second language
- Wayne Turner for the innumerable hours spent on my behalf in admirable typing of the text on computer
- my dear family who gave their prayerful support and many a time lovingly put up with a preoccupied husband and father
- my wife Ulrike for reserving time in her busy schedule to assist with the proof-reading
- those relatives, friends and colleagues of mine who undergirded the project with their intercession and encouragement
- God, above all, without whose gracious enabling withness the task would never have been finalized.

Foreword

This is a book about Jesus.

For any person who is fascinated with Jesus, who is interested in His life, who wants to know more about how He impacted people, this book is for you.

Besides the Bible, this is the most important book that I have read in twenty-five years. Günter Krallmann has captured the essence of what it means to be a follower of Jesus Christ; that is, he has focused not on just the message of Jesus, but on an equally important truth - <u>how Jesus imparted His life to others.</u>

Günter Krallmann emphasizes that we are given the task of discipling others as we follow Jesus. This is at the heart of the gospel. The good news is not just for us; it is people imparting life to other people, and through their association and friendship with them, showing them the way to be a disciple of Jesus Christ.

This book is a thorough, extremely well-documented, and inspirational study of the life of Jesus as a discipler of men and women. We gain insights into the cultural and religious environment in which Jesus was raised and how that influenced Him.

A careful look is given to His family upbringing and how that contributed to His skills and wisdom as the Master Discipler. We gain insight into the relationships that Jesus had with His disciples: whom He called and why; His selection standards; how He motivated them to follow Him and to change; and the skills that are essential for us to follow the example of the Lord Jesus in selecting, recruiting, and enabling men and women to become fruitful followers of Jesus Christ.

A book on this subject can make us feel that mentoring or discipling is only for the experts. After putting this book down, I didn't have that feeling at all. It is an inspirational manual for every Christian who wants to be involved in helping others grow and reach their potential in Christ. Not only is it informative and inspirational, it is practical as well because it fleshes out the principles of godly mentoring.

At times a book like this can be overwhelming in its detail, but that is not the case with "Mentoring for Mission". It gives you the big picture of what's on God's heart concerning leadership development principles and relationships, and then it illustrates those truths with Scriptural insight and example.

What better way could there be for us to inform ourselves and to build faith in our hearts for the discipling process which we are commissioned and commanded by our Lord Jesus to be involved in? (Matthew 28:19-20, 2 Timothy 2:2)

I am already using this book as a study guide with a small group of interns that I am working with, and I encourage every committed lay person, church leader, educator, evangelist, and missionary to use it as a guide in reproducing themselves in the lives of others. After all, that's what Christianity is about - one believer enabling another believer, through the power of the Holy Spirit, to reach others and in turn enable them to be all that God wants them to be.

May God bless you as you commit yourself to this task.

Floyd McClung Jr.

Table of Contents

Introduction   13

I THEOLOGICAL DELIBERATIONS: ASSOCIATION AS A FUNDAMENTAL PRINCIPLE IN JESUS CHRIST'S DISCIPLING OF THE TWELVE

1 Jesus Christ's Experience of With-ness before Discipling the Twelve

1.1	His Exposure to Spiritual Parenting	19
1.2	His Recipience of Vocational Apprenticing	23
1.3	His Cognizance of Rabbinic Tutoring	29
1.4	His Enduement with Divine Anointing	36

2 Jesus Christ's Utilization of With-ness in Discipling the Twelve

2.1	His Call to Observation	44
2.2	His Call to Consociation	50
2.3	His Call to Imitation	59
2.4	His Call to Continuation	66

3 Jesus Christ's Pursuit of Witness through the Twelve

3.1	His Desire for Authentic Witness	75
3.2	His Desire for Alternative Witness	80
3.3	His Desire for Worldwide Witness	85
3.4	His Desire for Empowered Witness	91

II MISSIOLOGICAL IMPLICATIONS: ASSOCIATION AS AN INDISPENSABLE PRINCIPLE FOR ALL DISCIPLING EFFORTS

4 Jesus Christ's With-ness Approach as Prototype

4.1	Jesus Christ as the Motivation	102
4.2	Jesus Christ as the Master	108
4.3	Jesus Christ as the Model	115
4.4	Jesus Christ as the Mentor	122
4.5	Jesus Christ as the Method	131
4.6	Jesus Christ as the Measure	138

5 Jesus Christ's With-ness Approach as Consummate Witness Strategy

5.1	The Dimension of Affiliation	148
5.2	The Dimension of Exemplification	157
5.3	The Dimension of Contextualization	166
5.4	The Dimension of Integration	178
5.5	The Dimension of Multiplication	188
5.6	The Dimension of Impartation	198

Appendix: Essentials of Jesus Christ's Discipling Model. A Survey   211

Endnotes   215

Bibliography   231

Index of Persons   247

Select Subject Index   252

"Let us also remember that, while in undertaking the momentous task committed to us, we should by the study of the Scriptures, prayer for divine guidance, and comparison of our varied views and experiences, seek to know what is the best method of work, still the best method without the presence of our Master and the Spirit of all truth will be unavailing."

John L. Nevius [+]

Some Remarks on the Design of the Text

Like the author's two earlier works "Following Jesus" and Leading with Jesus", the material at hand has been prepared in the form of a handbook. It addresses everyone who shares a deeper interest in the process by which the Lord Jesus Christ developed leaders. Expressly it seeks to assist those actively involved in spiritual leadership training, particularly within missionary contexts.

The text lends itself to individual and group study, and special care was taken to facilitate its utilization as a teaching tool. Consequently
- numerous Bible references have been included in the running text
- a broad spectrum of direct quotes can be resorted to as an additional substantiation resource
- essential elements of content have been highlighted through bold print
- central truths have been reiterated
- the appendix presents a survey of chief characteristics of Jesus Christ's discipling model in outline form
- separate indexes for persons and subjects have been added to help the reader localize specific information speedily.

To simplify the identification of missionaries, past and present, among the persons referred to, their first names have been spelled out and for the most part some brief background information has been added.

More widely interested readers are encouraged to avail themselves of the supplementary data contained in the endnotes and to turn to the bibliography consisting of the sources quoted and further titles recommended for the pursuit of more extensive personal research.

Introduction

Extensive personal experience in mission work has made me acutely aware of the immense need for the development of Christian leaders. A shortage of competent leadership can not only be discerned in secular society but has also surfaced in the Body of Christ at large and the mission enterprise in particular. As the centre of gravity in church growth and missionary advance has increasingly shifted to the Two-Thirds World, C.P. Wagner's pronouncement, "Many mission specialists believe that leadership selection and training is the single most crucial issue in the spread of the gospel throughout the world today,"[1] bears out the urgent necessity for raising up spiritual leaders, especially such of non-western backgrounds.

In my handbooks "Following Jesus" and "Leading with Jesus" I conveyed a number of basic insights as regards attributes of a disciple of Jesus Christ and qualifications for the exercise of leadership on his behalf. Complementary to those earlier manuals, the treatise on hand provides a detailed analysis of the procedure of building leaders as exemplified by Jesus Christ. It was devised from a missionary perspective for missionary practice. It was written out of the keen desire to render a deeper grasp of fundamental aspects of his training methodology fruitful for missionary endeavour, most of all when undertaken in cross-cultural settings.

The Gospel records furnish ample evidence that in his discipling of the Twelve the Master attached eminent importance to association, i.e. companionship, the cultivation of close relational ties. On the basis of such with-ness he generated a dynamic process of life-transference which was meant to foster wholistic maturity in his friends and to facilitate them towards effective leadership at the same time. While being trained to follow, they were actually groomed to lead. In fact Jesus Christ never saw reason to draw a clear distinction between discipling and leadership development. His perception and practice of discipling were so comprehensive that they encompassed essential connotations of current designations like 'mentoring', 'leadership training' and 'coaching'. Therefore the ensuing portrayal of his association with the Twelve will use these terms interchangeably.

Those engaged in rearing Christian leaders ought to be aware that their concept of leadership determines their mode of operation. Whether, for instance, a leader is preoccupied with personal goals rather than with his followers' progress or leans more toward privileged rulership than sacrificial servanthood, will undoubtedly show in how he carries out his responsibilities. From a Biblical point of view, however, the only legitimate focal point for all spiritual leadership aspirations is Christlikeness.

As we are going to see, the Lord Jesus challenged his disciples repeatedly with this absolute standard, and the Scriptures attest that leaders like Simon Peter, John and the apostle Paul made it the yardstick for their lives and ministries. We cannot do better today. The pursuit of Christlikeness is still the most intelligent, most responsible and most effective use of one's leadership capacity. P.T. Chandapilla advised so well when he wrote that "the method of training and producing Christian leaders is first to understand the method of Christ and then to put it into faithful and productive practice."[2]

Jesus' training of the Twelve established once and for all the consummate and normative paradigm for Christian leadership development. Evidently though, no one can follow Christ's blueprint without first paying the price of studying it assiduously. Neglect in this regard will make us vulnerable to either acting according to our own inclinations or to embracing secular leadership patterns. Both approaches, while they may be sanctioned by human approval, are nevertheless in dissonance with the purposes of God as revealed in Jesus Christ and will hence fall short of full divine confirmation and blessing. In the final analysis, every shortcoming in Christian leadership can be traced back to failure in following Christ's example.

The Master, furthermore, mentored for mission. He, whom the Father had sent as a missionary into the world, instilled in his associates a global vision, entrusted them with the commission to be his representatives to all the world and promised the Holy Spirit's enabling for the accomplishment of this task. Just as in king David's person leadership and witness were intertwined (cf. Isa 55:3.4), the Lord Jesus, in the atmosphere of his with-ness, prepared his disciples to exercise their future leadership roles as his witnesses. No less are Christian leaders in our day expected to fulfill their respective functions in a way that bears accurate testimony to the one who enlisted them for his cause. It stands to reason that leadership status creates most favourable opportunities to serve as an influential witness for Jesus Christ, yet also entails all the greater responsibility to do so.

Although Jesus identified thoroughly with the cultural context he lived in, his mentoring mode nevertheless displayed essentially supracultural traits, that is to say, it revealed principles which as absolute and timeless constants transcend cultural differences. PART I of the book outlines major influences that shaped Jesus' training strategy, describes the significance of his with-ness approach for the grooming of the disciples and unfolds his intention that they would become instrumental in leading a worldwide witnessing movement energized by the Holy Spirit.

PART II concentrates on vital implications which Jesus Christ's prototype enjoins for mission work today. Special attention is reserved for delineating a number of supracultural non-negotiables for leadership training, whose faithful and Spirit-activated application will unleash the intrinsic power of mentoring according to the Master's pattern. It is my hope that the insights provided in this respect will in some way aid to remedy the helplessness noticeable in various mission circles in connection with leadership development across cultural borderlines.

*

To research the topic in question has proved a truly enriching experience. I feel privileged to have received deeper revelation concerning the matchless strategy Jesus chose for discipling the Twelve. As I sought to retrace the way he walked with his friends, I have been challenged and inspired, re-oriented and convicted, have also been led to a new measure of gratitude for the sublime leadership model he supplied.

If a kindred response is evoked in the readers of the following pages, I will regard my labours as richly rewarded.

Günter Krallmann

I

THEOLOGICAL DELIBERATIONS:

ASSOCIATION AS A FUNDAMENTAL PRINCIPLE IN JESUS CHRIST'S DISCIPLING OF THE TWELVE

"I am more than ever convinced that if we were to take the directions of our Master and the assurances He gave to His first disciples more fully as our guide, we should find them to be just as suited to our times as to those in which they were originally given."

J. Hudson Taylor *

1 Jesus Christ's Experience of With-ness before Discipling the Twelve

On studying the Gospel records, we discover that the four evangelists veiled Jesus' childhood and education largely in silence. This however should not really take us by surprise.

Evidently, it was not the authors' leading interest to present a detailed biography of Jesus the man; rather, they primarily desired to outline the relevant circumstances and significance of the life, death and resurrection of Jesus the Christ. Furthermore, their reticence seems to suggest that Jesus' educational development occurred within the perimeter of the ordinary Jewish upbringing of the day.

Jesus' experience of various kinds of association from his early childhood days up to the beginning of his public activities was of profound formative relevance for both his life-style and future ministry. Therefore the necessity arises to start our quest for understanding the nature and implications of the essential with-ness principle by inquiring into some major aspects of Jesus' Jewish upbringing. In fact, as G. Vermes succinctly pointed out, "if we are to understand him, it is into the Galilean world that we must look".[1]

1.1 His Exposure to Spiritual Parenting

When Jesus was born around the year 6 BCE,[2] he was born into a devout Jewish home.

In fulfillment of the Law[3] (cf. Gen 17:9-14, Lev 12:1-3), Joseph and Mary had Jesus circumcised eight days after his birth (Lk 2:21). At the same time - rather than following the tendency of some of their Galilean countrymen to choose a Greek name - they gave Jesus the then common Hebrew name of *Yeshua*,[4] in obedience to the divine direction received earlier (Lk 1:31, Matt 1:21). Not only do we find Mary complying with the requirements laid down for her purification (Lk 2:22-24, cf. Lev 12:6-8), but we also see her and her husband travel to Jerusalem to dedicate their first-born in the Temple, a journey that was not obligatory according to the Law, nevertheless undertaken by pious Jews. Luke sheds further light on the devotedness of Jesus' parents through the information that they made it their habit to go on an annual pilgrimage to the capital (2:41).

Growing up in close association with such a godly father[5] and mother, we may wonder in which areas of Jesus' life formative parental influence became particularly apparent.

A first and most natural learning sphere was the realm of language acquisition. As Jesus spent much time with his parents and started to imitate words that he heard them utter, he gradually developed a command of **Aramaic**, to be more exact, of the Galilean dialect of West Aramaic. That Jesus made use of Aramaic as his first tongue can be concluded from a number of Aramaisms recorded by Mark.[6] In addition, Luke 4:16-19 presupposes that Jesus also knew **Hebrew**, which was the sacred language of the scrolls read in the services in the Jerusalem Temple as well as in the synagogues all over Palestine. Under the tutelage of such devout Jewish parents, it is most probable that at quite an early stage in his life already Jesus was not only introduced to the Aramaic colloquial, but to the sacred language of his forefathers as well.

It appears that spiritual education in a Jewish home began as soon as a child was able to speak (cf. Ps 8:2, Isa 28:9). During his earliest years, parental influence into Jesus' life came largely from Mary's side. Like every Jewish mother, one of the first things she taught her son was the simple **prayer**, "Into your hands I commit my spirit . . . ." (Ps 31:5), spoken nightly before going to sleep.

When Jesus turned four or five years old his father became the leading figure in the spiritual instruction process. Joseph was expected to fulfill the high responsibility of teaching Jesus the *Torah* both by precept and personal example. Through questions and answers, but even more by a strong emphasis on memorization (cf. Prov 7:1-3), a Jewish father sought to implant the **Word of God** into his son so that the latter would be led to know and remember but also to obey it. The foremost Scripture portion any Jewish boy would be taught was the *Shema*,[7] consisting of the passages Deut 6:4-9, 11:13-21 and Num 15:37-41, which was recited at the commencement of the daily morning and evening prayer times[8] as well as of every synagogue service. Time and again Jesus would be graphically reminded of the pre-eminence of God's Word as he observed his father pass through the door of their home, touch the *Shema* parchment fixed on the frame with his fingers and then raise them reverently to his lips.

Through his parents Jesus was also introduced to a number of religious customs. **Sabbath observance** had been a paramount ordinance ever since the beginning of God's dealings with his people (cf. Gen 2:2.3, Ex 20:8-11, 31:14-17). From his boyhood days Jesus would hear three trumpet blasts shortly before sundown on the sixth day of each week. Produced on a ram's horn at the local synagogue, they rang over the roof-tops of his hometown to announce the approaching Sabbath. The day of rest, climaxing with a **synagogue service** the next morning, lasted till Saturday sunset. Already at an early age, children accompanied their parents to this gathering.[9]

Interspersed throughout the year there were various festivities. These provided occasions to remember God's miraculous and gracious actions of the past and to offer him thanksgiving, but also to experience times of joyful fellowship. Among those **yearly festivals** the greatest was the Passover, celebrated at the Temple in Jerusalem. After preparations on the preceding afternoon it commenced at sunset of the fifteenth day of Nisan in springtime and lasted for a week. The distance of a several days' journey separating Nazareth and Jerusalem rendered it inexpedient for Joseph and his family to regularly take part in the festivals at the capital. The prominent Passover festivities at the Temple, however, Joseph and Mary attended every year, and it was on one of these occasions that they were joined by their son who had now reached the age of twelve (Lk 2:41.42).

In connection with the circumstances of this episode, Luke brings to our special attention that Jesus was obedient to his parents (2:51). Of course, by this stage of his life Jesus would have received a lot of teaching from the *Torah* on the necessity and blessings of **obedience** to parental authority (cf. Ex 20:12, Lev 19:3, Deut 5:16). But particularly, this instruction had been enforced over the years through the visible example of his father. Scriptural evidence suggests to us that Joseph provided an outstanding model in this respect, as his relationship to God was characterized by utmost obedience (cf. Matt 1:20.21.24.25, 2:13.14, 2:19-21, 2:22.23).

Finally, Jesus' experiences at home imprinted indelibly upon his life an understanding of and an appreciation for close **relationships**. Every recital of the *Shema* would remind him of the supreme importance of intimate fellowship with God. At the same time, his parents' godly family government allowed him to experience daily the foundational significance of attitudes like love, acceptance, humility, forgiveness and patience for the establishment of meaningful human relationships. In addition, the very living conditions of the time, i.e. for a family commonly to dwell in a small house under one roof, were also conducive to Jesus' development of close association and resulting intimate relational ties with his parents as well as with his four brothers and at least two sisters (cf. Matt 13:55.56).

Jesus' adult life offered striking evidence of how profoundly he was impacted by the godly direction received at home. On the basis of close with-ness, Joseph and Mary practised spiritual parenting that contributed decisively to the formation of their son's thinking, character, and life-style.[10]

Once Jesus has entered upon the stage of public ministry, we recognize him as a man of prayer (cf. Lk 3:21, 5:16, 6:12, 9:16.18.29, 11:1, 22:41-43, 23:46, 24:30.50) as well as a man of the Word who enriches and enforces his preaching and teaching through frequent references to the Scriptures.[11] On the Sabbath, we find him attend the synagogue service, because it is his custom (Lk 4:16); furthermore, we see him take part in annual festivities (cf. Jn 2:23, Matt 26:18, Jn 7:2.3.10). Obedience, first learned in regard to his earthly parents, now finds its fullest expression in joyful and absolute obedience to his heavenly Father (cf. Jn 4:34, 5:30, 6:38). The high value which he attributes to interpersonal relationships does not only surface in his love for his mother (cf. Jn 19:25-27) and his appreciation for children (cf. Matt 19:14.15, Mk 9:36), but especially in his companionship with the disciples (cf. Lk 22:15, Jn 13:33, 21:5).

In all, the spiritual parenting Jesus experienced during his formative years by means of association produced rich fruit in his later life. It helped mould him into a man of great love for God, his Word and communion with him; moreover, it contributed towards shaping him into a man of great love for people, fellowship and meaningful relationships.

1.2 His Recipience of Vocational Apprenticing

Of Palestine's major provinces, Galilee was the most northern. Lower Galilee, providing most of the sites playing a significant part in the Gospel events, was favoured with a pleasant climate, good watering conditions and very fertile soil. Fields and pastures interchanged with orchards and vineyards. The land was adorned by a diversity of trees, yielded a variety of crops as well as vegetables, and offered a multiplicity of fruits, among them grapes, figs, dates, nuts, almonds, olives and citrons.

That **Galilee** was the richest part of the country, was also due to the fact that it possessed a bustling fishing industry. In fact, the hub of activity in the province was the area around the Sea of Tiberias. Home of countless fishing boats, the lake teemed with all sorts of fish, and thus secured the livelihood of thousands of fishermen, many of whom were resident in the villages thickly dotting the western shore in particular.

Although, generally speaking, Galilee was predominantly an agricultural region, it nevertheless harboured a considerable number of handicrafts. You could find basket weavers, mat makers, potters and blacksmiths together with tanners, leather workers and dyers.

The northern province was densely populated; according to the Jewish historian Josephus there were "two hundred and forty cities and villages in Galilee".[12] In the countryside, the inhabitants were mostly Jewish, the towns, however, were largely Gentile. Besides, the fact that "Galilee, although an essentially Jewish territory, was in close contact with Greek cities on all sides",[13] helps explain why many Galileans were bilingual, conversing in their mother tongue of Aramaic and in Greek.

Tucked away in a valley in the foothills of Lower Galilee lay the city of **Nazareth**. Situated 1,300 feet above sea level and twenty miles from the Sea of Tiberias, Nazareth was surrounded by wheat-fields, olive groves and vineyards. In the vicinity two important roads of commerce traversed the province, the one linking Damascus with Egypt, the other leading from Phoenicia to the Euphrates.

From the summit overlooking the town a spectacular

panorama would meet the eye: to the east, wooded Mount Tabor; looking southward, the fertile plain of Esdraelon with the mountains of Ephraim in the background; towards the west, the Carmel ridge on the Mediterranean; and in a northward direction, Mount Hermon, sometimes capped with snow.

Such was the environment in which Jesus grew up. During these years, spiritual parenting at home was not the only influence that conduced to a thorough religious education and ensuing character formation. Rather, the instruction was further complemented in the local synagogue.

Of devout family background, Jesus frequented the synagogue of his hometown, in order to take part in the services (cf. Lk 4:16). But, according to the custom of the day, the synagogue as the local community centre also housed the elementary school, and it was an incidental duty of the "attendant" (Lk 4:20) to run it. Therefore it is most probable that, from his sixth or seventh year, Jesus underwent **formal education** at the Nazareth synagogue.

As within Jewish culture the educational interest was exclusively spiritual, the only text-book used was the *Torah*. Oral instruction was given primary importance, and great emphasis was placed upon the dominant method of internalizing truth in antiquity - memorization, facilitated through various mnemotechnic devices.[14]

Presumably at the age of fifteen, Jesus became a full-time apprentice in Joseph's workshop. Apart from teaching his son the Law, it was a Jewish father's second duty to teach his son a trade. Whereas in the question of Jesus' school education our assessment of his development cannot reach beyond conjecture, in the case of his **vocational education** we are able to draw upon clear Scriptural evidence; Matt 13:55 names Jesus as "the carpenter's son", and Mk 6:3 calls him "the carpenter".

The fact that both evangelists make use of the Greek

term *tekton* is revealing. This word, commonly translated **'carpenter'**, actually has a wider connotation. It could also be rendered 'artificer in wood, wood worker', and therefore imply, for instance, the activities of a joiner. W. Barclay pointed out that *tekton* designates "a craftsman who could build a wall or a house, construct a boat, or make a table or a chair, or throw a bridge across a little stream";[15] and J.I. Packer went so far as to say "*tekton* could equally mean "mason" or "smith". . .; or it could mean that Joseph and Jesus were builders, so that both carpentry and masonry would have been among their skills".[16]

Thus we can imagine that Joseph and his son not only repaired and made farm tools, e.g. goads, threshing-flails, winnowing-forks, harrows, ploughs and yokes, but also pieces of furniture like stools, chairs, tables, beds and storage chests. Moreover, in the realm of house construction, they may have provided wooden locks and keys, frames for doors and windows, posts and roof beams. Among the tools they would have used were axe and adze, chisel, plane and file, bow drill, mallet and stone-headed hammer.

For almost half his life, it seems, Jesus worked with his hands as a carpenter. In the Jewish community different trades were regarded as honourable professions, among them also carpentry. Many rabbis had that very vocational background, and carpenters were considered as especially learned. This could not merely be attributed to the fact that their business connections often made a certain command of Greek indispensable. But, even more significant, many carpenters were respected for their sound Scriptural knowledge.

Usually a trade in Palestine was a family enterprise. As there was no institution for vocational training, the son would learn the trade through being taught by either his father or another male relative on the basis of **apprenticeship**.

Undoubtedly Joseph trained Jesus in this way too. Time

and again during the countless hours they spent together in the workshop, Joseph would explain and demonstrate, while Jesus listened, observed and imitated. Through close and extensive with-ness in the shared working environment Jesus gradually advanced in knowledge, skill and experience, until he became a proficient carpenter himself.

In C.H. Dodd's estimation,[17] Jesus' words in Jn 5:19.20 imply a recollection of the former workshop situation at home. The passage reads:

> ... the Son can do nothing by himself; he can only do what he sees his Father doing, because whatever the Father does the Son also does. For the Father loves the Son and shows him all he does ....

This Scripture portion indeed summarizes the main elements of the apprenticing process Jesus must have undergone in the workshop; on the one hand Joseph desiring to train his son out of a commitment of love, demonstrating by his personal example everything pertinent, on the other hand Jesus depending on his father for learning, imitating whatever the latter shows, in the end performing also what the father did before.

During the silent years which Jesus devoted to carpentry, the workshop proved to be an excellent place of preparation, where he could learn lessons of great value for his public ministry in years to come.

By doing manual labour he was able to closely identify with the life-style of the working majority. To be able to help his fellow-men later he first had to understand them. While he earned his own living through hard work and came into contact with customers from diverse walks of life - some undoubtedly easier to deal with than others -, he gained deeper insight into the daily routine, views, feelings, aspirations, concerns and joys of the common people as well as into the complexity, strengths and weaknesses of **human**

nature (cf. Jn 2:24.25). And there was another aspect of interhuman relationships which Jesus could learn in his daily close association with his father, namely, what it takes to develop and maintain a good **working relationship** with another person.

Numerous conversations with Joseph about spiritual issues and many occasions for meditation over routine projects enabled Jesus to acquire an ever increasing understanding of **Scriptural truths** and his own future mission.

From various **observations** linked to practical carpentry work Jesus derived insights which surfaced again in his preaching and teaching in the form of graphic illustrations.[18]

The ongoing necessity to produce quality work required and enhanced the **development of character traits** such as dedication, faithfulness, patience and commitment to excellence (cf. Mk 7:37).

Working as a carpenter lends itself in unusual degree to the furtherance of **strategic thinking**. Time and again in connection with various assignments Jesus would find opportunity to first determine the desired end product, then select the best suited raw material, next apply the proper tools and finally pursue the most effective procedures to bring about the result originally envisioned. As will become apparent, Jesus' approach for choosing and discipling the Twelve moved essentially within an identical strategy perimeter.

Furthermore, Jesus was able to gain certain **managerial expertise**. The need to set goals, prioritize, schedule, budget and evaluate would have become even greater when, in all probability, at a later stage he had to take over the workshop.[19] This, we can imagine, not only added the responsibility of becoming the breadwinner for the large family, but also opened up a remarkable new opportunity, namely to apprentice his younger brothers. It gave Jesus the chance to utilize the association principle in a working context, to reproduce his knowledge, skill and experience on a trade level, - a kind of preliminary training exercise for what he would undertake later on a spiritual level when focusing his attention on the discipling of the Twelve.

1.3 His Cognizance of Rabbinic Tutoring

During the time of Jesus, various parties and movements exerted a powerful sway over Jewish society.

A first dominant group were the **Sadducees**. For the most part of priestly background, representatives of this aristocratic party held the majority in the seventy-one member *Sanhedrin*, which was the most authoritative council in the nation, wielding both supreme court and legislative powers. Besides, the Sadducees always furnished the high priest out of their ranks. They had made their peace with the overshadowing presence of the Romans as well as with the rule of the Herodian dynasty, and their outlook was essentially secular and materialistic. In fact, their leading interest seems to have been political rather than religious.

This immediately rendered them diametrically different to the **Pharisees**, who were religious separatists and nationalists at the same time. Numbering not less than 6,000 in Jesus' day, they were organized as a fraternity and pursued strict adherence to the Law as they perceived it, viz. in the form of 613 ordinances, 365 prohibitions and 248 commandments. The Pharisaic party, whose followers could be found in towns as well as in the countryside, included a number of priests, but primarily laymen like merchants, farmers and especially craftsmen. The strong religious influence of this pious movement, however, was mainly due to those of its members who were scribes (cf. Lk 5:30).

Unlike the Sadducees and Pharisees, the **scribes** could be considered neither a political nor a religious party, instead, they more strongly resembled a guild. To facilitate the pursuit of their calling, scribes cared for their own livelihood, be it through running a business or through manual labour. Apart from that they studied, copied, interpreted and taught the Law, the latter encompassing also the expounding of Scripture in synagogue services. It was their special desire to see the many facets of the *Torah* understood and applied within the context of everyday existence. Their study and teaching concentrated on the Word of God but also on "the tradition of the elders" (Matt 15:2). Because of their intimate familiarity with the Law, scribes functioned as jurists, too. In the light of their varied activities they were regarded as "doctors of the law" (Lk 5:17, AV), "lawyers" (Lk 7:30, AV), "teachers of the law" (Mk 2:6) and sages. Their fellow-men addressed them with "Rabbi" (cf. Matt 23:7), a special title of honour.[20] Most of the scribes joined the Pharisaic movement, a step which doubtlessly served to bring their intentions and convictions to bear upon larger segments of their contemporary society.

The picture would be incomplete though, if mention were not made of two other currents that put their stamp on first century Judaism. The first were the **Zealots**, fervent patriots violently opposed to the Romans. Their movement which had been founded by Judas the Galilean had its home base in the province of Galilee, in fact, the members of this rigorously nationalistic group were even named 'Galileans'.[21] As to their doctrinal persuasion, the Zealots identified with the Pharisaic position.

The second was the ascetic movement of the **Essenes**, in the time of Jesus at least 4,000 strong, a considerable number of whom were a part of the desert community of Qumran near the Dead Sea. Although the Essenes, who liked to call themselves 'sons of light', are not mentioned in the New Testament, their influence appears noticeable, particularly in the life-style and ministry of John the Baptist. The adherents of this monastic group were committed to high ethical standards, welcomed strong discipline, a lot of them embraced celibacy, they emphasized prayer, ritual washings and communal living. On the whole, in their quest of a life of purity, they were even stricter than the Pharisees.

During his years of silent preparation, while the strategy for his God-given mission gradually evolved into sharper and sharper contours, Jesus must undoubtedly have taken note of the distinct aspirations and activities of the parties and movements just sketched. One of these groups, however, offered him a particularly rich reservoir of strategic insight, namely the scribes, in their **concept and practice of rabbinic tutoring.**

When a Jewish boy in Jesus' day had finished elementary school at about fifteen years of age and desired to proceed to secondary education he could go to a scribal college. In Jerusalem hundreds of students attended the many rabbinic academies[22] which operated either in the house of the presiding rabbi or on the Temple premises. Some of the most outstanding rabbis whose activities overlapped with the time span of Jesus' life were Hillel, Shammai, Johanan b. Zakkai and Gamaliel the Elder, who counted Saul of Tarsus amongst his students (cf. Acts 22:3). Hillel, "this greatest of Pharisees",[23] and Shammai were the heads of the two most influential academies, the former representing a more liberal, the latter a more conservative outlook on the Law.

In those days apprenticing was a well-established mode of training in the vocational realm, as we have previously seen, but in the intellectual too. Actually, the **teacher-disciple relation** had already been observable in Greek society where Socrates, Plato and Aristotle each had their students and was a familiar phenomenon within Judaism as well. The rabbinic *talmîd*, i.e. 'pupil, scholar, disciple' (cf. 1 Chr 25:8), was seen as "the one who gives himself (as a learner) to Scripture and to the religious tradition of Judaism".[24]

At the academy the rabbi was seated on a low platform,

his students in a semicircle around him on the ground. The teacher was desirous to pass on his heritage in the form of lessons from Scripture and tradition,[25] the pupils were frequently engaged in debating theological issues, especially those relating to the proper interpretation and application of the *Torah*. Although note-taking was practised,[26] **the instruction method was essentially oral**, with a strong emphasis on memorization. The transmission process was governed by two basic guidelines, **authenticity** and brevity.

The ideal of rabbinic learning was not that a *talmîd* would be required to present his master's thoughts in newly developed phraseology or to summarize them. Instead proficiency was seen in the pupil's ability to reproduce from memory the rabbi's original words as accurately as possible. The precept "a man must use the manner of speaking of his teacher " (M Eduyoth 1,3) was followed conscientiously. So we read Rabbi Joshua's assertion, "I have received as a tradition from Rabban Johanan b. Zakkai, who heard from his teacher, and his teacher from his teacher . . . ." (M Eduyoth 8,7). Nor is it a surprise that rabbinic students, along with the asking of questions and discussing, were occupied with numerous mnemonic drills. While, as B. Gerhardsson remarked, "the teacher, by constant repetition, "recorded" . . . on the memories of his pupils",[27] the student in turn had to internalize the rabbi's very words through consistent repetition on his part. The goal of the *talmîd* was to become similarly accomplished as Rabbi Eliezer b. Hyrcanus, one of Rabbi Johanan b. Zakkai's disciples, who was praised as "a plastered cistern which loses not a drop" (M Aboth 2,8).

Furthermore, the rabbinic pedagogical maxim, "A man should always teach his pupil (orally) in the shortest way",[28] indicates the masters' preference for **brevity**. Their use of catch-words, condensed and pregnant phrases, images and parables for instance, helped make their utterances "like goads" and "like firmly embedded nails" (Eccl 12:11), thus greatly enhancing the intended memorization effect.

So far, our investigation into the character of rabbinic tutoring was firstly directed towards features relating to **with-ness for information**, i.e. association for the purpose of knowledge acquisition. Now attention must be given to a second dimension, **with-ness for formation**, i.e. association for the purpose of character development. Corresponding to the Scriptural observation, "He who walks with the wise grows wise . . . ." (Prov 13:20), a keen Jewish student would seek, beyond formal instruction offered at the academy, to avail himself of the formative influence stemming from intimate association with a rabbi of his choice for a certain period of time.

For a *talmîd*, his rabbi was not merely an intellectual and theological authority, he served as a living example, too. He influenced his student through what he said and what he did, impacted his life through teaching and conduct; in fact, as M. Friedeman articulated, "The words of the rabbi were precious, his example, more precious still".[29] Whereas on the level of association for information the rabbi taught primarily for the aim of memorization and his pupils were expected to listen and remember, on the level of association for formation the rabbi exemplified for the aim of imitation and his students were in addition expected to observe and emulate.

To facilitate this process of **imitation** a disciple entered into a life-sharing companionship with his rabbi. He would accompany him to the synagogue service or to the law-court, when the latter was involved in meritorious activities or complemented theoretical instruction with further life-related lessons in the field or market-place. In short, the student was constantly with his teacher. Furthermore, the disciple was envisioned to assume the role of a servant to his master, performing menial tasks like e.g. carrying loads, buying food, preparing meals or taking care of various other errands. The close association established between teacher and pupil generated in the disciple growth in understanding as well as character.

While the *talmîd* followed his rabbi simultaneously in a literal and a moral sense, he adjusted more and more to his ways, became more and more like him. Similar to two tributaries flowing into one river, the two forms of association - with-ness for information and with-ness for formation - converged into one powerful impact moulding the disciple into an authentic replica of his master's prototype. To provide an illustration from rabbinic history, a Talmudic record of certain characteristics of the famous Rabbi Johanan b. Zakkai concludes with the remark, "and so did his disciple R. Eliezer conduct himself after him" (BT Sukkah 28a). **Such imitation enabled and qualified the disciple to become his teacher's reliable witness**, personifying the validity of the precept "a man's agent is like to himself" (M Berakoth 5,5); at the same time such emulation assured and preserved the efficiency of rabbinic tutoring.

One further aspect of rabbinic training requires mentioning, and that is the focus on **multiplication**. In accordance with the challenge, "raise up many disciples" (M Aboth 1,1) and the Talmudic advice, "Form groups for the purpose of study, for Torah can be acquired only in a group",[30] it was normal for a rabbi to gather around himself a group of students, for example "Hillel the Elder had eighty disciples . . . ." (BT Sukkah 28a). This brought certain group dynamics into play which the Word of God delineates in the principle, "As iron sharpens iron, so one man sharpens another" (Prov 27:17). The disciple who was considered as moving along the road of excellence of rabbinic learning was not only the one who repeated accurately what he had heard and learned in order to teach others, but also the one who made his teacher wiser (cf. M Aboth 6,6).

Of course, the question arises to what extent Jesus would have been familiar with rabbinic thought and practice.

A significant hint can be gleaned from Jn 7:15, where Jews marvelling at Jesus asked, "How did this man get such learning without having studied?" In other words, these Jewish observers certified that **Jesus had never undertaken any studies at a rabbinic academy**, never sat at the feet of one of the revered masters.

From what sources then did Jesus derive his learning which, once he embarked on his public ministry, was so unmistakably evident that his fellow-men quite naturally tended to address him as "Rabbi" (cf. Jn 1:38.49, 3:2)?

Here it is helpful to remember our earlier discovery that the major formative influences on Jesus' life stemmed from his godly home. By the time he was twelve and on the threshold of *bar-mitzvah*, - the age of full personal accountability before the Law -, his religious education was so thorough that even teachers in Jerusalem were amazed (Lk 2:46.47). Incidentally, it is telling indeed to realize that the favourable acceptance which Jesus received from the notabilities on that occasion indirectly attested him **an outstanding grasp of rabbinic knowledge, thinking and debating.**

This remarkable understanding would most probably also have been enhanced by different learning experiences at the local synagogue. While Jesus attended elementary school there, the attendant could have made use of recurrent occasions to explain traits of Jewish theological training to his pupils. During worship services the sharing of itinerant rabbis, usually accompanied by several disciples, would have served to further complete the picture in Jesus' mind.

It seems moreover only logical that over the years Jesus came into contact with a number of scribes who evidently could be found in every Galilean village (cf. Lk 5:17). By means of his personal acquaintance with them he attained a deeper perception of their scribal profession and its rabbinic linkages.

Especially, a fourth source of information must not be overlooked. Jesus' repeated visits to Jerusalem, where the leading rabbis and their disciples could be observed in the Temple precincts, must have provided him time and again with firsthand opportunities to expand his comprehension of the rabbis' views as well as their methods of teaching, debating and last, but not least, tutoring.

All these different insights matured towards greater depth and clarity during the hidden years. Finally, as we shall see, in his discipling approach with the Twelve, Jesus **utilized the form** of rabbinic tutoring, **refined its content** and **redefined its end result**.

1.4 His Enduement with Divine Anointing

When eventually Jesus emerged from the shadows of his secluded carpenter's existence into the limelight of public activity, he was about thirty years of age (Lk 3:23), reminding us of Joseph and David who both at thirty moved into positions of influential leadership (Gen 41:46, 2 Sam 5:4).

Advancing in total obedience to God, it was not until the very moment when God's perfect timing was fulfilled, that Jesus appeared among the crowds flocking into the Jordan valley to John the Baptist. The event of **Jesus' baptism** through the revival preacher (cf. Lk 1:16.17) was evidently of major importance, as can be concluded from the observation that it is recorded in each of the four Gospels (Matt 3:13-17, Mk 1:9-11, Lk 3:21.22, Jn 1:32.33). Indeed, the attendant circumstances were charged with both public and personal significance.

For John, the encounter marked a climax in his ministry, because it created for him the occasion to reveal the

Messiah[31] to the multitude (cf. Jn 1:29.31.41). For Jesus, beyond the general recognition received through John, the act of baptism offered the opportunity to openly identify (though without sin himself) with the sinners he had come to save. The incident furthermore supplied him with strong personal assurance. The words "You are my Son, whom I love; with you I am well pleased" (Mk 1:11) attested Jesus' divine Sonship, and at the same time confirmed to him his heavenly Father's love and approval.

Unlike the many others John the Baptist ministered to, Jesus encountered water baptism and **a special enduement with the Holy Spirit** concurrently. In Luke's statement "Jesus, full of the Holy Spirit, returned from the Jordan" (4:1), it is noteworthy that the word "full" (Gk. *pleres*) "seems intended to describe a permanent condition",[32] which is in keeping with John's testimony that the Spirit of God descended and remained on Jesus (Jn 1:32).

The experience of being particularly endowed with the Holy Spirit to facilitate his God-assigned mission placed Jesus into the succession of numerous Old Testament leaders who were granted a special divine enduement for the respective tasks God had allocated to them. The anointing of priests (cf. Ex 29:7) focused on their consecration to serving God. When a prophet was anointed (e.g. 1 Kgs 19:16), it served to qualify him to minister as God's mouthpiece. The kingly anointing (e.g. 1 Chr 29:22) imparted authority.

Occasioned through his baptism, Jesus Christ personified the threefold anointing of priest, prophet and king (cf. Heb 3:1, Acts 3:22, Jn 18:36). As a result his life and ministry displayed in unprecedented measure the enabling and confirming power of God through the Holy Spirit. This very power equipped Jesus to fully be and do what God intended and gave to his words and actions their utmost effectiveness for the advancement of the kingdom of God.

Mark, the Gospel author who took a special interest in

portraying Jesus as a man of action, only briefly indicates **the fact** of Jesus' enduement (1:10), but then devotes the larger part of the remaining chapter to procuring **the evidence** of the remarkable anointing resting upon Jesus Christ. The evangelist presents him as exercising power in dealing with people (vv. 16-20), in teaching (vv. 21.22), in deliverance (vv. 23-27, 32-34, 39) and in healing (vv. 29-31, 32-34, 40-42).

The unquestionable reality and the extraordinary results of Jesus' enduement arouse interest in the question of how one is to understand its essential **nature**. Simon Peter, while delivering his message at the home of the Roman centurion Cornelius, provided the answer when in retrospect he disclosed the secret underlying Jesus' anointing in this way:

> You know what has happened throughout Judea, beginning in Galilee after the baptism that John preached - how God anointed Jesus of Nazareth with the Holy Spirit and power, and how he went around doing good and healing all who were under the power of the devil, because God was with him. (Acts 10:37.38)

According to Simon Peter's understanding,[33] it was this **divine with-ness** that ultimately explained the anointing evident in Jesus' life-style and ministry. Moreover, we do well to recognize that only once, at the beginning of his public activity, viz. when he quoted Isa 61:1 in reference to himself, Jesus Christ spoke of being "anointed" by the Holy Spirit (Lk 4:18). Instead, it seems, he rather preferred to emphasize that God was with him (Jn 8:29, 16:32).[34]

Whereas due to God's omnipresence, his **general with-ness** encompassed all his creation (cf. e.g. Jer 23:24, Ps 139:7-10, Prov 15:3) and was concentrated with marked interest and commitment on his people (cf. e.g. Isa 41:10, 43:2, Ps 91:15), there was obviously furthermore his **special with-ness** in operation, which he sovereignly bestowed on his chosen leaders, pre-eminently upon his Son.

This joint characteristic linked Jesus even more with outstanding leadership personalities of Old Testament days. It is astounding indeed to realize how many times the Word of God condenses and focuses the secret of these significant leadership careers into the simple yet profound formula of God's being with them. For example, the Scriptures state explicitly that God was with:

Abraham:	Gen 21:22	Samuel:	1 Sam 3:19
Isaac:	Gen 26:3.24	Saul:	1 Sam 20:13
Jacob:	Gen 28:15, 31:3	Solomon:	2 Chr 1:1
Joseph:	Gen 39:2.3.21.23	Asa:	2 Chr 15:9
Moses:	Ex 3:12, 33:14	Jehoshaphat:	2 Chr 17:3
Phinehas:	1 Chr 9:20	Hezekiah:	2 Kgs 18:7
Joshua:	Josh 1:5, 3:7	Job:	Job 29:5
Gideon:	Judg 6:12.16[35]	Jeremiah:	Jer 1:8.19

However, king David, in some respects an Old Testament forerunner of Jesus Christ, is the Biblical leader to whom the Scriptures assert special divine with-ness more often than any other Bible character.[36] As we investigate his life and the biographies of other anointed leaders amongst the Israelites, we can discern **a broad spectrum of blessings**, all associated with special divine presence operative in their lives. We find, for instance, that God's with-ness effected:

protection:	Gen 28:15	courage:	cf. Judg 6:33.34
victory:	cf. 1 Chr 18:6.13	faith:	cf. 1 Chr 12:18
provision:	cf. Ps 23:1-4	rest:	cf. 2 Sam 7:1.11
knowledge:	cf. Ex 31:3	help:	2 Chr 32:8
understanding:	cf. 1 Chr 28:12.19	success:	Gen 39:23
wisdom:	cf. 1 Kgs 3:28	honour:	cf. 2 Chr 18:1
skill:	cf. Ex 31:3	wonders:	cf. Judg 6:13

In a similar way, when at the time of his baptism Jesus entered into a further release of God's with-ness into his life, he in a new measure acquired access to the vast storehouse of God's abundant resources available through the anointing presence of the Holy Spirit.

It was this divine association pervading the physical, emotional, intellectual and spiritual dimensions of his life which equipped Jesus Christ with the supernatural means and abilities prerequisite to the accomplishment of his calling. It was this divine association that furnished him with the **supernatural adequacy** so crucial to living a holy life, preaching and teaching with authority, moving in spiritual gifts, attracting and impacting followers, as well as to inspiring faith in God.

Thus the Holy Spirit endowed him with all the indispensable qualifications for effective service and supplied him with **the divine unction needful for his specific function**, in short, gave him power. Concerning God's very enabling with-ness through his Spirit, J. Denney aptly concluded, "power - that is, the presence of God, who can do what men cannot do - is the fundamental note of the Spirit . . . ."[37]

Conscious of the anointing and power he had received (cf. Lk 4:18.19), Jesus moved with confidence towards the immense challenges lying ahead, neither worried about lack nor success, rather resting in the awareness of God's abundant provision through his enabling with-ness. At the same time, the supernatural power evidenced in Jesus' life and unfolding ministry brought to his contemporaries a new sense of God's nearness (cf. Lk 7:16, Matt 9:8). They entered into the personal experience of the truth contained in the angel's announcement (Matt 1:23) that Jesus would be called *Immanuel*, meaning "God with us". So we realize that whereas the name *Jesus* focused on his saviour role, and *Messiah* emphasized the aspect of his anointing, *Immanuel* elucidated another vital facet of his mission - to introduce his fellowmen to a new manifestation of God's presence in their midst.

Before Jesus would be released to fully embark on that

mission, however, there was one more step he had to take. Led into the desert by the Holy Spirit (Mk 1:12), Jesus was tempted by Satan in all respects like common man (Heb 4:15). The divine anointing resting upon him did not exempt him from being **tempered in the furnace of temptation**.[38] But, not only did he by means of prayer, faith and God's Word overcome the enemy's onslaught, he even emerged spiritually enriched from this period of severe testing (cf. Lk 4:1.14).

*

A closer inquiry into Jesus Christ's experience of with-ness up to the point when he commenced his public ministry, discloses that he became acquainted with three types of **human association**: spiritual parenting, vocational apprenticing and rabbinic tutoring. Each of these patterns exerted profound formative influence on his life.

Still a fourth decisive determinant of the strategy he would pursue in his discipling of the Twelve arose from his familiarity with **divine association**, the special divine with-ness as released through the Holy Spirit's anointing. This supernatural endowment, more than any other factor, qualified and empowered him for the God-assigned mission before him.

2 Jesus Christ's Utilization of With-ness in Discipling the Twelve

At the beginning of the Letter to the Hebrews we read that in the past God spoke through his prophets in various ways but at last through his son (1:1.2). That is to say, God's dramatic endeavour to woo man into re-transferring his affection upon his Maker, eventually culminated in the ultimate step of God's sending his own Son into the world (cf. Mk 12:6). The evolving plan of redemption for mankind showed God once again and in particular measure as a God of strategy.[1]

Jesus Christ stressed it was his desire to do God's will (Jn 6:38), and he could undertake only what he saw his Father doing (Jn 5:19). Therefore, sent on his mission by God the Father (cf. Jn 3:16) and operating in obedience to the leading of the Holy Spirit (cf. Matt 4:1), Jesus attended to the implementation of his divine charge with **utmost strategic awareness**. In his pursuit of two pre-eminent concerns - to procure salvation for man through his propitiatory death, and to provide leadership for a movement taking its rise from those who would come to appropriate his work on the cross by faith and to submit to his Lordship - Jesus advanced neither in haphazard nor bewildered or hesitant fashion. On the contrary, his every step was marked by single-minded purposefulness, deep assurance and supreme efficiency.

After investigating in the first chapter Jesus' exposure to different forms of with-ness before he set out to train disciples, the second will examine the utilization of these experiences in his discipling of the Twelve. This inquiry will bring to light how Jesus' growing affiliation with these men developed within the framework of a fourfold call.

2.1 His Call to Observation

With regard to the realization of his divinely appointed task, the envisioned end determined Jesus' strategy, and in his case, the assertion "the wise heart will know the proper time and procedure" (Eccl 8:5) proved singularly true. We recognized in the preceding section how "the proper time" for Jesus' emergence from the shadows of obscurity disclosed itself through the occasion of his baptism. To ensure 'the proper procedure' to inaugurate and establish his ministry, Jesus chose to take on the role of a teacher.

His fellow-men instantly discerned and accepted this then familiar function, as can be concluded from the naturalness and ease with which they accosted him both as "Rabbi" (cf. Jn 6:25, 3:2; 9:2, 11:8; Mk 9:5, 11:21) and as "Teacher" (cf. Matt 12:38, 19:16; Mk 4:38, Lk 21:7; Mk 9:38). Even more telling, Jesus repeatedly described himself as a teacher (Matt 26:18, Jn 13:13.14).

Like the rabbis of his time, we can picture Jesus Christ before our minds' eyes as wearing sandals, clothed with a tunic and a tasselled cloak (cf. Mk 6:56, M), his sun-tanned face framed by a beard. His public activities gave evidence of a threefold emphasis: preaching, teaching and healing (cf. Matt 4:23, 9:35).

Jesus launched his **preaching** in Galilee with the tidings, "Repent, for the kingdom of heaven is near" (Matt 4:17), the very same message with which John the Baptist had claimed people's attention (Matt 3:2). In unison with his herald, Jesus challenged his listeners towards a change of heart and life-style, because "the kingdom of heaven" - a Jewish transcription for the "kingdom of God" (Mk 1:15), which essentially signifies the rule of God in the human heart (cf. Lk 17:21) - had drawn close. The Gospel records of the synoptists in particular show that the concept of the kingdom of God formed a pivotal theme of both Jesus' preaching and teaching (cf. e.g. Matt 13:1-52).

Although Jesus tallied with John in his initial proclamation emphasis, preached in the open as he did and also led people to baptism, there were nevertheless significant differences. While John was an ascetic, stressed judgement and basically limited his attention to the nation of Israel, Jesus was a man of the people, proclaimed salvation and was guided by a worldwide perspective.

Having studied the Word of God, Jewish culture, nature, as well as the character and needs of man for about thirty years, Jesus burst forth with **teaching**[2] that filled contemporary observers with utter amazement (cf. Mk 1:22.27).

The subject matter he covered had much in common with rabbinic thought.[3] Furthermore, certain forms of speech he made use of, e.g. pregnant sayings, proverbs, questions, images, illustrations, comparisons and especially parables,[4] also brought Jesus into resemblance with his rabbinic counterparts.

There was, however, a most striking dissimilarity which Matthew captured into the contrast, "he taught as one who had authority, and not as their teachers of the law" (7:29). Where did the obviously so mighty impact of Jesus' teaching spring from?

Firstly, Jesus had for years been in close touch with the common people and was therefore thoroughly acquainted with their existence and mindset. Consequently he was in a position to adjust his communication efficiently to his hearers, addressing them in relevant, simple, clear, practical and impressive terms. Secondly, he directed his instruction at his listeners' intellect, emotions and will, evoking a response. Jesus never sought, thirdly, to substantiate his teaching through resorting to rabbinic tradition, instead he derived authority directly from his intimate relationship with God. And lastly, the anointing of the Holy Spirit resting upon him endowed his words, which at times carried prophetic undertones, with such power that they pierced the hearts and minds of his audience in unprecedented manner.

The divine confirmation of Jesus' ministry, already recognizable in the unique authority symptomatic of his teaching, became particularly visible in the numerous **healings** which accompanied his activities. Of course, these healings represented only one segment of the broader spectrum of miracles which Jesus performed throughout his public career.

Jesus himself regarded miracles not only as an integral part of his divine commission (cf. Lk 4:18), but also as one of its prominent credentials. When John the Baptist's disciples approached Jesus in order to gain for their by then imprisoned master further substantiation whether the Teacher from Nazareth was indeed the Messiah, Jesus gave them the answer:

> Go back and report to John what you hear and see: The blind receive sight, the lame walk, those who have leprosy are cured, the deaf hear, the dead are raised, and the good news is preached to the poor. (Matt 11:4.5)

Whereas miracles, last not least the curing of various diseases, were an outstanding trait of Jesus' work, the Gospels do not mention any miracles in connection with John the Baptist (cf. Jn 10:41), nor - as A. Schlatter identified[5] - were any performed by the renowned rabbis Hillel, Gamaliel the Elder and Johanan b. Zakkai. Evidently then, Jesus' moving in the realm of the miraculous added a further distinctive feature to his unequalled ministry.

We have so far considered the threefold emphasis characteristic of Jesus' involvement with the public. Now we need to give attention to another major component of his appearance in the role of a teacher. J. Klausner pointed out, "It was a common sight then in Palestine to see teachers ("Rabbis") attracting disciples in large numbers . . . .";[6] deviating from this familiar pattern, **Jesus called a nucleus** of disciples to observe his life and service.

After catering to a large audience at the outset, as time went on Jesus focused more and more on the recruiting and training of a core group of men who would later be able to help him accomplish God's far-reaching purposes. Parallel to his former frequent experiences in the carpentry workshop, where he first envisioned a certain desired end product and then moved on to select the right raw material, tools and production procedures, Jesus now set out to enlist the right calibre of men who would be best suited to be discipled for leadership responsibilities within the expanding kingdom of God. What type of men did Jesus go after, which criteria did he follow?

To begin with, **Jesus decided to win men who were unlearned**, a label by the way which clung to the disciples even beyond the days of their association with Jesus (cf. Acts 4:13, AV). That Jesus would seek to attract men who presumably had attended elementary school and gained vocational expertise but would definitely not have undergone any rabbinic tutorial training, should not amaze us.

John 7:15 seems to suggest the conjecture that Jesus himself had avoided rabbinic tutoring.[7] If he had attached himself as a disciple to a rabbi, he would have run the risk of being influenced to heed human wisdom rather than the leading of the Holy Spirit, to emulate a human prototype rather than his heavenly Father, to adhere to binding human traditions rather than the liberating principles of divine Scripture, to move towards increasing independence rather than closer dependence on God. Understandably, Jesus would have been concerned about excluding such potential interference with the discerned intentions of God both in his own life and in the lives of his potential followers. Therefore he preferred to recruit men who did not have to unlearn much respecting the ways of man, but had the desire to learn much respecting the ways of God.

Jesus' decision to make Galilee his primary field of operation, was a move of highest strategic significance. This was, first of all, the area which he knew best, because he had grown up in it. Besides, it was the most densely populated region in Palestine and hence promised to his itinerant ministry approach a broad spreading of his teaching and personal influence. Pharisaic opposition, furthermore, needed to be suspected much less in the conservative northern province than in the vicinity of Jerusalem.[8] Especially though, Galileans were a unique brand of people, admirably fitted for the enterprise Jesus had in mind.

Galileans could be quickly recognized by their strong accent (cf. Matt 26:73), which included their confounding the guttural sounds.[9] They had the reputation of being impulsive and hot-tempered. But more noteworthy, they were known as pious, vigorous, tough and courageous; they were forward-looking, according to Josephus "ever fond of innovations, and by nature disposed to changes . . . ."[10] Amongst these unsophisticated and zealous people Jesus found the most receptive hearts, the warmest welcome (cf. Jn 4:45), his staunchest supporters, and - especially - the majority of recruits for his mission. In fact, the group of the Twelve was all Galilean (cf. Acts 1:11), except apparently for Judas Iscariot who hailed from the Judean village of Kerioth.[11]

Over and above Jesus showed a preference for Galilean **fishermen** in particular. From Mk 1:16, Matt 4:21 and Jn 21:2.3 we may infer that Simon Peter, his brother Andrew, the two Zebedees John and James, Nathanael, Thomas and at least one other disciple belonged to this category. Their occupational background had moulded them into men who were circumspect, used to hard work, prepared to take risks, inclined to persevere and experienced in team-work (cf. Lk 5:7.9.10).

So we have seen that Jesus went after simple men, who were open-minded, energetic and easy to motivate, men who had graduated from the demanding and practical school of real life. The leading motivation on Jesus' side for his contact with these men over the first fourteen months[12] was to offer them **ample opportunity for observation.**

In R.E. Coleman's estimation, during this phase "these early disciples really did not do much more than watch Jesus work...."[13] In truth, this observation was their very training, because it afforded all the insights Jesus desired them to glean. Ever since his initial invitation to John and Andrew, "Come and you will see" (cf. Jn 1:39), Jesus consciously gave his adherents access to receive understanding, convince themselves, gain first-hand experience and thus learn as they witnessed his life-style, words and actions.[14] The men around Jesus at that stage were occasional companions, part-timers, who for certain periods accompanied him (cf. Mk 1:38, 2:23), but now and then also returned to their jobs and homes (cf. Jn 1:40-42, Lk 5:1-11). This situation also offered them repeatedly the chance to ponder the implications of a potential long-range commitment to Jesus Christ.

One ingredient of Jesus' contact with the emerging core group needs added elucidation, namely the fact that beyond his role as teacher **he related to them as leader.** The task of providing redemption for mankind did not presuppose spiritual leadership status on Jesus' part, the task of creating a movement to promote God's global cause, however, certainly did.

As a leader seeking "to influence a specific group of God's people toward God's purposes",[15] Jesus sensed a deep concern for the deplorable state of the multitudes who "were harassed and helpless, like sheep without a shepherd" (Matt 9:36).[16] **His desire was to raise up qualified leaders who could serve as catalysts for the release of people's latent spiritual capacity for the things of God.** To secure this end, a nucleus of certain men would be his method.

As a leader Jesus was able to captivate the attention of

prospective followers by articulating his sense of direction into **a clear plan of action**. Mark recorded it in the words, "Come, follow me, and I will make you fishers of men" (cf. 1:17). Appealing to their vocational understanding, Jesus promised to disciple them into men who would attract others to God. Expressing his confidence in their potential, Jesus at the same time instilled an inspiring vision and purpose. Actually, right at this point he already planted the seed of the Great Commission into their hearts and minds.

As a leader Jesus knew that the success or failure of his mission would decisively depend on the selection of the right helpers. Thus **he took the initiative in calling men** to become disciples (Matt 4:19, 4:21, 9:9), a step as unprecedented in rabbinic tradition as the fact that he called them **to follow not just his teaching but him as a person** (Mk 1:17, Jn 1:43, also Jn 21:19.22).[17] Jesus did not merely recruit them for their intellectual benefit or for a task, he recruited them for a relationship.

2.2 His Call to Consociation

Without any doubt the development of events reflected in Mk 3:13.14 signalled a decisive moment in Jesus' correlation with his adherents:

> Jesus went up on a mountainside and called to him those he wanted, and they came to him. He appointed twelve - designating them apostles - that they might be with him and that he might send them out to preach

Jesus sensed the time had arrived when it became necessary to narrow the larger number of possible candidates down to a smaller band of full-time companions. Consequently he **"called to him those he wanted"**(v. 13). This indicates that once again the initiative lay completely on his side, and that he sovereignly reserved to himself the freedom to hand-pick those whom he regarded as best suited for being trained to first assist and later continue his mission.

Luke's account of this momentous incident (6:12.13) lets us know that Jesus spent a whole night in prayerful preparation for the crucial decision to be taken. Waiting on God for specific direction seemed all the more imperative in view of the possibility of getting side-tracked through mere human inclinations, as we can infer from Samuel's Old Testament experience (cf. 1 Sam 16:6-12). Besides, Luke emphasized by his use of the term 'choose' (Gk. *eklego*, v. 13) that Jesus carried out a deliberate selection (cf. also Jn 15:16.19). Under the guiding presence of the Holy Spirit Jesus made his choice of the very individuals God intended for him (cf. Jn 17:6.9).

Among those whom Jesus Christ invited to form the core group of the Twelve was, to start with, Simon Peter, a man of considerable leadership aptitude. His brother Andrew, an inconspicuous server, was the one who initially introduced him to the Teacher from Nazareth; Andrew had formerly been a disciple of the Baptist, together with John, son of Zebedee. Jesus nick-named John and his brother James "Sons of Thunder" (Mk 3:17). Like their impulsive fishing partner Simon, these two hotspurs were typical specimens of the true Galilean stock. In addition Jesus called Philip from Bethsaida, who had previously made Bartholomew (Nathanael) aware of the Messiah's emergence, along with James, son of Alphaeus, Thaddeus (Jude) and Thomas, who appears to have shared a somewhat sceptical outlook with Bartholomew (cf. Jn 11:16, 20:24-29; 1:46.48). Another member of the group was Matthew (Levi) whose background as a tax collector and therefore collaborator with the Romans debased him in the eyes of any patriotic Jew, especially a fervent nationalist and revolutionary like Simon the Zealot (Cananaean). Finally, there was Judas Iscariot, marked by a materialistic bias (cf. Jn 12:4-6, Matt 26:15.16), who in the end would betray the Master.

As far as the Gospels indicate, Simon Peter was the only married person in the party (cf. Mk 1:30). Bearing in mind that in Jewish society the marriageable age for men was eighteen, J.S. Stewart's evaluation "Christianity began as a young people's movement",[18] sounds apt, the more so if we heed the fact that Jesus himself addressed his disciples as 'lads' (Jn 21:5, M).

Hence there is good reason to assume a good number of the Twelve to have been comparatively young when Jesus called them. We also have to realize that this nucleus of men embodied a microcosm of the multiplicity of human character. Obviously Jesus' perspective in choosing them was not so much focused on who they were at the outset, but rather on who they could become under his leadership and influence (cf. Jn 1:42). Conscious of their evident deficits and weaknesses, Jesus was at the same time aware that he could build upon their teachability and dedication. Totally convinced that God had entrusted to his care these very Twelve, Jesus embarked on their training with confidence, single-minded determination and a clear strategy.

The key principle of Jesus' approach is intimated in Mark's statement that Jesus selected the Twelve "**that they might be with him**" (v. 14). Over the next twenty months,[19] Jesus provided his newly appointed disciples constantly and consistently with opportunities to share in his life and ministry. Together with Jesus they walked and talked, ate and drank, worked and rested; they accompanied him to the synagogue, the Temple, into the fields and onto the Sea of Galilee, to villages and to Jerusalem; they were with him at a wedding and a funeral, when he visited friends and sick people, when he dealt with multitudes and individuals, women and children, religious leaders and outcasts, Jews and Gentiles, rich and poor; they heard him pray, preach and teach; they saw him heal and deliver; they experienced Jesus in public and in private, as joyful and saddened, thirsty and tired.

To put it in another way, Jesus opened up to them countless occasions to move with him in **consociation**. According to Webster's dictionary,[20] the word 'consociation' - derived from the Latin root elements *com-* ('together') and *socius* ('joined with') - expresses "intimate union of persons; fellowship; alliance; companionship; association". Even more strongly than the latter term it accentuates the aspect of together-ness.

Jesus regarded consociation with him as the most fertile soil for his disciples' growth relative to character, understanding and skill. Hence he made the experience of his with-ness the pivot of their training. "Jesus had no formal curriculum", D. Watson declared, "no planned course of instruction, no classroom syllabus. Instead, he called his disciples to be *with him*".[21] And R.E. Coleman emphasized, "Truth was not taught in abstract doctrines or regulations; it was caught in the experience of their shared life".[22] Through the disciples' continual exposure to who he was, what he did and said, Jesus intended them to discern and absorb his vision, mindset and mode of operation. He desired them to become so saturated with the influences arising from his example and teaching, his attitudes, actions and anointing, that every single area of their lives would be impacted towards greater likeness to himself (cf. Matt 10:25). The approach he decided on was simple and informal, practical and wholistic. The totality of shared life experiences made up the disciples' classroom, and their teacher's words merely needed to further elucidate the lessons already gained from his life.

With **consociation as the heart and the secret of the Master's training method**, it is not surprising to observe that Jesus not only spent a lot of time with his protégés, but even did so increasingly over the ensuing months. This realization suggests our consent to Coleman's conclusion, "The time which Jesus invested in these few disciples was so much more by comparison to that given to others that it can only be regarded as a deliberate strategy".[23]

The Gospels mention 'being with Jesus' not just in connection with certain activities which the disciples undertook together with their Master (e.g. Matt 26:20.36, Mk 3:7, 8:10, 11:11, Lk 6:17, 7:11, 8:1, 9:18, Jn 3:22, 6:3, 11:54, 18:1.2). Moreover it appears that the same terminology was used as a synonym for being a disciple of Jesus (e.g. Matt 26:69.71, Mk 16:10, Jn 18:26) and that the two-sided with-ness existing between the Master and his disciples was referred to as an equivalent for Jesus' technique of training the Twelve (Mk 3:14; cf. also Lk 22:28, 24:44, Jn 7:33, 13:33, 14:9.25, 16:4, 17:12).

Utilizing the consociation concept for this process served more than one purpose though. It was more than a **pedagogical** principle applied to secure effective influence on the basis of close with-ness, for Jesus Christ saw in this approach the best vehicle to ground his contact with the Twelve on a solid **relational** footing.

We may recall how Jesus' earlier experiences in his parents' godly home and in the carpentry workshop had led him to understand, appreciate and develop meaningful interpersonal relationships. And after he engaged in public ministry, Gospel evidence leaves us in no doubt that **Jesus was strongly people-oriented** and regarded his relationship with the Twelve in particular as a matter of highest priority. Jesus made himself more readily available to them than to anyone else (cf. Mk 9:30.31), took a special interest in their understanding of his teaching and mission (cf. Mk 4:34, Matt 16:21) and exercised remarkable patience with their slow growth (cf. Mk 8:17-21). He displayed great concern on their behalf (cf. Jn 18:8), expressed his love for them (Jn 15:9), told them he longed for their fellowship (Lk 22:15) and was especially committed to them in intercession (cf. Jn 17:6-19, Lk 22:31.32).

There is one area, however, which affords most astonishing insight into the nature and depth of Jesus' relationship with his disciples, and that is **his intimate communication with them**. To T.W. Manson we owe the noteworthy discovery that the language Jesus used with the Twelve showed certain unique features.[24] A perhaps even more amazing clue is the fact that while the word 'disciple' is found in the Gospels 225 times in reference to Jesus' followers,[25] he himself addressed the Twelve directly with this term on only two occasions (Jn 13:35, 15:8). Evidently the Master himself did not share the same preference for the word as the four evangelists in general - why?

Jesus, it seems, rather favoured to call his disciples "my brothers" (Matt 12:49, 28:10, Jn 20:17) and to address them as "children" (Mk 10:24), "my children" (Jn 13:33), "friends" (Jn 15:15, 21:5) and "my friends" (Lk 12:4, cf. also Jn 15:14). The Greek text of the Gospel records indicates that Jesus employed two different words for 'friend', viz. *philos* and *hetairos*, the former being an affectionate term, the latter denoting "comrade" or "partner".[26] It is telling indeed to realize that in talking to the Twelve Jesus always used *philos*, but resorted to *hetairos* when accosting Judas at the moment of betrayal (Matt 26:50).

All the different expressions of endearment just listed imply close fellowship, intimacy, heart bonding.[27] They offered themselves as more appropriate to capture the essence of Jesus' consociation with the Twelve than the common term 'disciple', because it stood in danger of being misinterpreted along the lines of certain rabbinic connotations, among them especially a stronger intellectual than relational orientation.[28] Yet Jesus did not go about establishing an academy, **he went about establishing a fellowship**; he first majored on making friends and only later on sending out apostles (cf. Mk 3:14).

Due recognition must also be given to the fact that the strong relationship emphasis which we have discerned in Jesus' dealings with the disciples was inseparably linked to his theological perspective, more specifically, **his theology of leadership**.[29] Theocentric Jewish epistemology did not leave any room for the conception of a humanistic philosophy of leadership. Jesus derived his view of spiritual leadership in general and his personal function as a leader in particular from his theological perception, which essentially centred around "the truth of God's Fatherhood" as "the inspiring and ruling thought in all His work".[30] His inimitable experience and grasp of this truth became singularly evident in his intimate and affectionate address of God as *"Abba"* (Aramaic for 'my Father', 'Daddy'), which in that form was totally without parallel in rabbinic tradition.[31]

Jesus' exercise of spiritual leadership shows that it was a real desire on his part to reflect the quality of his close and loving relationship with his Father in heaven in the quality of his personal and warm relationship with his disciples on earth (cf. Jn 15:9); even more, he regarded it as a vital element of his mission to display the Father to them through his life (cf. Jn 14:8-10). With God as the Father of all men continually before his eyes, it was only natural for Jesus Christ to envisage the disciples as brothers and to set the stage for his contemplated leadership training through founding a brotherhood on the basis of consociation.

As outlined earlier on, over his preparatory years Jesus became acquainted with a number of groups and movements which all left their mark on the Jewish society of his day. Of the various forms of interdependence between leaders and followers which he was able to identify, **Jesus gave preference to the rabbinic tutoring pattern as a model for training the Twelve.** However, while he took over the outer form, he modified the inner content significantly.

K.H. Rengstorf pointed out that the New Testament usage

of the word 'disciple' (Greek *mathetes*) "always implies the existence of a personal attachment which shapes the whole life" and that there exists "no doubt as to who is deploying the formative power".[32] This was specifically true in the case of Jesus Christ and the Twelve, so true in fact that Rengstorf even spoke of "this wholly non-Jewish relation of Jesus to His disciples".[33]

Different to rabbinic practice, Jesus took the initiative in calling his disciples. He summoned them to himself as a person and claimed the right to be their only teacher. He did not prepare them for ordination but to bring forth much spiritual fruit, not for a career of public recognition but to deny themselves. He informed them that working on his behalf would require a willingness to suffer. He did not enlist them for a limited period only but challenged them to a lifelong commitment.

So we find Jesus availing himself of the familiar format of rabbinic tutoring, yet in view of his unprecedented intentions **revising its substance**, last not least by **fine-tuning it through a strong relationship linkage to himself.** To quote Rengstorf once again, "Jesus binds exclusively to Himself. The rabbi and the Greek philosopher are at one in representing a specific cause. Jesus offers Himself".[34]

Jesus conceived of discipling as a dynamic process of shaping his trainees' mindset and life-style progressively after his own. The favourite image and the technical term Jesus chose for this action-charged procedure was 'to follow' (Greek *akoloutheo*) him as Master (cf. e.g. Matt 10:38, 19:28, Mk 2:14, 8:34, Lk 9:59, 18:22, Jn 1:43, 21:19.22). He viewed discipling as life-transference through the channel of relationship, and not as mere intellectual absorption of certain theoretical precepts. Thus we understand why **he never spoke of the abstract concept of 'discipleship'**,[35] even though - as G. Kittel put forward[36] - the term *akolouthesis* could have been employed for that purpose.

The passage Mk 3:13.14 makes us also aware that in his desire to create a most conducive learning environment for the disciples, **Jesus opted for a team setting**. This decision brought certain group dynamics to the fore which he took advantage of. A team milieu provides a sense of belonging and security, facilitates mutual encouragement, stimulation and challenge. It creates a favourable atmosphere for relational bonding and accountability. Within a circle of like-minded persons it is easier to keep vision alive, maintain motivation and commitment, smooth away character edges and compensate one another's weaknesses. Group backing enhances performance, producing better results through co-operation than would be achievable through solitary endeavour (cf. Eccl 4:9-12, Lev 26:8). Generally speaking, the team context served to reinforce and broaden the 'vertical' formative influence emanating from Jesus' person and instruction by way of the 'horizontal' communication and interaction amongst the Twelve (cf. Prov 27:17).

The precise objective of starting a worldwide movement for the expansion of the kingdom of God Jesus pursued with a clear agenda which helped him to exclude unproductive undertakings. His strategy was to provide for this coming movement qualified leadership through discipling based on consociation. For his twelve hand-picked candidates Jesus had the desire that, "they were to learn, in the privacy of an intimate daily fellowship with their Master, what they should be, do, believe, and teach, as His witnesses and ambassadors to the world".[37]

Jesus himself summed up this very purpose when he notified the Twelve "you also will bear witness, because you have been with Me from the beginning" (Jn 15:27, NKJV). These words disclose his utter confidence in the validity and efficiency of the **consociational discipling model** employed under his leadership. And was not this confidence afterwards fully justified and strikingly affirmed when the members of the *Sanhedrin* in their encounter with individuals he had trained "took note that these men had been with Jesus" (Acts 4:13)?

2.3 His Call to Imitation

In view of his aim to rear "fishers of men" (Mk 1:17), Jesus mobilized suitable aspirants in order to channel them into appropriate training. Wishing them to undergo high quality preparation for their future capacity, Jesus decided to keep their number small enough to assure the effectiveness of the procedure he had in mind. Accordingly he selected a nucleus of only twelve men to receive and benefit from his intensive discipling endeavours.

As we have seen, Jesus made his close relation with the Twelve the cornerstone of their training. We also realized that he treasured this warm companionship so much that he sought to avoid addressing them directly with the rather technical term 'disciples', because they were not academic students on their way to become scholars of exegesis and rabbinic tradition but his friends, intimately linked with him in a life-sharing experience. A dynamic process of this nature, furthermore, could not be aptly delineated in static terminology, thus the abstract concept of 'discipleship' found no place in Jesus' vocabulary.

At the core of the formative effect which he desired to exert on his protégés was **the power of his personality**. "Now the influence of personality," E. Griffith-Jones wrote,[38] "can never be adequately transmitted by any other means than through personality itself." Consociation was the avenue which Jesus created to unleash the full impact of his character, actions and words upon the Twelve. To impress his personality on his disciples through association with them, was a simple and inconspicuous educational technique, yet at the same time the most natural, profound and powerful method of influencing them for his purposes.

E. Stanley Jones once stated, "Christianity is not merely a conception; it is also a contagion".[39] For his training of the Twelve, Jesus made use of this element of **contagion**, which W.L. Duewel called "the secret of all great leadership, of whatever kind".[40] Facilitated by their intimate relationship, Jesus and his disciples reached a point of closeness where his spirit touched their spirits, his heart imparted to their hearts, so that, for example, vision was birthed, motivation inspired, commitment instilled, concern aroused and faith kindled, - in short, **beyond truth taught, attitude was caught**. Because it was not Jesus' intention to provide the Twelve with theoretical **information** alone, but to produce in them actual character **formation**, he, through his with-ness, brought to bear upon them his words and his example, too. The many occasions on which the Twelve witnessed the totality of Jesus' life and activities, added up to one all-inclusive textbook from which they could learn both on cognitive and experiential level all the key lessons pertinent to their future engagement for the kingdom of God. For them the observation of Jesus' example in a multiplicity of real life situations both clarified and verified; it provided them with visual proof of the practicality of the principles he shared and afforded them with a prototype which they could later on recall and reproduce in other settings.

The basic leadership role which Jesus adopted for the process of discipling the Twelve was not one of a task-oriented supervisor, but rather a **person-oriented mentor**. As such he exhibited greatest care for his trainees' well-being and development. Conscious that it required a high and wise time investment to establish and maintain sound relationships, he watched carefully over the quantity and quality of the time he spent together with his entourage.

One distinguished feature of Jesus' various encounters with people was his estimation of meal-times as extraordinary opportunities for relationship building and communication in a relaxed atmosphere. We observe this in his contacts with the public (cf. Lk 5:29-32, 7:36-50, 10:38-42, 14:1-23, 19:5-27, Jn 2:1-11) and also with his disciples (cf. Jn 13:2-17:26, 21:9-19, Acts 1:4). In addition, on certain occasions he took the Twelve aside (cf. Mk 4:34, 4:35.36, 10:32, Lk 10:23, 18:31). At other times he considered it indispensable to ensure the privacy needful for their further instruction and growth through retreats (cf. Mk 8:10, 9:30.31, Lk 9:10, Jn 11:54).

Quite naturally, the fact that Jesus on his part was intent on presenting to his disciples the living example of what he wanted them to become, called for a commitment on their part to imitate him. This important focus of their learning relation to Jesus was also implied in the latter's favourite image for discipling, the idea of 'following him'.

W. Barclay explained how in classical Greek the verb *akoloutheo* occurred with various shades of meaning. It was employed for instance in reference to a soldier following his commander and a slave accompanying his master; it could express obedience to the law and to someone's advice.[41] In rabbinic context, 'following' described the student's 'walking behind' his teacher at a respectful distance, but the expression also carried the figurative connotation of 'being a disciple', which included the patterning of one's life after the respective rabbi. Relative to Jesus' discipling practice, the use of the term was narrowed down further to signify the intimate consociation between Jesus as a person, and his followers, for **the distinct purpose of their being progressively conformed to his model.**

It was the disciples' sole profession, A. Schlatter declared, to follow Jesus.[42] Their doing so was both an instructive and a liberating experience. While Jesus' example gave visual evidence of what needed to be learned, his coaching witness was geared towards proper implementation and rendered devices like a fixed curriculum, manuals, rules and regulations completely superfluous. The disciples, because of their friendship relation with Jesus, were desirous to please him, accept his leadership, submit to his guidance and obey his instructions. As they followed in this manner, Jesus "stamped His own image on them. It was this that made them the men they became".[43]

Of special relevance is the observation that even in regard to what 'following' truly meant, Jesus furnished his disciples with the supreme example, for **he himself focused his existence on following God**. Linked to his heavenly Father in unique intimacy, he made it his expressed aim to please him (Jn 8:29), glorify him (Jn 12:27.28) and obey him (Jn 6:38, 4:34) in all things. He looked upon God's moral excellency as the applicable standard for himself (cf. Matt 5:48) and placed his Father's priorities in his own life first as well (cf. Matt 6:9.10, 6:33). Jesus did God's works (Jn 5:19.36, 14:10, 17:4) and passed on God's words (Jn 8:26.28, 12:50, 14:24, 17:8.14). Among numerous other godly attributes he displayed God's love (cf. Jn 15:9), compassion (Matt 9:36, cf. also Lk 13:34), righteous wrath (cf. Mk 11:15-17) and willingness to forgive (cf. Lk 23:34). In short, through his exemplary likeness to his heavenly Father, he exhibited God in consummate manner (cf. Jn 1:18, 10:30, 12:45, 14:9).

From the model which the Master supplied by his being, doing and speaking, his disciples were able to benefit respecting knowledge, skill and character growth. Without any doubt, it was the last-mentioned area to which Jesus devoted his primary attention. Actually, according to the Gospel records, Jesus' communication relating to practical ministry issues was surprisingly scant, as L. Eims noticed, "it is amazing how *little* Jesus spoke to His men on ministry skills. He majored on the man rather than on ministry methods".[44] Jesus concentrated his instruction more on those **attitudes and spiritual principles** which underlie and determine conduct, relationship building, skill application and ministry performance.

The Scriptures set forth a picture of the disciples which is both realistic and honest about certain flaws they betrayed, foremost in the realm of character. We are shown that they were men of little faith and slow learning, sometimes impulsive, impatient, argumentative; we see them as fearful, sceptical and prejudiced. Jesus' loving and patient commitment to them did not entail his condoning their failures in silence. On the contrary, he quite clearly addressed various weaknesses, among them one which he regarded as singularly detrimental - pride, "for what good could these disciples do as ministers of the kingdom so long as their main concern was about their own place therein?"[45] It is indicative of Jesus Christ's affectionate and considerate mentoring that he never explicitly criticized the Twelve for being proud. Rather, he devoted extraordinary effort to repeatedly pointing out to them the antidote - humility.

In Matt 11:29 Jesus challenged, "learn from me, for I am gentle and humble in heart". The wider denotations of the two Greek words *praÿs* ("gentle") and *tapeinos* ("humble") suggest that Jesus here advocated his listeners should imitate him relative to a meek, mild, considerate attitude on the one hand and a lowly, unassuming, self-effacing heart disposition on the other. This challenge undoubtedly touched a sore spot in the disciples' lives, because they lacked both meekness (cf. e.g. Matt 19:13, Lk 9:49, 9:54, Mk 10:41) and humility (cf. e.g. Mk 9:33.34, 10:35-37, Lk 22:24).

Their tendency towards pride Jesus endeavoured to counteract in several ways. He took up the issue in his general teaching (Matt 23:12, Lk 14:7-11, 18:9-14), then also in his training talks with the Twelve (cf. Mk 9:35, 10:42-44), turning their attention to himself as their example (Mk 10:45).[46] Further, he gave them a visible illustration (Matt 18:1-4). When in the end he sensed that they still had not fully grasped his intent, he followed up with a personal demonstration, graphic and drastic at the same time, when he engaged in the menial task of washing their feet (Jn 13:1-12). In this extremely humbling setting Jesus reiterated **the prototype function of his life-style** with the exhortation, "I have set you an example that you should do as I have done for you" (Jn 13:15).

Jesus' discipling labours targeted his disciples' response of imitating him in word, deed and attitude. His repetition of vital truths (e.g. Matt 13:44-46; 25:14-30, Lk 19:11-27; Jn 14:16-26, 16:7-15; Mk 8:31, 10:32-34) as well as the usage of impressive and poetic language helped the Twelve remember his words.[47] Not only did they learn by **hearing**, however, but also by **doing**, as Jesus gave them opportunities for application (e.g. Jn 4:2, Matt 10:5-8, Mk 6:39-43, 14:12-16). Moreover, they learned by **seeing**, with the Master's transparent life leaving the strongest imprint of all (cf. e.g. Lk 9:18, 11:1; Jn 13:34, 1 Jn 3:16; 1 Pet 2:21-23; 1 Jn 1:1-3).

As we recognized earlier on, Jesus adopted the conventional form of rabbinic tutoring, but then took to honing its content. Now it is essential to notice further that Jesus visualized and defined a different end result. A key passage opening up insight in this regard is Matt 23:1-36.

The observer could at first sight be misled to interpret this portion of Scripture as a downright condemnation of all scribes and Pharisees. Yet we do well to bear in mind, firstly, that Jesus addressed the multitudes and his disciples (v. 1) and did not launch a direct verbal attack against the religious leaders in question. Secondly, it is gainful not to overlook A. Finkel's assertion that Jesus' polemics was "directed at the zealous Pharisees, the disciples of Shammai's academy," whereas the position of "the disciples of Hillel's school - their humbleness, restraint, clear argumentative reasoning and liberal stand - was close in spirit to that of the teacher of Nazareth".[48] Doubtless Jesus saw reason to denounce specific aberrations manifest in the lives of certain scribes and Pharisees; at the same time this backdrop threw into much sharper relief those characteristics which he longed to see in his adherents.

Jesus warned his audience that these Jewish leaders were not worth imitating, because they did not put their words into practice (v. 3). He deplored the fact that they burdened people with legalism (cf. v. 4), were ostentatious in their religious performance (v. 5), loved public recognition and honour (vv. 6.7) and oppressed the poor (v. 14). Likewise he discerned them as lacking in a sense of proportion (cf. v. 23) and in congruity (cf. vv. 25.28). Consequently Jesus looked upon them as disqualified for the exercise of true spiritual leadership, even more so because they were "blind" (vv. 16.17.19.24.26) and "hypocrites" (vv. 13-15.23.25.27.29).

Of course the implication of these denouncements was that Jesus wished his disciples to be void of such deficiencies. Instead they were to lead lives of **humility**, **love** and **integrity**, of inward godliness rather than outward legalism. Emphatically Jesus rejected for them the title of honour 'Rabbi' (v. 8). Neither did he desire them to fall into the trap of self-aggrandizement, nor did he want the Twelve to disregard the fact that in their case confidence for future ministry effectiveness could never rest upon human ordination[49] but solely on **divine authorization**. Over and above Jesus underscored his position as their one and only Master and Teacher whom alone they were to follow and thus imitate.

With the words, "everyone who is fully trained will be like his teacher" (Lk 6:40), Jesus summarized the overall aim of his consociational discipling method. Why did he focus his coaching of the Twelve on **reproducing in them replicas of himself**?

Firstly, Jesus purposed to launch a movement which would advance by virtue of reproduction. For any such process the prototype to be recreated would be crucial. In God's eyes, nobody but his own Son was qualified to serve as the consummate model needed (cf. Matt 3:17, 17:5).

Secondly, Jesus abstained from establishing a college or organization, from devising a programme or handbook; he preferred to disseminate the truth by means of human personality, through his followers. By precept and especially by exemplar Jesus sowed what he aspired to reap later on in their lives and ministries: "The first and probably the greatest aspect of their training was personal association with him and learning through example and imitation".[50] On the basis of their emulation, his with-ness was to produce likeness which in turn was to secure authentic witness in the future.

Yet this overriding goal of the disciples' reflecting their Master would never be achievable by mere striving in the energy of the flesh to copy him. Rather, it would require remaining in close fellowship with him (cf. Jn 15:4.5), made possible through the constant presence of the Holy Spirit effecting progressing transformation into the likeness of Jesus Christ (cf. 2 Cor 3:18).

2.4 His Call to Continuation

In Matt 10:27 Jesus challenged his disciples, "What I tell you in the dark, speak in the daylight; what is whispered in your ear, proclaim from the roofs". This charge uncovered the Master's desire to see his **hidden training** of the Twelve bring on their involvement in **public ministry**. More specifically, he intended them to in the future continue and lead the mission which he had come to initiate.

While Jesus was with his chosen core group of followers, he repeatedly announced his forthcoming suffering, death and resurrection (Mk 8:31, 9:31, 10:32-34). Especially during the last opportunity for extended fellowship with the disciples before his betrayal through Judas Iscariot, Jesus sought to direct their attention to his impending departure (Jn 13:33, 14:2.4.12.28, 16:5.7.10.16.28, 17:11.13). A closer look at several key concepts which Jesus utilized in connection with the Twelve, however, reveals with particular clarity that **he actually prepared his companions all along with the perspective of their carrying on his work.**

At the outset, he stated his goal to disciple them into "fishers of men" (Mk 1:17), to develop them into such men who could attract multitudes to his Father. When he invited the Twelve into close consociation, he did so "designating them apostles" (Mk 3:14), because the training they were about to undergo was designed to qualify them to be sent out to represent his divine cause to mankind. Recurrently Jesus portrayed before their minds' eyes the image of a harvest (Matt 9:37.38, 13:30, Mk 4:29, Jn 4:35), indicating their future role in reaping souls for God. During the Last Supper the Master made the amazing pronouncement that those who believed in him would accomplish "even greater things" (Jn 14:12) than the works he performed while on earth, thus encouraging his friends with the prospect of God's using them in new and mighty ways to establish his kingdom.

It is essential to note though that in envisaging the future involvement of his disciples, Jesus Christ did not anticipate only a continuation of his ministry, but he foresaw growth, expansion, multiplication, - in short, **the rise of a movement.** "We do not mean to assert", D. Flusser wrote, "that Jesus wanted to found a church or even a simple community, but that he wanted to start a movement",[51] and in J.H. Charlesworth's opinion the Teacher from Nazareth "certainly set in motion the Palestinian Jesus Movement".[52]

A number of the Master's sayings leave us in no doubt that this picture of an evolving movement, which he worked for but could only envision by faith during his walk among men, was a prominent facet of the strategy he pursued. It is reflected in the parable which Jesus regarded as cardinal to the understanding of his parabolic teaching in general (Mk 4:13), viz. the parable of the sower, where the seed that fell on good ground yielded a multiple crop of thirty, sixty or a hundred times the amount originally sown. It shines through his comparison of the extension of the kingdom of God with the growth of a mustard seed (Matt 13:31.32). It is evident in the principle he pointed out in Jn 12:24 that any single grain of wheat which dies will generate many new seeds. Furthermore we see it surface in his high priestly prayer, when he visualized and included in his intercession all those who would come to believe through the disciples' words (Jn 17:20).

The message which Jesus came to deliver, the glad tidings of God's sacrificial love for a world lost in sin (cf. Jn 3:16), was of such momentous significance that it must not remain the privilege of a select few but had to be shared universally. Therefore Jesus set out to start a movement, establishing its starting-point and foundation through his intensive training of the nucleus of the Twelve. Its future growth would depend upon and stem from the ministry the disciples would exercise in the days to come.

Acutely aware of the multitudes' need for proper direction (cf. Matt 9:36), **Jesus prepared his closest followers thoroughly for future leadership responsibilities** within the prospective movement. He did so, as we have already seen, primarily through his **modelling** (cf. Matt 11:29, Jn 13:15), yet he also provided them with **teaching** on specific leadership issues (e.g. Mk 10:42-45, Lk 16:10-12; Jn 21:15-18). In addition he gave them **opportunity to practically apply** what they had learned.

Exceptionally illuminating in this respect is the example found in Matt 10:1-42. After the disciples had been able to observe for an extended period of time how Jesus carried out various ministry activities, he led them to become an answer to their own prayers (cf. Matt 9:38) by sending them out on an assignment. The latter was restrictive, as the Twelve were commissioned to make their Jewish fellow-men their only target group (Matt 10:5.6), as well as imitative, because they were to move out emulating their Master's ministry (cf. Matt 10:7.8).

As he delegated authority to his trainees (cf. Matt 10:1) and sent them on their way, these twelve "apprentice missionaries",[53] as A.B. Bruce called them, underwent "an educational experiment".[54] They were able to gain experience by putting their theoretical knowledge into practice, could acquire further ministry skills, had the chance of learning in areas like personal reliance upon God, shouldering responsibility and accountability. Altogether they were enabled to progress in maturity and to get a foretaste of what their future existence as apostles would hold in store for them.

Just like consociation and exemplification, delegation facilitating implementation formed another major ingredient of Jesus' leadership development approach with the Twelve. Closing the Last Supper gathering with his friends by prayer, Jesus conveyed to his heavenly Father the remarkable evaluation, "I have brought you glory on earth by completing the work you gave me to do" (Jn 17:4). Without a doubt a vital component of this entrusted work was the mentoring of the Twelve, upon which Jesus at this point in time could look back with a sense of fulfillment.

The disciples themselves were conscious of Jesus' efforts to prepare them for spiritual leadership. Apart from teaching they received along these lines, they could not escape the observation that even within their twelve member core group Jesus established still closer **circles of influence**. From a perspective not of spirituality but of suitability, he invested himself particularly into the lives of Simon Peter, John and James. There were certain outstanding experiences which he granted solely to these three (Mk 5:37-43, Matt 17:1-9, Mk

14:33-42). Moreover, it became obvious that he gave special attention to Peter's development (e.g. Matt 17:25-27, Lk 22:31.32, Mk 16:7, Jn 21:15-19). Interestingly enough, it was he who in retrospect showed distinctive awareness of the Master's grooming his followers for leadership (cf. Acts 1:20).

Commenting on the venture but also the wisdom inherent in Jesus Christ's rearing the Twelve to continue his mission, R.E. Coleman reckoned, "He literally staked His whole ministry upon them. The world could be indifferent toward Him and still not defeat His strategy".[55] One must recognize though, Jesus' confidence in the effectiveness of the approach he had taken (cf. Jn 15:27, AV) did not rest on the natural aptitude of the candidates he selected nor on his mentoring endeavours alone. Despite the best leadership development ever offered to man, i.e. the one Jesus had made available to the Twelve, the Master nevertheless did not consider them sufficiently equipped yet to take up the leadership responsibilities he desired and anticipated for them. This became singularly apparent during his extended discourse at the Last Supper, when, dwelling predominantly on what would sustain the disciples after his imminent departure, **he elaborated with noteworthy emphasis and detail on the character and role of the Holy Spirit.**

From the four Gospels we can gather ample evidence as to how essentially and intimately the Holy Spirit was involved in Jesus' life and ministry (cf. e.g. Matt 1:18, 3:16, Mk 1:12, Lk 4:14.18, Jn 1:33). Whereas the synoptists furnish only sparse teaching on the Holy Spirit (cf. e.g. Lk 11:13, Mk 3:28.29, Matt 10:20, 28:19), John supplies us with comprehensive instruction on the personality and work of the Third Person of the Trinity (e.g. Jn 3:5-8, 7:39, 14:16-18.26, 15:26, 16:7-15).[56]

Soon after Judas Iscariot had withdrawn into the night (Jn 13:30), Jesus started explaining to the remaining Eleven how in the future the Holy Spirit would be with them (cf.

Jn 14:16) and help them in various ways. As "the Spirit of truth" (Jn 14:17) he would be their teacher (Jn 14:26), in fact guide them "into all truth" (Jn 16:13) and bring to their remembrance everything Jesus had told them (Jn 14:26). He was going to convict of sin as well as convince of righteousness and judgement (Jn 16:8). Besides he would testify about Jesus (Jn 15:26) and glorify him (Jn 16:14). In essence the Holy Spirit would reveal to the disciples the fullness of Christ and keep their focus on him.

Of great relevance is the fact that Jesus stressed to the Eleven the role of the Spirit as "Counselor" (Jn 14:16.26, 15:26, 16:7). The Greek word employed in these instances, *parakletos*, literally meaning "called to one's side, i.e., to one's aid",[57] was in classical usage primarily a forensic term and stood for "the adviser of a defendant, or his representative and counsel in a court of law".[58] Actually then, Jesus let the disciples know that after his departure the Holy Spirit would draw near to represent his cause **first to them** and **then through them** to the world; the Holy Spirit would come to their assistance as advocate, comforter and exhorter.[59]

Likewise it is significant indeed that in Jn 14:16 Jesus spoke of "another Counselor". Once again recourse to the Greek taps additional insight, for *allos* ("another") expresses a mere numerical distinction and not a difference in quality,[60] designating a further specimen of the same kind. In other words, the Eleven received from Jesus, who himself is called *parakletos* in 1 Jn 2:1, the pledge that **the Holy Spirit would come to replace him**, "would take exactly the same place with them in the unseen realm of reality that Jesus had filled in the visible experience of the flesh . . . .",[61] to exercise a ministry on behalf of the disciples which in nature would be parallel to the one Jesus carried out while he was with them.

One remark which presumably stunned the disciples was Jesus' affirmation, "But I tell you the truth: It is for your good that I am going away . . . ." (Jn 16:7). How could it be advantageous and profitable for them to witness their beloved Master's departure? Jesus provided the answer, pointing out that the Spirit would be not just with them but in fact in them (Jn 14:17). His own temporary presence would soon be superseded by the Spirit's abiding presence in their hearts. Jesus' physical consociation, restricted through time and space, was about to be replaced by the universal divine consociation of the Holy Spirit. Mediated through the Spirit's with-ness, the disciples would be enabled to experience and draw on Jesus' with-ness, anywhere and any time.

This mediator role of the Holy Spirit would be absolutely crucial to the continuation and success of Jesus' mission in the future. Only in this way his promise, "surely I am with you always . . . ." (Matt 28:20) would become a living reality to them; only in this way the Spirit's abiding presence would release into their lives the supernatural qualifications to carry on and adequately represent Christ's global cause, to properly follow his example and to give capable leadership to the movement he had birthed.

Jesus did not hide from his friends that they were still in need of further instruction: "I have much more to say to you, more than you can now bear" (Jn 16:12). Yet he was confident the Holy Spirit would furnish the necessary training. True, the Spirit's taking over **would change the person of the mentor but not the programme**. There is no disparity in purpose amongst the members of the Trinity, and the Holy Spirit, Jesus informed the Eleven, "will not speak on his own; he will speak only what he hears . . . ." (Jn 16:13) and "will take from what is mine and make it known to you" (Jn 16:15). J. Denney put it well when he formulated, "the Spirit is the *alter ego* of Jesus".[62]

The Master's declaration, "I have come to bring fire on the earth, and how I wish it were already kindled!" (Lk 12:49) intimates **his yearning for a powerful worldwide movement.**

"The fire was there in Jesus's ministry", F.F. Bruce said, "but the earth had not yet caught fire".[63] Recognition that Jesus' expression 'bringing fire on the earth' can be interpreted as "revolutionizing the world",[64] strengthens the impression of Jesus' longing for a mighty outpouring of the Holy Spirit's power to set the world aflame for God.

With utmost wisdom and care **Jesus ahead of time fostered the leaders who would be needed** to channel such an arising movement according to divine purposes. Were they going to cope with the forthcoming challenges? Would the quality of their leadership performance reflect the excellence of the leadership development they had been privileged to enjoy? Of course, after Jesus' nearing departure they would be able to fall back on their past learning experiences under his mentorship. Yet this would not be their only source of assistance, because they would also be in a position to benefit from Jesus' future consociation facilitated through the Holy Spirit's abiding closeness. As Jesus' with-ness had shown itself totally sufficient in the past, so it would do in the days to come, provided the disciples fulfilled their part in maintaining an intimate relationship with Jesus. No wonder the Master explicitly challenged the Eleven to remain in him (cf. Jn 15:4-10).

After his resurrection Jesus supplied his disciples with further teaching on the kingdom of God (Acts 1:3) and defined their commission (cf. e.g. Matt 28:19.20, Mk 16:15). In addition he exerted distinctive effort to make them understand the power source which alone would qualify them for the accomplishment of this very commission (cf. Lk 24:49, Acts 1:8). He desired his followers to obtain the same blessing which had become precious to him, and announced **they needed what he himself had experienced as indispensable**. Hence he charged them to wait and not leave Jerusalem (Acts 1:4, Lk 24:49) until they had been endued with the Holy Spirit.

However, the release of this enabling and empowering divine with-ness into the lives and ministries of his followers had to be ushered in by prayer. "And I will ask the Father . . . ." (Jn 14:16), Jesus committed himself, and his final action before his ascension was to bless the disciples (Lk 24:50.51), who in turn also gave themselves to prayer (Acts 1:13.14).

With the ground thus prepared, on the day of Pentecost the disciples "were filled with the Holy Spirit" (Acts 2:4) and in this way equipped to embrace and embark upon the task for which Jesus had appointed them: to go into all the world as his witnesses.

3 Jesus Christ's Pursuit of Witness through the Twelve

In training his chosen disciples, Jesus Christ did not aspire to turn the Twelve into well-read scholars, shrewd theologians or brilliant orators. The function intended for them he specified by stating:

> ... On account of me you will stand before governors and kings as witnesses to them. (Mk 13:9)
> And you also will bear witness, because you have been with Me from the beginning. (Jn 15:27, NKJV)
> You are witnesses of these things. (Lk 24:48)
> ... and you will be my witnesses in Jerusalem, and in all Judea and Samaria, and to the ends of the earth. (Acts 1:8)

To secure the continuation of his mission, Jesus needed to raise up representatives of his cause. Hence he selected a group of followers who not because of intellectual capacity or academic background, but by reason of character and attitude, qualified to serve this very purpose. Their teachability, simplicity, honesty and zeal singled them out as uniquely eligible for becoming his spokesmen. What, however, was the distinct significance of Jesus' outlining their future role as witnesses?

3.1 His Desire for Authentic Witness

The original and typical environment in which **a witness** (Gk. *martys*) operates, is a court of law. *Martys* "is used in the classical sense for one who gives testimony on the basis of observation, or who in the legal sense is enlisted to confirm a state of affairs, an agreement".[1] The Old Testament provides a very instructive example in this regard through

Boaz, who made sure that he acquired a piece of property and Ruth as his wife-to-be in the presence of certain witnesses (cf. Ruth 4:1-11).

A witness recalls previous observations and describes what he has seen and heard (cf. Matt 11:4). As he shares a firsthand report from a personal standpoint, his testimony shows some autobiographical colouring. He is able to confirm facts or events because of his personal knowledge and experience of persons, circumstances and occurrences (cf. Jn 3:11).

When Jesus stated **his disciples would act as witnesses**, he foresaw them giving testimony because of their status as eye-witnesses of his life and ministry, his death and resurrection.[2] One must realize though, sheer cognizance of Jesus' words and deeds alone did not automatically qualify the disciples to bear effective testimony; there were others who observed Jesus' activities but never became his witnesses (cf. Lk 23:48).

Rather, what motivated his chosen men later on to engage in witnessing, was firstly **their intimate and intensive association with him** (cf. Jn 15:27, AV). While being with Jesus, they were impacted by his personality. They became his close friends and thus, in T.B. Kilpatrick's words, "capable of bearing witness, not merely to a series of His acts, but to His character and to His influence; having an understanding not merely of His doctrine, but of Himself".[3] Secondly, it was their awareness that they had been **specifically chosen** to testify (cf. Acts 10:41) **and even commanded** to do so (cf. Acts 10:42).

Jesus' announcement in Acts 1:8 contains the salient expression "my witnesses". Close examination of the original Greek text strongly suggests the view that with this phrase Luke was not so much aiming at conveying whose witnesses the disciples would be as on whose behalf they would testify. Therefore it seems more appropriate to render the English translation 'witnesses of me' or 'witnesses to me'.[4]

More was expected of the disciples than a mere handing down of their Master's ideas and teachings. According to M. Griffiths they "were to bear authentic testimony not only to what Jesus said, but also to what he did. He both commanded in words and indicated by example what they should say and do".[5] They were to testify of Jesus' historicity and reality, of their past and present experience of his ongoing with-ness. Their witness was not meant to be a presentation of a theological system, but a **pointing to Jesus as the Christ**. Just like the witness in a Greek law-court would unite "his mental powers with the person for whom he is testifying, in order to help him to victory, thus interceding more for the person than - in the strict sense - for the case",[6] a true disciple of the Master primarily focused on bearing witness to the person of Jesus.

He represented Jesus through word and deed, backed up his message by his life. The totality of his witness comprised **what he was, did and said for Christ**. The Master prepared his disciples, D.L. Guder wrote, "to be credible witnesses, people whose whole lives make their communication authentic and powerful", and added that the messengers and their message cannot be divided.[7]

This inseparability makes **the character of the witness a matter of crucial importance**. Scripture warns against false testimony (Ex 20:16, 23:1) and does not only state explicitly that God hates evil witness (Prov 6:16.19) but also points out its devastating effects (Prov 25:18; cf. 1 Kgs 21:8-14). On the other hand the trustworthy witness of a person of honesty and integrity is a great blessing (Prov 14:25, 25:13).

Relative to truthful witnessing neither originality nor inventiveness are desirable, they are actually obstructive. In this connection it is profitable to recollect such characteristics of rabbinic tutoring as were sketched earlier in section 1.3, where we saw how strong emphasis was placed on the student's incorporating the words and adopting the ways of his teacher. With-ness, both for information and formation, was intended to shape the *talmîd* into an authentic replica of his rabbi, endorsing by his life's witness the principle "a man's agent is equivalent to himself" (BT Berakoth 34b).

Following the rabbinic precedent **Jesus spared no effort in his mentoring of the Twelve to train them in a way that their future witness would be reliable and accurate.** Ever since he called them initially to observation, then to consociation and later also to imitation, his overruling coaching goal was to mould them into his likeness (cf. Lk 6:40). To be able to testify of him authentically, they first needed to get to know him intimately, to acquire in-depth knowledge of his thinking, actions and character; otherwise they would never develop the capacity to reflect his prototype correctly. Jesus' consociational discipling approach which drew particular attention to emulating his example, prepared his followers so thoroughly that - in resemblance to the rabbinic precept just quoted - he assured the Twelve, "He who receives you receives me . . . ." (Matt 10:40, cf. Jn 13:20) and the Seventy-Two, "He who listens to you listens to me . . . ." (Lk 10:16).

One of the pillars of Biblical law was the multiple witness principle. We read for instance in Deut 19:15: "One witness is not enough to convict a man accused of any crime or offense he may have committed. A matter must be established by the testimony of two or three witnesses." That is to say, for someone to be convicted for a capital crime, at least two witnesses (cf. also Num 35:30, Deut 17:6) had to give evidence before a decision could be taken. Circumstantial evidence alone was regarded as insufficient, eye-witnesses had to testify; neither was a written statement acceptable, the testimony had to be oral. Furthermore, L. Coenen remarked, "The idea of testimony or of a witness derived from uncertifiable subjective convictions is not known in the OT, and also has no place in Judaism."[8]

John the apostle applied this principle of multiple witness to the person of Jesus Christ, taking great care to consolidate Jesus' testimony for himself (Jn 8:14.18, 18:37) through the substantiating witness of the Father (Jn 5:37, 1 Jn 5:9.10), the Holy Spirit (Jn 15:26, cf. 1 Jn 5:6), the Scriptures (Jn 5:39, cf. 19:36.37), the works Jesus did (Jn 5:36, 10:25), John the Baptist (Jn 1:15.34, 3:26), disciples of Jesus (Jn 1:41, 6:69) and other observers (Jn 4:39.42, cf. 12:17).

Jesus himself referred repeatedly to the necessity of **multiple authentication** (Matt 18:16, Jn 5:31.32, 8:17.18) and particularly made the Eleven aware of its relevance for the validation of their witness to him. The full credibility of witnessing undertaken on his behalf, he let them know, would be established only through **the combination of their testimony with the additional testifying of the Holy Spirit** (cf. Jn 15:26.27).

The Spirit's contribution to the witnessing process is both vital and manifold. Fundamentally one must understand that, as J.R. van Pelt put it, "the effectiveness of the word of testimony is absolutely conditioned upon the operation of the Holy Spirit".[9] The latter is the chief agent in the procedure and only his enabling with-ness renders any disciple competent to carry out Christ's commission to be a witness.

It is the Holy Spirit who motivates to testify (cf. Acts 4:18-20) and grants boldness (cf. Acts 5:29). As "the Spirit of truth" (Jn 14:17) he normatively protects the testimony of Christ against oblivion (cf. Jn 14:26) and contamination (cf. Jn 16:13), reveals the very words appropriate for a specific situation (cf. Lk 12:12), serves as advocate of the truth communicated (cf. Jn 16:7-11) and energizes the message so that it pierces people's hearts (cf. Acts 2:37). Besides, the Spirit is the one who furnishes supernatural objective evidence to confirm the spoken testimony (cf. Mk 16:17.18, Acts 4:14.16).

Through their experience on the day of Pentecost, the Eleven were brought into a close and powerful co-operation with the Holy Spirit, whose authentication significance the apostles indicated soon afterwards in their response to the *Sanhedrin*, "We are witnesses of these things, and so is the Holy Spirit, whom God has given to those who obey him" (Acts 5:32).

With reference to witnessing **Jesus once again exemplified by his own life-style what he purposed his disciples to be.** The apostle John called him "the faithful and true witness" (Rev 3:14) and depicted him in his Gospel, to use J.M. Boice's terminology, as "the witness par excellence".[10] Whereas the Baptist witnessed to Jesus as the Messiah (cf. Jn 1:6-34), Jesus' own testimony was primarily directed towards his heavenly Father (cf. Jn 1:18), testifying of what he heard and saw in intimate relationship with him (cf. Jn 3:11.32, 5:19.20). In short, Jesus' life, words and works bore witness to the presence, character, purposes and power of God.

To equip his disciples for a similar role in the world at large, the Master subjected them to intensive mentoring based on association. Underlying his training endeavour was the specific interest to see them exercise that role as alternative witnesses.

3.2 His Desire for Alternative Witness

Without question the Teacher from Galilee stood out in bold relief against his Jewish contemporaries and that for a number of reasons.

His unique position was first of all due to **his godly life-style**, of which one dominant trait was his total submission to the will of God. Jesus gave himself willingly into accountability to God, made his Father's purposes the sole guidelines for his activities and practised joyful obedience.

Out of his deep love for God he established the maxim to please his heavenly Father in all his undertakings (cf. Jn 8:29). Besides he displayed complete trust in God; unbelief, as he observed it in some of his fellow-men, filled him with astonishment (Mk 6:6). The lifeline for his unswerving faith in God's character and Word was his persistent communion with him. In fact his ministry on earth was, as Luke's Gospel in particular brings to the fore, bathed in an atmosphere of prayer from beginning to end.

Secondly, there was **Jesus' remarkable authority over satanic influence** in its various forms. After he had vanquished the devil's climactic onslaught in the wilderness, the evil one "left him until an opportune time" (Lk 4:13). But whenever Satan threw out the net of temptation afresh,[11] Jesus overcame victoriously. By his ministry of healing and deliverance (cf. Lk 4:18) Jesus time and again conspicuously demonstrated the superiority of divine power over any satanic schemes, effects and bondages.

Moreover, Jesus deviated from rabbinic practice of the day in that **he freely associated with all strata of society**. His desire to seek out the lost made him go after all those in dire need of God, including the despised and outcast. He did not shy away from touching the leper or eating with tax collectors, he was actually accused of being a friend of publicans and sinners alike (cf. Matt 11:19). If Jesus crossed social barriers, he did the same with cultural boundaries, reaching out to persons of Samaritan, Roman and Greek backgrounds as well.

Another divergent feature of the Master was **his attitude towards women**. His largely itinerant ministry mode brought him into contact with a broad spectrum of people. One especially telling incident was his encounter with the Samaritan woman at the well, laid out in the fourth chapter of John's Gospel with uncommon detail. If the fact that Jesus travelled through Samaria already defied customary Jewish thinking (cf. v. 9), the disciples were further amazed to find their Master conversing with a woman in public (cf. v. 27). At a time when ladies were neither allowed to testify as witnesses in court nor get actively involved in the synagogue,[12] when the rabbis thoroughly resisted the *Torah* being taught to women,[13] and one out of their midst, Jose b. Johanan, warned, "talk not much with womankind" (M Aboth 1,5), the Master contravened cultural and social taboos in order to meet a Samaritan woman's spiritual needs. As if this were not enough, in Jerusalem he came to the defence of an adulteress against her rabbinic and Pharisaic accusers (cf. Jn 8:3-11). Indeed he went so far as to welcome females into the wider circle of his followers (cf. Lk 8:1-3, Mk 15:40.41), a step without any precedent among contemporary Jewish teachers.[14]

Last but not least, there was **Jesus' teaching** which shattered the mould of traditional views and expectations. More than any other Gospel portion, the Sermon on the Mount (Matt 5 to 7) contains a number of essential principles which were to delineate the alternative kingdom life-style of God's people, to characterize the divine counterculture destined to oppose, invade and overcome the kingdom of darkness. As representatives of this alternative culture, Jesus taught, his disciples should e.g. be meek (5:5) and pure in heart (5:8), function as peacemakers (5:9), love their enemies (5:44) and refrain from judging others (7:1); they ought to avoid being ostentatious in their spirituality (6:1-6.16), put God's concerns first (6:33), do his will (7:21) and lay up treasures in heaven (6:20). In addition, the Master employed a series of contrastive statements to mirror the distinctive nature of the kingdom of God against worldly precepts and standards,[15] underlining in the outreach instructions for his chosen protégés, "Whoever finds his life will lose it, and whoever loses his life for my sake will find it" (Matt 10:39). Finally, Jesus' admonition to the Twelve,

"Not so with you" (Mk 10:43), marked his servanthood-oriented concept of spiritual leadership as diametrically opposed to the preoccupation with position and dominance so typical of certain secular leadership perspectives.

The observations presented up to this point elucidate that Jesus Christ, while moving among men, exemplified an alternative witness. He led a holy life, i.e. a life of separation from sin, set apart unto God. The testimony of his godly life-style, entailing a standing accusation against all unholiness around him, was so powerful that some people could not bear his presence in their midst (cf. Matt 8:34). Jesus kept God's moral perfection as the desired norm for human living before his eyes and summoned his disciples to do the same (cf. Matt 5:48). His exemplification of an alternative witness was meant to stimulate his disciples' imitation; as he encapsulated succinctly in his high priestly prayer, he wished them to be in the world but nevertheless not of the world (Jn 17:11.14.16). For their practice of an alternative witnessing mode of life, the Master gave his followers various directives. Of those, three challenging and two affirming pronouncements will be briefly considered.

Jesus commanded his disciples to **love** one another (Jn 13:34, 15:17). They were familiar with the obligation to love others (cf. Matt 22:39) but he introduced a new emphasis through the requirement that they were to love one another as he had loved them (Jn 15:12), viz. unselfishly, unconditionally and sacrificially. The movement he initiated through his consociational discipling of the Twelve, would only be able to survive and grow by means of sound relationships based on love. And this mutual love, Jesus asserted, would be the hallmark of his disciples before all the world (Jn 13:35).

A further challenge was implied in his longing to see his followers live in **unity** (cf. Jn 17:21), that inner harmony which in final regard could only be brought about by the

Holy Spirit's gracious assistance. Yet the disciples on their part would have to work at preserving this unity, for example through taking the first step to restore broken relationships (cf. Matt 5:23.24) and through extending forgiveness (cf. Matt 6:12, Mk 11:25). Besides, the experience of corporate oneness would presuppose individual humility (cf. Matt 11:29). Complete unity amongst his disciples, the Master underscored, would certify to the world the divine commission he had received from his Father (Jn 17:23).

During the Last Supper discourse, Jesus told his friends he selected and appointed them to bear **fruit** (Jn 15:16). Previously he had warned against producing bad fruit (cf. Matt 7:17-19) or none at all (cf. Matt 25:24-30). Now he challenged them to bear much and lasting fruit (Jn 15:8.16). If they did, manifesting the fruit of the Holy Spirit[16] in their lives, doing good like their Master (cf. Acts 10:38) and acting as "fishers of men" (Matt 4:19), they would prove themselves as his true disciples (Jn 15:8).

At quite an early stage of their association, Jesus voiced his confidence in the disciples with the affirmation, "You are the salt of the earth" (Matt 5:13). **Salt** possesses the power to lend flavour, halt corruption, purify and fertilize. It makes its absence or presence known, influences quietly, takes effect as it is dispersed, exerts a potent impact. In other words, Jesus commented on the powerful and cardinal roles the disciples were to play in society, including the function, to borrow R.V.G. Tasker's phrase,[17] of "a moral disinfectant" among sinful and therefore perishing mankind (cf. Jn 3:16).

"You are the light of the world" (Matt 5:14), Jesus declared, assuring his disciples once more of his trust in them as change agents. In the same manner as **light** contrasts darkness, the disciples were going to personify an alternative holy witness in an unholy environment. As light dispels the dark, renders visible, guides, warns of danger and gives life, so Jesus anticipated his followers to have a similarly vital influence on the world around them. John's Gospel makes repeated reference to the dualism of light and darkness,[18] and the apostle introduces Jesus as the light that came into the world (cf. Jn 1:8.9, 3:19). Against the backdrop of the Master's self-disclosure, "I am the light of the world" (Jn 8:12, 9:5), his affirming word to the disciples in Matt 5:14 projected their reflecting him as the real source of light. S. Briscoe's assertion, "disciples prove they are disciples by the way their lives show something of the characteristics of Christ Himself, as His life shines through theirs",[19] has been true ever since the first disciples were assigned to serve as the Master's substitutes on earth. Further still, Jesus' declaration reiterated his ardent interest in their emulating his example; W. Barclay verbalized it this way: "When Jesus commanded His followers to be the lights of the world, He demanded nothing less than that they should be like Himself".[20] No doubt, as Christlike lights dispelling the surrounding darkness, they were inevitably going to present an alternative witness and impact the world for God.

3.3 His Desire for Worldwide Witness

The profound truth accentuated by D.J. Bosch, "God is a missionary God....",[21] enunciates a core element of Biblical revelation. In Genesis 12:2.3 God gave Abraham this far-reaching promise:

> I will make you into a great nation and I will bless you; I will make your name great, and you will be a blessing. I will bless those who bless you, and whoever curses you I will curse; and all peoples on earth will be blessed through you.

Ever since God announced to Abraham that he would first bless him and then make him a blessing to all peoples, God's global concern surfaced time and again in the Old Testament. Compelling Scriptural evidence[22] refutes the erroneous tendency to regard God's missionary interest as a solely New Testament prerogative. One would have to agree with W.G. Scroggie's conviction that "The Bible is essentially a missionary book" and that "the missionary purpose dominates revelation".[23]

As a missionary God, the Creator not only sent his Word but also his Son (Jn 3:16.17). The Gospels, especially the fourth, make us realize **Jesus' deep consciousness of doing his work among men as God's emissary**; over and over again he alluded to the fact that his Father sent him (e.g. Matt 10:40, Mk 9:37, Lk 4:18, 10:16, Jn 5:23.24.30.36-38).[24] While Jesus left no doubt that his mission was primarily geared towards his Jewish fellow-men (Matt 15:24), he also called attention to its worldwide relevance and ramifications.

Marking out the extent of the divine assignment he had received and embarked upon, Jesus spoke repeatedly of the world (e.g. Matt 13:38, 24:14, Mk 14:9, Jn 6:33, 12:46.47, 17:21.23). On other occasions he linked his undertaking on earth with the future destiny of the nations (e.g. Mk 13:10, Lk 21:25, Matt 25:32). Did the Master's communication already challenge his disciples to develop **a global perspective**, then his mode of operation did so no less.

With the objective before him to establish a worldwide witness, Jesus did not carry out his activities in seclusion. He differed in this respect significantly from his rabbinic contemporary Johanan b. Zakkai, who, before he took up teaching in Jerusalem, spent eighteen years in the Galilean village of 'Arav (not far from Nazareth) with just one *talmîd* during that time.[25] **Jesus, in order to procure a broad impact for his endeavours, carefully selected his ministry environment** and laboured to a large extent under the eyes of the public. He preached in numerous local synagogues (Mk 1:39) and could later on be found daily teaching varying audiences at the Temple (Lk 19:47). In the open air he addressed big crowds, with Luke even speaking of "an innumerable multitude of people" treading on one another (12:1, AV).

Of strategic relevance, moreover, was the fact that for an extended period of time the Master made densely populated Galilee his primary field of operation and, in particular, the town of Capernaum on the northwestern shore of the Sea of Galilee his 'headquarters'. The move from Nazareth to Capernaum (Matt 4:13), which in the Scriptures became known as "his own town" (Matt 9:1), can not merely be attributed to the fact that people in Nazareth did not honour Jesus (cf. Matt 13:54-57). More important, Capernaum was situated in the region of Zebulun and Naphtali, singled out as an area of divine promise (cf. Matt 4:14-16). Besides, the town was a commercial centre on the major trade route connecting Alexandria with Damascus, and its convenient lakeside position rendered it easy to reach surrounding areas by ship. From the incident recorded in Matt 8:5-13 we may infer that Capernaum also accommodated a detachment of Roman soldiers, an opportunity for cross-cultural outreach which Jesus welcomed in his contact with the centurion.

Jesus ministered throughout Galilee (Matt 4:23), his itinerant approach, however, took him to Judea, Samaria, Perea, the Decapolis and Phoenicia as well. True, he consciously prioritized his labours on the people of Israel and conspicuously avoided working in Hellenistic towns, like Sepphoris and Tiberias for instance. Yet on the other hand, it seems, **the remarkable radius of his activities** indicated both the absence of any ethnocentric bias on his part and his openness for involvement across cultural barriers, should the Holy Spirit direct him that way (cf. e.g. Jn 4:4-26, Matt 15:21-28).

Through his exemplary course of action and his utterances

Jesus nurtured in the Twelve an increasing awareness that the mission he pursued had a worldwide dimension and they were meant to play a crucial part in its continued fulfillment. When he encouraged them with the affirmation that they were the light of the world (Matt 5:14), he simultaneously **placed upon them the same charge he was under.** As J.O. Sanders intimated, "in these pregnant words, the Lord of the harvest issued His Galilean call to world-wide witness. Their sphere of witness was to be nothing less than 'the world' ".[26]

Utmost clarity and emphasis characterize five postresurrection statements with which the Master comprehensively defined the worldwide witnessing assignment for which he had prepared his disciples. Closer examination brings into focus how **each of these five versions of the Great Commission carried a different accent** and thus shed additional light on the nature of the task Jesus committed to his friends.

Mk 16:15 reads:

> He said to them, "Go into all the world and preach the good news to all creation".

The Master's words made unmistakably clear the Great Commission was neither a mere human idea nor an optional project, but **a divine command** to be obeyed. The disciples were expected to take the initiative in delivering this charge of universal scope by way of **evangelism**, proclaiming the glad tidings of God's love for mankind to **every individual** on earth.

Additional understanding can be gained from Lk 24:46-48:

> He told them, "This is what is written: The Christ will suffer and rise from the dead on the third day, and repentance and forgiveness of sins will be preached in his name to all nations, beginning at Jerusalem. You

> are witnesses of these things".

Characteristically, this rendering of the Great Commission highlighted **the content of the message** the disciples would share. At the same time Jesus laid stress on their **role as witnesses** and let them know their global testimony would have its starting-point at Jerusalem.

In Acts 1:8 the third evangelist quoted Jesus further:

> But you will receive power when the Holy Spirit comes on you; and you will be my witnesses in Jerusalem, and in all Judea and Samaria, and to the ends of the earth.

Here Jesus gave his friends the essential promise of the Holy Spirit's coming, thus drawing their attention to **the indispensable power source** for the accomplishment of their task. This promise was "coupled with the setting forth of an action plan, with quite specific instruction as to its procedure and purpose".[27] Moreover he addressed the disciples' function as **witnesses of himself** and the worldwide as well as **cross-cultural span of their future labours**.

Jn 20:21 contains the fourth statement:

> Again Jesus said, "Peace be with you! As the Father has sent me, I am sending you".

Implied was not alone the fact that Jesus was commissioned by his Father, and now he in turn commissioned his followers. As the underlying Greek wording enables us to perceive more clearly,[28] the Master furthermore emphasized **the analogous manner in which the disciples were to continue the mission he had begun**. In other words, they were reminded of the necessity to imitate his example in their ministry approach (cf. Jn 13:15; 14:12).

Finally, there is Matt 28:18-20 to be considered:

> Then Jesus came to them and said, "All authority in heaven and on earth has been given to me. Therefore go and make disciples of all nations, baptizing them in the name of the Father and of the Son and of the Holy Spirit, and teaching them to obey everything I have commanded you. And surely I am with you always, to the very end of the age".

Once again a closer look at the original Greek is profitable, because there we discover the main verb for verses 19 and 20a is the imperative form *matheteusate* ('make disciples'). Subservient to this leading verb are three adverbial participles, viz. *poreuthentes* ('going'), *baptizontes* ('baptizing') and *didaskontes* ('teaching'). From this we can gather that actually Jesus commanded his followers to engage, as they were going out, in the making of disciples; he also told them baptizing and teaching would be fundamental to this very process. Hence the fifth version of the Great Commission at its core was not a challenge for the disciples to go into all the world,[29] but rather voiced their **obligation to make disciples** wherever they went. Divergent from the other evangelists Matthew alone - through "Therefore" in verse 19 - connected the commissioning of the disciples to Jesus' universal authority and concluded the delineation of the Master's strategy for reaching the world with the latter's reassuring **promise of his permanent with-ness**.

On comparing the closing portion of Matthew's Gospel with the outreach instructions given in Matt 10:5-8, two striking differences spring to the eye. Firstly, at that time the Twelve were directed to limit their efforts to their Jewish fellow-men. Don Richardson suggested the explanation, "Jesus most likely placed this temporary restriction upon His disciples, . . . because His disciples were still spiritually and mentally unprepared to undertake a cross-cultural mission".[30] Now, shortly before the Master's ascension, **they were**

summoned to target all peoples. Secondly, earlier on the Twelve were not entrusted with the responsibility of making disciples. Still under intensive training themselves, they were too wanting both in adequate understanding and sufficing personal experience of consociational discipling to take on a leading role in such a procedure. Now, however, **Jesus charged them to focus on reproduction and multiplication** through disciple-making. "Jesus knew that any movement had to have effective leaders in order to grow and spread to the entire world", M. Rush remarked.[31] So in view of his global intentions, Jesus commanded his followers to prioritize on the discipling of believers unto leadership, that all nations might be affected for God by the divine movement soon to burst forth through the empowering of the Holy Spirit.

3.4 His Desire for Empowered Witness

After Jesus was glorified, God sent the promised Holy Spirit (cf. Jn 7:39, 14:26). On the day of Pentecost Jesus' followers were "clothed with power from on high" (Lk 24:49), a monumental experience which absolutely revolutionized their lives.

They, who formerly had been selfish, weak of faith, fearful and unstable, were now turned into loving, trusting, courageous and effective achievers for God. In particular, they in new measure began to radiate Jesus' presence, to reflect his likeness. "By taking permanent hold of the waiting disciples as he had taken hold of Jesus," J.V. Taylor explained, "the Holy Spirit effected a kind of extension of the incarnation, bringing them into everything that could be available to them in Christ",[32] Bestowing on them, as A.B. Bruce specified, "enlightenment of mind, enlargement of heart, sanctification of their faculties, and transformation of their characters",[33] **the Holy Spirit equipped them to perform** the task for which Jesus had prepared them through **consociational discipling.**

Earlier on the Master had announced the Holy Spirit would <u>bear</u> witness of him, the disciples though would <u>be</u> his witnesses (Jn 15:26, Acts 1:8). Since their Pentecostal enduement this witnessing role became a prominent feature of their newly gained spiritual stature. Not that the Third Person of the Trinity did away with their respective God-given individuality, but he filled their being in such a way that henceforth the similitude of their Master shone unmistakably through their life-style and ministry (cf. Acts 4:13).

No wonder the standard designation for the men who had been with Jesus underwent a significant change as well. While they were learning in association with him, they were commonly referred to as 'disciples'; in the book of Acts, however, any member of the original core group is seen as an 'apostle', meaning "one sent as a messenger or agent, the bearer of a commission".[34] Enabled through the Holy Spirit's advent to tap into boundless divine resources providing them with new physical, intellectual, moral and spiritual power, the apostles moved out as their Master's delegates to continue and extend his mission.

Among these freshly endued witnesses **no one personified and utilized the manifold assets of the Spirit's gracious visitation more prominently and powerfully than Simon Peter.** He hailed from Bethsaida (Jn 1:44) and was married (cf. Mk 1:30). A typical Galilean, he was devout, energetic and brave, at the same time tending to be tempestuous. In fact his character showed not only complex but even conflicting traits: now he was full of faith (cf. Matt 14:28.29), then full of fear (cf. Matt 14:30); at one time he appeared determined (cf. Jn 18:10), at another weak-willed (cf. Matt 26:40.43.45); one moment he spoke as a herald of divine revelation (cf. Matt 16:17), the next as a mouthpiece of Satan (cf. Matt 16:23). J.O. Sanders appraised so aptly when he wrote, "Peter's vivid personality, forthright utterances and deep devotion combine with the greatness of his strength and the magnitude of his mistakes to make him an ideal test-case for the methods of the Master".[35]

Jesus discerned in Simon extraordinary leadership potential. Although the latter exhibited a volatile disposition at the beginning of their association, Jesus expressed already right then his confidence in the fisherman's future development, giving him the additional name of *Cephas,* which is the Aramaic equivalent of the Greek *Peter,* denoting 'rock' (cf. Jn 1:42, Mk 3:16). Along the way Jesus encouraged him further (cf. Matt 16:17-19, Lk 22:32) and concentrated more time and effort on Simon's coaching for subsequent leadership responsibility than on any other member of the core group.

With the unique grooming attention focused on Peter, Jesus' disappointment must have been the greater when the fisherman denied three times that he had shared in the privilege of the Master's with-ness, enforcing his denial even with an oath and curses (Matt 26:69-74). All the more amazing was Jesus' loving and considerate response to Simon's failure, granting his repentant friend the opportunity to settle this sad shortcoming in private, before only afterwards appearing to the other ten disciples (Lk 24:34, 1 Cor 15:5).

As a result of being filled with the Holy Spirit at Pentecost (cf. Acts 2:1-4), Peter's latent leadership capacity was fully released and brought to the fore. With his personality ignited through the Spirit's fire (cf. Matt 3:11), **his alternative lifestyle** (cf. Acts 4:19.20, 5:29) made him like a bright light to the world around him. Moreover, **the words of his testimony** took immense effect upon his listeners (cf. Acts 2:37), and he seems not to have skipped any favourable occasion to impress upon his audience the authenticating nature of the apostles' communication on behalf of the one who had commissioned them as his messengers:

> ... we are all witnesses of the fact. (Acts 2:32)
> ... We are witnesses of this. (Acts 3:15)
> For we cannot help speaking about what we have seen and heard. (Acts 4:20)
> We are witnesses of these things .... (Acts 5:32)
> We are witnesses of everything he did .... (Acts 10:39)
> ... by witnesses whom God had already chosen - by us who ate and drank with him after he rose from the dead. He commanded us ... to testify .... (Acts 10:41.42)

These Scriptures reveal how deeply Jesus' desire to see his disciples operate as his witnesses had permeated their thinking and ministry involvement. Especially the closing statement of Paul's words in Acts 13:31, "and for many days he was seen by those who had traveled with him from Galilee to Jerusalem. They are now his witnesses to our people", furnished striking evidence that the apostles did exactly what Jesus had prepared and proclaimed them to do, thus proving that with them he reached the very goal he had set for his mentoring efforts.

It was J. Stalker who expressed the insight, "No one will have power with men who has not power with God for men ...."[36] On studying the activities of the apostle Peter, one comes away with the impression he was guided by a kindred conviction, for undoubtedly he was a man of **prayer**. He could be found entering the Temple precincts at the afternoon time of prayer (Acts 3:1). In connection with the arising need in the Early Church to appoint assistants for the covering of certain responsibilities, Simon emphasized the apostles' two highest priorities, viz. "prayer and the ministry of the word" (Acts 6:4). God's direction for him to engage in cross-cultural ministry in Cornelius' home was ascertained while praying (cf. Acts 10:9-23). The fact that after one prayer meeting, which Peter was part of, the ground shook and a fresh filling with the Holy Spirit occurred (Acts 4:31), served as a memorable intimation of the powerful prayer atmosphere he lived in.

More frequently the spiritual might generated and maintained through prayer (cf. Acts 4:30) became visible in supernatural manifestations attached to Peter's ministry. The book of Acts reports a situation in which he employed words of knowledge (cf. 5:1-10), he was God's tool for the healing of Aeneas (9:33.34) and of a cripple (3:1-8). The extraordinary anointing resting upon Peter was such that "people brought the sick into the streets and laid them on beds and mats so that at least Peter's shadow might fall on some of them as he passed by" (5:15). God further glorified himself by bringing Tabitha back to life in answer to Simon's praying (9:36-41).

God's confirmation through **the miraculous** was of vital significance for the reception of Peter's witness. The divine with-ness so obviously accompanying his work procured attention (Acts 3:11.12), established indisputable evidence (Acts 4:14.16), helped induce faith (cf. Acts 9:35.42), caused people to praise God (Acts 3:8.9, 4:21) and thwarted satanic interference (cf. Acts 5:3).

One recurrent feature of Peter's ministry approach calls for special comment. We observe he taught in the name of Jesus (cf. Acts 5:28), declared men could be saved by that name alone (Acts 4:12), spoke about forgiveness through Jesus' name (Acts 10:43), ordered baptism in the same name (Acts 10:48) and commanded healing by faith in Christ's name (Acts 3:6.16). Sent out by the Master as his messenger, representing his cause and witnessing on his behalf, Peter was only too aware he operated with delegated authority (cf. Lk 9:1, Matt 28:18.19) and with inherited power (cf. Jn 14:26, Acts 1:8). He understood the secret to his effectiveness for God to lie in Jesus' permanent enabling with-ness, which the latter had promised to the Eleven before his ascension and which now through Pentecost had become such a mighty reality for all of them.

Under the energizing influence of the Holy Spirit **the global harvest force Jesus had initiated through his selection and discipling of the Twelve broke forth as a visible movement**, gaining momentum at breath-taking speed. In response to Simon Peter's anointed message on the day of Pentecost about 3,000 new believers were won (Acts 2:41), and God kept on adding to them every day (Acts 2:47). Quite soon the number of men who had decided to follow Jesus Christ soared to approximately 5,000 (Acts 4:4). The movement of the Way, as it became known,[37] broadened further in Jerusalem (Acts 5:14, 6:1.7), spilled over into Judea, Samaria as well as Galilee (Acts 9:31) and spread to Damascus (Acts 9:19), Phoenicia, Cyprus and Antioch (Acts 11:19). It was there that Jesus Christ's disciples were named Christians for the first time (Acts 11:26).

The filling with the Holy Spirit[38] preserved the inner dynamic and secured the outer expansion of the developing movement. As Jesus had been endued with divine power at his baptism and then bequeathed the Holy Spirit's anointing on his followers (cf. Acts 2:33), so members of the Way movement acted likewise (cf. Acts 8:14-17, 9:17). Doing so they passed on, as it were, not merely a baton but a torch, kindling reproduction and multiplication of Christlike witness wherever they went.

*

Thus the stage was set for the further expansion of the Way movement into the world at large. God's choice instrument to take up that challenge was Saul of Tarsus. His Jewish background, theological training under the famous rabbi

Gamaliel, his Roman citizenship, his conversance with the Greek culture and language, his zeal, determination and courage fitted him uniquely for this awesome task. Converted after a dramatic encounter with the risen Christ on the road to Damascus (Acts 9:3-6), called to apostleship (Ro 1:1, cf. Acts 9:15) and filled with the Holy Spirit (cf. Acts 9:17), he emerged as the unsurpassed pioneer missionary amongst first century Gentiles.

In the first part of this publication we reflected upon association as a fundamental principle in Jesus' discipling of the Twelve. Proceeding now to consider in the second part certain missiological implications of this investigation, special attention must be reserved for the apostle Paul's ministry, as he was the first to on a large scale apply Jesus Christ's global strategy and his consociational discipling approach in particular within cross-cultural context.

II

MISSIOLOGICAL IMPLICATIONS:

ASSOCIATION AS AN INDISPENSABLE PRINCIPLE FOR ALL DISCIPLING EFFORTS

"As we aim at being fruitful, we find our need of intelligent understanding of the Divine methods, in order that we may apply them in our own work."

J. Hudson Taylor *

4 Jesus Christ's With-ness Approach as Prototype

In Matt 12:30 Jesus declared: "He who is not with me is against me, and he who does not gather with me scatters." This sobering statement brings to light that in mission work, as in any other sphere of spiritual endeavour, there is no room for a 'neutral' strategy; either our efforts serve the purposes of God or they promote the interests of the powers of darkness. At the same time, Jesus' words are a solemn warning against the fateful proneness to plan and execute missionary activities solely on the basis of human striving. It was J. Hudson Taylor, founder of the China Inland Mission, who raised the question of concern: "Has not the failure of many of our efforts been due to our attempting to do God's work in man's way - aye, and sometimes even in the devil's way?"[1]

Looking towards the future of mission work in general and of the development of leaders in particular, we have to acknowledge that we will only be able to achieve significant progress, if our strategies have been sharpened through proper orientation gained from the past. "What the modern missionary movement needs above everything else," J.H. Kane challenged, "is to get back to the missionary methods of the early church."[2] Actually we must go back even one step further and first seek to grasp **the nature and significance of Jesus Christ's supreme paradigm for missions**. Without question no New Testament writer helped us more to fathom the relevance and missiological implications of Jesus' prototype than the apostle Paul, who - as trailblazer of the cross-cultural Christian enterprise - both interpreted and implemented the principles of the Master's consociational discipling model.

Regarding Paul's approach to leadership development it is noteworthy that the apostle, notwithstanding his intellectual brilliance and extraordinary theological qualification, did not assume any liberty to design a pattern of his own, instead he faithfully followed the Master's precedent. Consequently, in our desire to shed additional light on the applicability of Jesus' method in cross-cultural settings, we will combine the further analysis of salient traits of his technique with supplementary insights derived from Paul's ministry and writings.

4.1 Jesus Christ as the Motivation

Absolutely foundational to Jesus' relationship with God was the reality of his heavenly Father's love for him. Not only was it publicly and objectively affirmed on the occasions of his baptism (Matt 3:17) and transfiguration (Matt 17:5), but also subjectively Jesus was deeply conscious of his Father's affectionate, tender and caring commitment to him (cf. Jn 5:20, 10:17, 15:9, 17:24.26). This awareness imbued Jesus with a profound sense of acceptance, identity, assurance and security.

The divine love thus bestowed on him met with a wholehearted loving response from his side (cf. Jn 14:31). Once a certain scribe inquired which of all the commandments the Teacher from Nazareth considered the most relevant:

> "The most important one," answered Jesus, "is this: 'Hear, O Israel, the Lord our God, the Lord is one. Love the Lord your God with all your heart and with all your soul and with all your mind and with all your strength.' The second is this: 'Love your neighbor as yourself.' There is no commandment greater than these." (Mk 12:29-31)

Without doubt the immediacy with which Jesus supplied his initial reply in form of a quote from the *Shema*, illustrated afresh his familiarity with and adherence to traditional Jewish thinking. More important though, "the first and greatest commandment" as Matthew's parallel text labelled it (22:38), tersely comprised the principal focus of Jesus' outlook, attitude and actions. By the totality of his life **he uniquely exemplified what it means to love God with one's whole being**.

During the Last Supper discourse Jesus told the Eleven: "As the Father has loved me, so have I loved you . . . ." (Jn 15:9). That is to say, he made his personal experience of God's love the standard for the manner in which he expressed his benevolent concern for his trainees. His love for them was active: he protected, instructed, encouraged and served them; he modelled, interceded and sacrificed for them. The selfless and compassionate love which he extended towards the disciples, motivated them to associate with him, dispelled their fears, set them free to be themselves, nurtured their self-esteem, inspired trust, opened up a way for them to come into their own in God. No wonder that under such caring tutelage the learning process the Master wished his protégés to undergo proved not a laborious ordeal, but, on the contrary, a joyful adventure.

While Jesus placed love for God as paramount requirement before his contemporaries (cf. Matt 22:37.38), he added to his demand a new element with reference to the Twelve: "Anyone who loves his father or mother more than me is not worthy of me; anyone who loves his son or daughter more than me is not worthy of me" (Matt 10:37). In other words, **next to their prime love for God, Jesus claimed their higher affection and radical commitment for himself**.

This really should not evoke surprise. "Discipleship is determined by the relation to Christ himself . . . .", D.J. Bosch emphasized.[3] And we do well to remember that ever since Jesus challenged potential disciples with the words 'follow me', he did not invite them to just link up with a certain system of thought or project, but to commit themselves to him as a person; he did not call them to a mere programme but into a life-transforming relationship.[4]

Apart from impressing the familiar greatest commandment on his disciples' minds, Jesus also faced them with a fresh charge: "A new command I give you: Love one another. As I have loved you, so you must love one another" (Jn 13:34, cf. 15:12). Unquestionably the thought that they were to love others was not new to the eleven Galileans. For one, the *Torah* had already outlined that moral obligation clearly (cf. Lev 19:18.33, Deut 10:19). Besides, Jesus had addressed the issue repeatedly in his teaching, not least through the graphic parable of the good Samaritan (Lk 10:25-37).

What was new to the disciples, however, was the command that they should love each other with the quality of love Jesus had exhibited towards them. Just as the Father's love for the Son had become the model for the Son's love for his disciples (Jn 15:9), so the Son now charged his disciples to take his love for them as the model for their love for each other (Jn 13:34). This train of thought prompts the formulation of a cardinal leadership development principle: From a Biblical perspective, **any mentor is to mirror in his relation to his mentorees the kind of love which God displayed towards his Son and which the latter in turn exemplified in his coaching of the Twelve; the same type of love is to govern also the mentorees' interrelation.**

Of course the question arises what specifically constitutes this love. The Greek term used in the New Testament to denote keen benevolent concern for someone else's welfare is the word *agape*. According to W. Günther and H.-G. Link *agape* has been recorded only once outside the Scriptures.[5] The unique quality of love signified by *agape* can be looked upon as the distinctive feature of all genuine followers of

Jesus Christ (cf. Jn 13:35).

The apostle Paul accentuated *agape* as the core of the Christian life-style (cf. Col 3:14, Eph 5:2, 1 Cor 16:14) and defined in 1 Cor 13:4-7 with greater detail than any other Bible passage the character of true love:

> Love is patient, love is kind. It does not envy, it does not boast, it is not proud. It is not rude, it is not self-seeking, it is not easily angered, it keeps no record of wrongs. Love does not delight in evil but rejoices with the truth. It always protects, always trusts, always hopes, always perseveres.

Each of these characteristics Jesus Christ personified in consummate fashion. Therefore it appears adequate and profitable to concur with T. Campolo's working definition that "love is a decision to do for the other person what Jesus would do for that person if He were in your place."[6]

Both God's and Jesus Christ's love for mankind Paul saw especially demonstrated in God's sending of his Son (cf. Gal 4:4) and the Son's dying on the cross (cf. Rom 5:8). A revelation of this sacrificial divine love, totally unmerited by man, should call forth as natural response an attitude of love towards the Godhead as well as one's fellow-men. *Agape*, however, cannot be produced by man himself, it is **not a human creation but a divine donation**, for "God has poured out his love into our hearts by the Holy Spirit, whom he has given us" (Rom 5:5). Through the Spirit's mediator role we are enabled to draw on God's supernatural resources, to partake of his divine love; Gal 5:22 names love first among the components of the fruit of the Spirit.

Inherent in *agape* emanating from the Trinity is a directive influence which the apostle Paul articulated when he pointed out that "Christ's love compels us . . . ." (2 Cor 5:14). Alternative translations of the verb *synecho* enhance our understanding of the phrase as setting forth that the love of Christ captivates, controls, constrains and urges forward.

Put differently, **Christ's love exercises both a motivating and a regulating function**, it seeks to keep us within the orbit of God's purposes.

Time and again in the course of mission history, individuals have followed God's call to the ends of the earth and given themselves to dedicated service, because the love of Christ mastered them. W.G. Blaikie closed his biography of David Livingstone, the well-known missionary and explorer, with the words, "... it was the love of Christ that constrained him to live and die for Africa".[7] And J. Hudson Taylor underlined, "One thing, and one only, will carry men through all, and make and keep them successful; the LOVE OF CHRIST, constraining and sustaining, is the only adequate power."[8]

Reflecting further upon Paul's concept of "Christ's love", it is significant to realize that it can be understood as designating concurrently Christ as the subject as well as object of this love;[9] to put it differently, the expression combines the aspects of Christ's love for us (cf. Rom 8:35) and of our love for Christ (cf. 1 Cor 16:22).

It is in this merger of love received and love reciprocated (cf. 1 Jn 4:19) that all missionary involvement, leadership development included, should find **its rightful motivation**. His gratitude for the divine love personally experienced, linked with the divine *agape* transmitted into his heart through the Holy Spirit, ought to urge the missionary forward to devote himself to God for self-denying service among men. Neither the awareness of man's neediness and lostness nor the challenge of obedience to the Great Commission represent the supreme motivation for missions, but rather the thankful response of fervent love to the incomparable *agape* first shown in God's sending of his Son, who laid down his life on the cross as the Saviour for mankind. There is a need to be mindful that our engagement for the fulfillment of God's worldwide purposes is always a product of and not a substitute for our love for Christ; Jesus must first become the focus of our affection before he becomes the focus of our commitment.

Loving devotion to Jesus Christ secures **a sacrificial motivation**, too. The founder of the Heart of Africa Mission, Charles T. Studd, became known for his motto: "If Jesus Christ be God and died for me, then no sacrifice can be too great for me to make for Him."[10] James Chalmers, missionary pioneer to the South Pacific, declared he earnestly desired "to spend and be spent among the heathen."[11] Of Toyohiko Kagawa, the outstanding Japanese Christian and social reformer, his biographer W. Axling recorded: "The love of Christ and a passion to befriend the poor and make Jesus' way of life a solvent of the problem of poverty led Kagawa to dedicate his life to the slums."[12]

Finally, true love for Christ also provides **a burning motivation**. Count Zinzendorf, the leading figure in the Moravian Revival of 1727, affirmed: "I have one passion - it is He, and He alone."[13] About James Gilmour, pioneer to Mongolia, we read that "his soul was aflame with love to the Saviour and to the perishing heathen."[14] "Had I a thousand lives", J. Hudson Taylor disclosed, "China should claim every one. No, not China, but Christ! Can we do too much for Him? Can we do enough for such a Saviour?"[15]

Relative to the proper motivational basis for mentoring in the context of missions, we do well to heed the exhortation: "If it is true that the quality of your spirit is the essential thing you bring to your leadership task, then the management of your *own* motivation must take top priority."[16] Before we launch out to inspire and equip others for the furtherance of God's global cause, we must first ensure the right motivational foundation in our own lives. We have to in all honesty deal with the question which the Master put three times to Simon Peter (cf. Jn 21:15-17) and still lays before every aspiring leader today: 'Do you love me?' Only ardent love for Christ as a person coupled with self-denying love for those around us will qualify us to approach the task of spiritual leadership in a God-pleasing and Christ-honouring manner. "Christian leadership is a leadership of love," W.L. Duewel epitomized and added, "As a Christian leader you lead in the name of Christ, on behalf of Christ, in the spirit of Christ, and for the glory of Christ. This can be done only as you lead with a Christly love."[17]

4.2 Jesus Christ as the Master

Closer investigation reveals that the English word 'Master', so often associated with the person of Jesus Christ, may actually occur as translation of five different terms used in the original Greek text of the Gospels.

The first of these is *"rabbi"* (e.g. Jn 3:2, Mk 11:21, Jn 9:2),[18] literally 'my great one'. That Jesus was approached with this title of honour for teachers of the Law with such matter-of-factness, illustrates how excellently he blended in with his cultural environment through adopting the familiar role of a religious teacher instructing both the public and a selected group of followers in the things of God.

More frequent though is the vocative *"didaskale"* (e.g. Matt 8:19, Lk 18:18, Mk 4:38). *Didaskalos*, meaning 'teacher', is simply the Greek equivalent of the Hebrew *rabbi* (cf. Jn 1:38). Seemingly Matthew took an interest in emphasizing the different relationship between Jesus and his disciples as compared to the contemporary Jewish rabbis and their students. Hence, while making repeated use of *didaskalos*, the evangelist employed *rabbi* merely twice - as the way in which Judas, who by then had distanced himself from the Master, addressed the latter in connection with the betrayal (26:25.49).

Besides, only Matthew utilized *"kathegetes"* (23:10), whose original meaning of 'leader' and 'guide'[19] sheds further stimulating light on the translation "Master" furnished in the

Authorized Version.

The underlying allusion to Jesus' leadership status is brought out even more forcefully in a fourth term, which in turn was chosen only by Luke. As Hellenist he discarded the Hebrew *rabbi* for "*epistates*" (5:5, 8:24.45, 9:33.49, 17:13). To its original signification of 'chief', 'overseer',[20] W. Barclay offered notable additional insight: "It is the word in Greek for a headmaster, and in particular for the man who was in charge of the *ephebi*, the cadets who were engaged in their years of national service of their country."[21]

However, the evangelists' favourite appellation of respect was the word '*kyrios*' (e.g. Lk 5:12, Jn 6:68, Matt 8:25). Already applied in politely addressing the earthly Jesus (cf. e.g. Mk 7:28, Jn 11:34, Matt 14:28.30), it above all became the predominant title of reverence for the resurrected Christ (cf. Lk 24:34, Jn 20:25, 21:7.15-17). According to H. Bietenhard the term denoted in classical Greek "lord, ruler, one who has control . . . .";[22] in the Gospel context it "also implies recognition of Jesus as a leader, and willingness to obey him . . . ."[23]

Considering the parallel texts Mk 4:38 / Lk 8:24 / Matt 8:25,[24] we observe how each synoptist through his specific terminology (*didaskalos/epistates/kyrios*) sought to convey his distinct perspective of the Master's multiple role. For the Gospel writers on the whole Jesus Christ was much more than just one *rabbi* among others; in fact Jesus himself underscored this very point: "You call me 'Teacher' and 'Lord', and rightly so, for that is what I am" (Jn 13:13). While during the time-span of his public ministry already certain individuals acknowledged Jesus' dignity and authority by calling him 'Lord', after his manifest triumph over death his dedicated followers all the more perceived him as the exalted *kyrios*, who merited to rule and lead, to be revered and followed.

A casual look into Paul's writings suffices to evince that

Lord' was also the apostle's preferred title for Jesus Christ. Right in his first encounter with the risen One, the zealous and radical Pharisee saw himself confronted with such divine authority that he was induced to ask, "Who are you, Lord?" (Acts 9:5; cf. 22:8, 26:15). It was this Lord who subsequently appointed him as his servant and witness (Acts 26:16) and called him to be an apostle (Rom 1:1). Moreover he entrusted Paul with the specific commission to share the Gospel among the Gentiles (Gal 2:7; cf. Acts 22:21).

Numerous statements in Paul's letters conjoin towards a rounded picture of Jesus Christ's Lordship. For instance, all things were created by him as well as for him (Col 1:16), and his name is above all other names (Phil 2:9). He is Lord over individual believers (cf. Rom 5:1), Head of the Church (cf. Eph 4:15.16) and King (cf. Col 1:13). He is Lord over the living and the dead (cf. Rom 14:9) and will judge all men (cf. 2 Thess 1:9.10). Jesus Christ as Lord grants peace (cf. 2 Thess 3:16), extends mercy (cf. 2 Tim 1:16), bestows ministry gifts (cf. Eph 4:11.12) and gives authority to those serving him (cf. 2 Cor 10:8). As the Lord, Jesus Christ has rightful claims on our bodies (cf. Phil 1:20), our activities (cf. 2 Tim 2:3.4) and our family relationships (cf. Eph 5:21-25).

So we can infer from our word study that for the early apostles to follow Jesus Christ included that **he was their teacher, guide, overseer, leader as well as Lord**, and as such he deserved and expected absolute obedience and unreserved accountability.

When God covenanted with the people of Israel, he gave them "the Ten Commandments" (Deut 4:13), - not 'Ten Recommendations' -, thus determining the desired human response to his divine direction as **obedience**. Correspondingly we see the Lord Jesus leading his disciples by commands (e.g. Matt 8:18, Jn 15:14, Acts 1:4). Should not the realization set us thinking that relative to decision-making the Gospels procure no evidence that Jesus in any case asked the Twelve for suggestions, at any time made himself dependent on their advice, ever went for group or majority resolutions? Instead, once he as the leader had under the Holy Spirit's direction discerned God's purpose, he communicated to his mentorees their need to obey. His strong personal commitment to execute his Father's will (cf. Jn 6:38, 15:10) and his intense desire to launch a dynamic movement guided and empowered by the Holy Spirit, left no room for mere human discretion and fleshly initiative.

Jesus' love for his chosen men established the basis from which he exercised authority over them. Whereas his love for the disciples motivated them to obey him, their obedience in turn, he let them know, would furnish proof of their love for him (Jn 14:15.21.23; cf. also Lk 6:46). The deep friendship which grew between Jesus and his disciples in the atmosphere of mutual love, did not exempt the Twelve from the Master's expectation of complete obedience on their part. In order to qualify to lead, they had first to learn to be led. They had to become aware that **no one will proceed to be a good leader unless he has first been a good follower.** Spiritual leaders cannot develop outside the perimeter of willing obedience. Small wonder then that God told Joshua his obedience would be crucial to a successful leadership career (Josh 1:7).

This fundamental and momentous import of obedience was assimilated right into the Matthaean version of the Great Commission, where Jesus obligated the Eleven to teach the disciples they were going to make "to obey everything I have commanded you" (28:20).

Down the centuries, unfortunately, the fulfilling of the Great Commission has often incurred harm through a twofold omission, viz. the neglect of making disciples (rather than just converts) and the neglect of teaching obedience (rather than knowledge only). Obviously it is easier to influence people to merely think right than to also make them act right. Yet Jesus had charged his Galilean friends to invest themselves into the expansion of a divine movement which was to reproduce and multiply within the confines of practical obedience to his normative teaching.[25]

Another non-negotiable in connection with mentoring spiritual leaders is the facet of **accountability**. That everyone will be held responsible for the way he lived and made use of what God trusted him with, was indicated by Jesus (cf. Matt 12:36, 25:19, Lk 19:15) and clearly reiterated by Paul (Rom 14:10-12). For leaders this prospect is all the more awesome because of Christ's announcement, "From everyone who has been given much, much will be demanded; and from the one who has been entrusted with much, much more will be asked" (Lk 12:48).

As God's stewards (cf. Tit 1:7), leaders should not only take 'vertical' accountability seriously but make themselves 'horizontally' answerable, too. The Master did no more than hint at the need to practise interpersonal accountability (cf. Matt 5:23.24, 7:3-5, 18:15-17); Paul, however, once again went into more elaborate detail.[26] True accountability involves the high cost of humility, openness and vulnerability. At the same time it pays the high dividend of providing **a haven** for fellowship, confidence, acceptance and encouragement as well as **a safeguard** against developing character flaws, unsound relationships, wrong priorities and unrighteous activities. Its motivational basis should be an honest desire to supply a channel for facilitating and maintaining spiritual progress, not a hankering after dominance and control.

The Biblical concept which incorporates the two requirements of obedience and accountability is **faithful stewardship**. Paul wrote in 1 Cor 4:1.2, "So then, men ought to regard us as servants of Christ and as those entrusted with the secret things of God. Now it is required that those who have been given a trust must prove faithful." That the proper criterion for evaluating the effectiveness of spiritual leadership is in the first place not outward success but faithfulness, can also be deduced from the Lord Jesus' words in Matt 25:21.23 and Lk 19:17 (AV), where the servants in the respective parables were praised for having been faithful,[27] and the aspect of success was not even brought to the fore.

To graphically illustrate to the disciples their need of being linked with their Master in an obedient and accountable manner, Jesus made use of a striking metaphor: he charged them to pick up and carry **his easy yoke** (Matt 11:29.30).[28] Transcending his professional expertise as a former carpenter that the bearing of a yoke can be rendered easier through the use of a not too heavy, carefully shaped and smoothed wooden bar, Jesus purposed to convey an essential spiritual principle. By commanding the Twelve to take his yoke upon themselves, he actually directed them to submit to his will, his rule, his discipling. "Accepting the yoke of Jesus or being his disciple," M. Maher elucidated, "means commitment to his Person, dedication to his service, a self-sacrificing love of the brethren and a desire to imitate the Master . . . ."[29]

Just as two draught animals would get a yoke placed on their necks, Jesus wished the disciples to fully come under his authority and leadership. On that condition, because of their consociation with him, their future existence would not turn out to be burdensome. Like two animals yoked together pulling side by side, first Jesus and later the Holy Spirit would occupy the place next to each of the disciples and through his loving, enabling and strengthening companionship share the load of their lives and ministries. Thus understood, being yoked to the Master would not alone be a privilege but even a dire necessity, for - as Jn 15:5 categorically asserts - apart from the Lord Jesus we can do nothing.

Inescapable then appears the conclusion that, as far as current experience and practice of leadership development are concerned, the boundaries of their value and efficacy are determined by the extent of our willing subordination to the Masterhood, and especially Lordship, of Christ. "When I call Jesus Lord," to cite Barclay once more, "I ought to mean that he is the absolute and undisputed owner and possessor of my life, and that he is the Master, whose servant and slave I must be all life long."[30]

Again and again godly men of the past have aligned their life-styles and labours for God with the far-reaching implications of **the complete submission and wholehearted commitment which the Lord Jesus rightfully deserves.** "Oh, let us trust Him fully," J. Hudson Taylor pleaded, "and now if never before, now afresh if often before, take Jesus as our Master and Lord, and with unreserved consecration give over to Him ourselves, our possessions, our loved ones, our *all*. He is infinitely worthy . . . ."[31] Henry Martyn, who followed God's call into pioneer mission work in India, professed, ". . . the Lord Jesus, who controls all events is my friend, my master, my God, my all."[32] The outstanding South Seas trailblazer John Williams wrote to his father, ". . . in the work of my Lord and Saviour I desire to live and to die. My highest ambition, dear father, is to be faithful to my work, faithful to souls, and faithful to Christ . . . ."[33] And John G. Paton, mightily used of God in the New Hebrides, succinctly remarked, "God gave His best, His Son, to me; and I give back my best, my All, to Him."[34]

Jesus desired totally committed followers, half-hearted enthusiasts he sought to discourage (cf. Jn 6:60.66). Experience in fostering spiritual leaders has shown that often dedication rather than giftedness finally decides on the quality of ensuing performance. B. Graham's estimation, "Salvation is free, but discipleship costs everything we have,"[35] still holds unabatedly true. Therefore, when recruiting and developing aspiring leaders for God's work, let us make sure we do not detract from the radical claims flowing from the Master's person and message. **He who did not spare himself for our** best, is not fully honoured unless we offer him our very best.

4.3 Jesus Christ as the Model

One of the remarkable features of Paul's writings is the frequency with which he referred to himself as an example to be emulated:

> Therefore I urge you to imitate me. (1 Cor 4:16)
> I plead with you, brothers, become like me . . . . (Gal 4:12)
> Join with others in following my example, brothers, and take note of those who live according to the pattern we gave you. (Phil 3:17)
> Whatever you have learned or received or heard from me, or seen in me - put it into practice . . . . (Phil 4:9)
> You became imitators of us . . . . (1 Thess 1:6)
> For you yourselves know how you ought to follow our example . . . . (2 Thess 3:7)
> We did this, not because we do not have the right to such help, but in order to make ourselves a model for you to follow. (2 Thess 3:9)
> What you heard from me, keep as the pattern of sound teaching . . . . (2 Tim 1:13)

What validated such a high claim? We are given the answer in 1 Cor 11:1, where the apostle summarized his discipling strategy in the concise guide-line, "Follow my example, as I follow the example of Christ."

Congruent with the Master's words to his disciples that he was God's visible representation on earth (Jn 14:9; cf. 1:14.18) and an example for them to follow (cf. Jn 13:15), Paul regarded Jesus Christ as "the image of God" (2 Cor 4:4) and commended him for imitation (cf. e.g. Rom 15:7, Eph 5:2.25, Phil 2:5, Col 3:13).[36] In this way, we can infer from various remarks in his letters, the apostle reproduced himself in his protégés Timothy (cf. 1 Cor 4:17) and Titus (cf. 2 Cor 12:18) no less than in Corinthian (cf. 2 Cor 3:2.3) and Thessalonian Christians (1 Thess 1:6). As these believers on their part became examples for others (1 Thess 1:7; cf. 1 Tim 4:12, Tit 2:7), the Lord Jesus' longing to see his movement spread on the basis of reproduction and multiplication was powerfully realized.

L. Eims aptly commented, "Paul knew he could not improve on the method of Jesus Christ. He knew what Jesus had done and he followed it as closely as he knew how."[37] While the Master was with the Twelve, **he exemplified before their eyes the totality of knowledge, skill and character which he considered the indispensable groundwork for their future authentic witness on his behalf.** Observing his model, they saw in him embodied the values, precepts and strategies he wanted them to be guided by. They recognized in his lifestyle and ministry performance the mode of operation he desired for their praying, preaching, teaching, working of miracles, soul-winning and disciplemaking. In him they perceived the attitudes he wished them to display towards all those whom God would send across their paths. The joint goal pursued by the Lord Jesus in all three areas was no other than that his likeness would become manifest in the Twelve.

The wholistic mentoring impact radiating from the Master's with-ness was aimed at developing his followers into genuine representatives of the culture of the kingdom of God. Both through teaching and 'imitation modeling'[138] Jesus endeavoured to rebuild the disciples' mindset and behaviour so that they would increasingly come to reflect the way he thought, felt and acted. Fully aware that **spiritual leadership influence in essence arises less from what you say and do than from who you are,** Jesus created through his consociational discipling technique the very atmosphere in which his personality could and would 'rub off' on his associates.

Out of the wide spectrum of character traits which Jesus

Christ consummately exemplified - among them love, faith, humility, meekness, obedience, compassion, patience, faithfulness, forgiveness and zeal -, two facets especially pertinent to the practice of leadership development require individual attention. The first of these is **living according to clear priorities**.

"Evidently everything Jesus did during his brief, intensive, focused, three-year career was done deliberately, to secure the beachhead which would eventually fulfil his long-range strategy to reach the whole world." With this estimation L. Ford[39] captured well the utmost purposefulness which characterized Jesus Christ's activities on earth.

His paramount concern was his relation to his heavenly Father (cf. Lk 2:49; Jn 8:29). Simultaneously he considered the interests of God's kingdom as of supreme relevance (cf. Matt 6:33.10). Robert Moffat, whose faithful and extended missionary labours in southern Africa were greatly blessed by God, followed the Lord Jesus' precedent when stating he regarded only such matters as worthwhile that stood in reference to the glory and expansion of the kingdom of God.[40] Moreover, in Jesus' pursuit of the affairs of the kingdom, relationships with people, and particularly with his twelve friends, occupied a high place (cf. Matt 19:13-15, Jn 4:4-26, Mk 9:30.31, Lk 22:15).

Singularly revealing was **the Master's strategic use of time**. The Gospels portray him as extremely busy but never in a hurry, under pressure but never losing his poise. Neither did he ever move ahead prematurely or act too late, nor give in to the tyranny of the urgent or waste time. He did not allow himself to get side-tracked into activities of subordinate relevance (cf. Lk 12:13.14, Mk 1:36-38), balanced work with rest (cf. Mk 6:31), handled interruptions wisely (cf. Mk 5:21-43, Matt 14:13-25) and did not neglect to ensure occasions for solitude (cf. Lk 5:16, 22:39; Mk 1:35, Lk 6:12).

Definitely correct was B. Hull when he accentuated that

"Christians never outgrow the need for basics."[41] Without doubt leading an existence marked by clear priorities belongs to the basic necessities of the Christian life, essentially so if leadership responsibility forms part of it. The perfect calm with which Jesus went about his demanding work among men, presents a permanent challenge to every leader. This challenge appears all the greater once we realize that at the same time he never disregarded the urgency of the kingdom (cf. Jn 9:4), that cardinal factor which Moffat elicited with his noteworthy exhortation, "We have all eternity in which to enjoy our victories, but only one short life in which to win them."[42]

The other facet demanding more elaborate inquiry is **the attitude of servanthood**. Jesus addressed it with singular emphasis in Mk 10:42-45, when he told his twelve friends:

> You know that those who are regarded as rulers of the Gentiles lord it over them, and their high officials exercise authority over them. Not so with you. Instead, whoever wants to become great among you must be your servant, and whoever wants to be first must be slave of all. For even the Son of Man did not come to be served, but to serve, and to give his life as a ransom for many.

To start with, the Master warned his trainees against adopting a secular model of rulership. The same danger still exists today, and E.J. Elliston rightly advised, "Christian leadership values and principles must come from a solid biblical base rather than just from a social science base. The beginning point ought to be revelation rather than management or secular leadership theory."[43] Then Jesus went on to outline his own design of servant leadership. What are some major traits of this "altogether new style of leadership", as J.R.W. Stott called it?[44]

By referring to the familiar roles of servant and slave Jesus intimated certain attitudinal features which he desired to be characteristic of his followers' forthcoming exercise of leadership. In fulfilling their respective functions both servants and slaves were expected to be attentive, dedicated, humble, obedient, faithful and selfless. Similarly Jesus wished his chosen men to practise their leadership not by authoritatively lording it over people from a position above them but by humbly serving **among them.**

The bases from which secular leadership on the one hand and spiritual leadership on the other operate are fundamentally different; to quote Stott once more: "The authority by which the Christian leader leads is not power but love, not force but example, not coercion but reasoned persuasion. Leaders have power, but power is safe only in the hands of those who humble themselves to serve."[45]

In verse 45 of the scripture cited above Jesus founded the requirement of servant leadership ultimately on the fact that servanthood was the very life-style he himself modelled.[46] This entails that everyone assuming Christian leadership responsibility automatically comes under the obligation to approach this task in a Christlike manner. **True spiritual leadership demands the leader's reflecting the attributes of Christ to those under his care.** Besides, one must recognize that Biblical servanthood offers **several built-in character protection mechanisms** of crucial importance: humility defeats pride, obedience averts independence, faithfulness checks irresponsibility, unselfishness neutralizes egotistic aspirations.

Of Jesus' theology of leadership, servanthood represented a quintessential component. Its principal focus was not the prospect of the leader's carrying out varied menial actions but rather of his displaying a servant heart, first toward Jesus as his Master and secondly towards those entrusted to him.

Genuine servanthood, however, can only be practised by means of divine enablement. Jesus Christ's permanent withness, promised in the Great Commission (Matt 28:20) and a powerful reality since the Holy Spirit's coming on Pentecost, turns the exercise of spiritual leadership into an inimitable experience: Jesus Christ's love renders it desirable to serve, his wisdom makes it reasonable, his example practical, his consociation possible, his Lordship a privilege.

Quite telling is the circumstance that throughout the Bible 'servant of God' appears as the preferred title for those functioning in spiritual leadership capacity. Abraham was designated as God's servant (Gen 26:24), so were Moses (Ex 14:31), Joshua (Josh 24:29), David (2 Sam 7:5), Hezekiah (2 Chr 32:16), Isaiah (Isa 20:3), Jesus Christ (Matt 12:18), Paul (Tit 1:1) and James (Jas 1:1). Ever since the requirement "be holy, because I am holy" (Lev 11:44) was pronounced, the challenge for every spiritual leader has been to undertake this responsibility not in his own way but in a godly way, with the status of servant of God as the means to secure that very end.

Through the coming of Jesus Christ the nature of spiritual leadership was further specified in that **those serving his cause as leaders are expected to do so as his authentic witnesses.** By their words and deeds they are to mirror in accurate fashion the paradigm observed in his exemplary life. Both with John and Simon Peter we observe an acute awareness of their responsibility to reproduce Jesus Christ's model. "Whoever claims to live in him must walk as Jesus did," John postulated (1 Jn 2:6), and Peter wrote for the recipients of his first letter, ". . . Christ suffered for you, leaving you an example, that you should follow in his steps" (2:21).

There can be no doubt that **the early disciples took their Lord's charge to emulate his prototype seriously.** With Simon Peter, for instance, we find clear evidence of how devotedly he followed Jesus' model concerning priorities (cf. e.g. Matt 5:48 and 1 Pet 1:15.16; Jn 9:4 and 2 Pet 3:12), precepts (cf. e.g. Matt 5:16 and 1 Pet 2:12; Matt 5:11, Lk 6:27 and 1 Pet 3:9) as well as ministry performance (cf. e.g. Lk 19:47 and Acts 5:42; Mk 2:11 and Acts 9:34; Mk 5:40-42 and Acts

9:40.41). And Simon was the one who commended Jesus' servant leadership style to fellow elders with the directives:

> Be shepherds of God's flock that is under your care, serving as overseers - not because you must, but because you are willing, as God wants you to be; not greedy for money, but eager to serve; not lording it over those entrusted to you, but being examples to the flock. (1 Pet 5:2.3)

Paul's declaration that Jesus Christ appeared to him in order to appoint him "as a servant and as a witness" (Acts 26:16), affirmed that he as well was only too conscious of the **double obligation** to combine the elements of humble servanthood and faithful testimony in his evolving labours for God. The convergence point for this twofold endeavour could be no other than the Lord Jesus Christ, the sole model suitable for and worthy of emulation.

"The church was charged not with the task of winning the whole world," R.H. Glover explained, "but of witnessing to the whole world; not with the responsibility of bringing all men to Christ, but of taking Christ to all men."[47] As mission workers, and specifically those with leadership roles, give themselves to the fulfilling of this mandate, they do well to bear in mind that the most powerful witness they can offer to the world consists in their setting a Christlike example.

Jesus Christ's sublime paradigm, which God in his wisdom ordained as the model to be demonstrated to mankind, possesses **a unique drawing power** (cf. Matt 4:18-22; Jn 12:32) and **a matchless inherent incentive towards imitation** (cf. Matt 14:25.28.29, Lk 11:1.2). Therefore the more our lifestyle, under the Holy Spirit's gracious enabling, approximates the Master's alternative example, the more effectively we will witness on his behalf and motivate others to follow him. "It is the character, values, attitudes, behavior, and commitment of the leaders, as they reflect Christlikeness," L.O. Richards and C. Hoeldtke pointed out, "that provide the compelling model."[48]

Our lives must first show a difference, viz. Christlikeness, before they can really make a difference. This helps us understand why spiritual leaders of days past have been gripped by a passion to become more and more conformed to the image of Christ (cf. Rom 8:29). In 1857 David Livingstone told an audience in Scotland his great object was to be like Jesus and to imitate him as far as possible.[49] James Gilmour, about three decades later, almost echoed his words when he wrote in Mongolia, "The great thought in my mind these days and the great object of my life, is to be like Christ."[50]

A contemporary of James Stewart, who did highly prolific mission work in southern and central Africa during the second half of the last century, honoured this remarkable man of God as "the first true living manifestation of Christ I ever knew . . . ."[51] When a leader's life evokes and justifies an evaluation of this kind, it certifies both the effectiveness of his witness and the glorification of the Master he serves.

4.4 Jesus Christ as the Mentor

A mentor in the Biblical sense establishes a close relationship with a protégé and on that basis through fellowship, modelling, advice, encouragement, correction, practical assistance and prayer support influences his understudy to gain a deeper comprehension of divine truth, lead a godlier life and render more effective service to God.

When exercising a mentoring role the leader essentially operates as facilitator. In order to further the full release of the trainee's personality and talents, he seeks to wholistically impact the latter through the totality of his shared life. As M.G. King explicated, "it is precisely this influencing of the whole being that no course, no seminar, no book can satisfy.

It takes life, it takes experience, it takes contact with a human soul, it takes example, and it takes emulation. In sum, it takes mentoring."[52]

Investigations up to now have unfolded that the Lord Jesus Christ fulfilled the function of facilitator for his twelve mentorees in matchless fashion. His servant approach uniquely illustrated W. Benniss' characterization of leadership as "not so much the exercise of power itself as the empowerment of others."[53] At this stage of our inquiry it seems profitable to furnish a review of key mentoring principles the Master applied. For a large part they were already given detailed attention and substantiated from the Gospels in the preceding sections; therefore only some of them will meet with further elaboration now. More specifically, the ensuing guide-lines will shed light on the groundwork, technique and results of mentoring carried out by the Lord Jesus.

The **foundation** of Jesus Christ's mentoring of the Twelve was laid through building-blocks like:

his total obedience to God
his anointing
his deep love for his followers
his intercession for them
his trust in God's work in them
his transparent with-ness
his primary concern for character development.

Corresponding to Jesus' pattern the apostle Paul also combined evangelistic endeavour directed at the crowds with leadership training geared towards individuals. That he pursued the latter aim on the same basis as his Lord, can for instance be deduced from his instructions to his esteemed disciple Timothy.[54]

Particularly notable appears the principal focus on character growth which we perceive with both Jesus Christ and Paul. This emphasis becomes all the more plausible once it is realized that more than anything else a leader's character serves as mirror for Christlikeness present or absent in his life and as crucial determinant for his actions. Besides, the firmer his character underpinning, the larger a ministry can prosper upon it. Flaws in character, however, will jeopardize or even ruin his efforts. Wong Ming-Dao, the great Chinese Christian also known as a 'Man of Iron', passed the potent verdict, "A person with a blemished character is a person unworthy to work for God."[55]

Among the significant aspects of Jesus' mentoring **technique** must be reckoned:
his approach was relational
his approach was informal
his approach was oral
his approach was mobile
he modelled
he taught
he enabled practical application
he encouraged
he corrected
he stressed the indispensability of divine empowering.

From the starting point that "real spiritual growth takes place primarily in the context of relationships,"[56] the Master devised a coaching programme which was informal and oral at the same time. He turned the entirety of everyday life experiences into one big classroom for the Twelve and wove the threads of his instruction most naturally into the overall pattern of ordinary events. Through training talks, dialogues, questions and answers as well as discourses, parables and proverbs Jesus committed to his disciples' memories those elementary precepts which were to govern their forthcoming engagement for the extension of God's kingdom.

An astute observer cannot help but recognize how immensely life-related, concrete and dynamic Jesus' leadership training mode was and that he consciously shunned any tendency to formalize, structuralize or institutionalize it,

- an inclination which in modern times unfortunately all too often has been yielded to, especially in the western world. Surprisingly enough, Jesus did not even see the need to draw up a manual or the like for his followers; instead he confined himself to implanting seeds of truth orally, leaving the provision of written records of his life, words, deeds and mission to the four evangelists. **Jesus made sure that the emergence and growth of the energetic global harvest force he initiated would not be stifled or even counteracted by a static recipe for the mentoring of its leaders.** He did not come to establish a well-structured organization but to engender a movement designed to be activated and advanced essentially not through human striving but the Holy Spirit's moving.

One of the Master's leading intentions in the coaching of his friends was that they would in the future remember and reproduce what they had learned through their association with him. "Effectively reproducing the behavior in appropriate situations," C.C. Manz and H.P. Sims, Jr. pointed out, "requires a mental model of the details of the desirable behavior to guide action."[57] Such a mental pattern to kindle successful behavioural transfer under different circumstances the Lord Jesus aimed to generate by resorting amply to the triad of modelling, teaching and implementation.

The pivotal relevance of Jesus Christ's modelling we have seen time and again. Application on the disciples' part provided both them and their Lord with recurrent opportunities to gauge their progress, faith, courage and knowledge as well as to probe their commitment, obedience, humility and faithfulness. As far as Jesus' teaching is concerned special mention has to be made of one simple yet powerful device which he utilized expertly and strategically also for the purpose of mentoring the Twelve - parables.[58]

For his trainees Jesus' example flowing from his constant with-ness was tantamount to a continual case study. In addition he drew their attention occasionally to other visible demonstrations of certain truths he wished them to learn (cf. e.g. Mk 12:41-44, Matt 26:6-13, 8:5-13). Apart from these observable real case studies **Jesus availed himself of parables as imaginary case studies to bring home certain relevant precepts and situational behaviour patterns** (cf. e.g. Matt 7:24-27, 25:14-30, Lk 10:30-37, 11:5-13, 12:16-21).

Why did Jesus make such conspicuous use of parables in his mentoring of the Twelve (Mk 4:33.34)? Unacquainted with intricate visual aids as they are accessible in many places today, he through parables effected internal visualization in his listeners. For them to follow his word pictures somewhat equalled watching a film before their minds' eyes. Simultaneously they were integrated into a learning process in which Jesus left room for their self-discovery of truth, aware that insight thus gained penetrates more deeply and is better retained. The striking and memorable form of his narratives, moreover, helped preserve the gist of his instruction. Through each potential life situation portrayed before their eyes the Master furnished his disciples with the opportunity to go on an imaginary test run, so to speak, sparing them the time-consuming alternative of learning the same lesson experientially on the basis of trial and error.

Thus we can notice that, on the one hand, Jesus extraordinarily materialized the pedagogical insight that "he is the best teacher who can turn the ear into an eye."[59] On the other, Jesus Christ's prototype demonstrated to all those involved in leadership development **the utmost value of imaginary case studies as a means to instil, cultivate, consolidate, accelerate and preserve both cognitive and behavioural learning**. Whoever desires to meet with success in his mentoring of others cannot afford to neglect either of those two pertinent lessons.

J. Stalker once stated, "To the Twelve the most valuable part of their connection with Christ was simply the privilege of being with Him - of seeing that marvellous life day by day, and daily receiving the silent, almost unobserved, impress of His character."[60] After their enduement with the Holy Spirit, the disciples truly manifested the remarkable **results** of Jesus' consociational discipling approach and its ensuing wholistic mentoring investment into their lives. We can recognize for instance:

    they were men of obedience and humility
    they were men of faith and prayer
    they were men of clear values and priorities
    they communicated what they had been taught
    they engaged in discipling others
    they operated as leaders
    they continued and extended their Master's cause.

May it once more suffice to merely add a few comments on some of the items just listed.

At one time while he fellowshipped with the Eleven after his resurrection, Jesus summed up all he desired them to be in only two words: "my witnesses" (Acts 1:8). They specified both the purpose and the end product he had mentored them for, namely that they would testify by their personalities, words and deeds authentically on his behalf as well as multiply their Christlike witness through the lives of others.

Paul drew the attention of his mentoree Timothy to the need of testifying for the Lord Jesus (cf. 2 Tim 1:8) and challenged him to reproduce and multiply his witness according to the brief formula, "And the things you have heard me say in the presence of many witnesses entrust to reliable men who will also be qualified to teach others" (2 Tim 2:2). At the core of this masterly strategy to secure reliable witness and genuine maturity over several spiritual generations was the element of teaching.

In this regard the apostle reiterated the directive included in the Great Commission (cf. Matt 28:20) that the contents of our shared testimony must be no other than the words Jesus commanded. As Paul, totally in line with the rabbinic tutoring he had experienced, felt obliged to pass on what he had received (cf. 1 Cor 11:23), so he encouraged Timothy to faithfully hold on to Christ's teaching (cf. 1 Tim 6:3) and praised the Corinthian believers for adhering to the instruction he himself had shared with them (1 Cor 11:2).

Judging from the twin perspective that a leader's greatness can be measured by the accomplishments of his followers and that success without successors is no true success, Jesus Christ without doubt was the greatest leader history has ever seen. **The unequalled genius of his mentoring approach was that by training good followers he actually raised outstanding leaders** who, once ignited, enlightened and invigorated by the Holy Spirit, turned into excellent achievers for their Lord.

The Old Testament already expressed the basic human need to be led in **the image of shepherding** (e.g. Num 27:16.17, Zech 10:2). P. Keller remarked that "it is no mere whim on God's part to call us sheep. Our behavior patterns and life habits are so much like that of sheep it is well nigh embarrassing."[61] Thinking of features like dependence upon being directed, fearfulness, mass mentality and even a certain disposition to stubbornness, this comment sounds only too appropriate.

John recorded in the tenth chapter of his Gospel how Jesus referred to himself as "the good shepherd" (v. 11) and intimated several telling parallels between a good herdsman and a good spiritual leader.[62] As the former knows his flock (cf. vv. 3.27), so the latter knows his followers well, for instance their cultural and social backgrounds, family situations, aspirations, strengths and weaknesses. It was the Palestinian shepherd's habit to walk ahead of his sheep (v. 4), in the same way the able mentor leads his trainees by setting for them direction and example.[63] Moreover, a good herdsman cares for his sheep (cf. vv. 11-13); a good spiritual leader loves those entrusted to him, encourages and comforts them.

Just like the responsible shepherd secures nourishment for his flock (cf. vv. 3.9), the conscientious leader nurtures by providing attention, personal contact, instruction, practical help and prayer support. While the dedicated herder regards it as part of his charge to protect his sheep (cf. vv. 11.12.28), the committed leader guards his followers against error, hurts or various attacks. Finally, the good shepherd gives himself for his sheep (cf. vv. 11.15); the good leader in analogous manner shares his life with his companions and is willing to sacrifice time, privacy, energy and personal means on their behalf.

Apart from the designation "good shepherd", we also find the Lord Jesus was called "great Shepherd" (Heb 13:20) and "Chief Shepherd" (1 Pet 5:4). This opens our eyes to the key realization that, as Chua Wee Hian put it, "Christ calls leaders today to serve as his under-shepherds,"[64] and such leaders will never be more than second in command, will never progress beyond the status of servants and stewards. **True spiritual leadership can only be exercised within the confines of Jesus' Masterhood.** He is the one who carries the final authority and responsibility, requiring from his sub-shepherds full obedience and accountability.

Relative to leadership development in particular then, the implication is obvious: all Biblical mentoring is under-mentoring. On the basis of his permanent with-ness (cf. Matt 28:20), communicated through the Holy Spirit (cf. Jn 16:13-15), Jesus Christ is the real and decisive agent in Christian mentoring. We cannot cause our trainees to grow, yet we can create conditions which are conducive to God's apportioning growth (cf. 1 Cor 3:7). Nor can we bring about change in our mentorees, yet we can influence them to be changed by Jesus Christ. Therefore we must not regard him as mentor of the past only but as mentor in the present as well. **Jesus' mentoring prototype is not merely a static blueprint of days past, it is operational as a formative power through the Holy Spirit today.** In our day and age the Master's promise, "Come, follow me, and I will make you fishers of men" (cf. Matt 4:19) has lost neither its validity nor its authority.

In his letters Paul traced with considerable detail Jesus Christ's current involvement in the lives of his followers. According to the apostle the Lord lives in them (cf. Gal 2:20), is in fact their life (Col 3:4); he encourages (cf. 2 Thess 2:16.17), protects (2 Thess 3:3), strengthens (Phil 4:13), gives understanding (cf. 2 Tim 2:7), makes the Christians' love increase (cf. 1 Thess 3:12), fosters blamelessness and holiness in them (cf. 1 Thess 3:13), gives them authority (cf. 2 Cor 10:8) and power (cf. 2 Cor 12:9).

"We need to relearn the principles taught and practiced by Jesus Christ and make Him our leadership mentor," M. Rush summoned.[65] By now we understand with greater clarity that **the Lord Jesus as our coaching model seeks more than our mere interest in him as a historical forerunner, he in fact claims our wholehearted trust in him as present enabler.**

If we commit ourselves in this way, we also can be mentors who facilitate their understudies into leading themselves. "Leading others to lead themselves," to call upon Manz and Sims, Jr. again, "is the key to tapping the intelligence, the spirit, the creativity, the commitment, and, most of all, the tremendous, unique potential of each individual."[66] More still, we can prepare our mentorees to effectively guide others into a release of their respective potential in God. Once a colleague said of Donald Fraser, missionary to Nyasaland, "There's no one in the world like Mr Fraser for getting the best out of people, and making them try to do their best. No one could work with him and not want to."[67] Would it not be wonderful if those under our tutelage could utter similarly appreciative words about us?

4.5 Jesus Christ as the Method

The overarching aim in Christian mentoring is to raise up leaders patterned after Christ's model. It would be a fatal fallacy though to think that this quest would allow an option between different roads or even short-cuts to reach the desired goal. As the African proverb, "The dawn does not come twice to awaken a man,"[68] so graphically expresses, there are certain processes and events which take place only once. God in his unsearchable wisdom resolved to make Jesus' consummate mentoring prototype once and for all the sole mode of operation to be followed in each and every succeeding generation.

Unquestionably it requires humility to willingly fall in with Jesus' paradigm. Man's proneness to pride and independence would suggest he resort to human intelligence and ingenuity rather than strictly abide by the normative course already plotted in the Scriptures.[69] This challenge is increased through the circumstance that Jesus' example did not display a broad spectrum of suitable procedures but only one approach. Moreover, he did not procure an abstract formula but a concrete method, in actual fact, as R.E. Coleman so succinctly phrased, "He was His method."[70] That is why in our efforts to train Christian leaders **we must concentrate primarily on seeing the present impact of Jesus Christ's person unleashed through the Holy Spirit's activity** and render the communication of theoretical precepts a secondary priority.

John the evangelist handed down a brief conversation between Thomas and his Master which arose during the Last Supper. When the concerned disciple asked, "Lord, we don't know where you are going, so how can we know the way?", he received the answer, "I am the way . . . ." (Jn 14:5.6). This momentous declaration is usually interpreted from an evangelistic viewpoint, highlighting **Jesus as the way to God for salvation**. More than that, however, the statement also discloses **Jesus as the way of God for service**. Not alone did Jesus provide the way by which one can be reconciled to God, he also showed the way in which men can most effectively work for God, not least in the realm of leadership coaching. Any mentor wishing fruitful results for his labours cannot set a better target for himself than John's maxim to walk as Jesus Christ walked (cf. 1 Jn 2:6).

Consider for instance Jesus' utterly positive mentoring attitude. Nowhere in the Gospels do we detect a hint at his telling the Twelve that whenever they would engage in coaching others they should act from an affirming stance. Instead, he just plainly illustrated this significant prerequisite through the way in which he handled them as his understudies.

He verbalized potential he envisaged (cf. Jn 1:42), thus revealing in his approach the utilization of a major mentoring principle which the famous German poet J.W. Goethe captured in the words, ". . . treat a man as if he already were what he potentially could be, and you make him what he should be."[71] Jesus encouraged his disciples (cf. Matt 16:17-19, Acts 1:8) and in this manner built their confidence and self-image. He corrected them where he saw the need (Matt 18:21.22, Mk 16:14) and patiently cleaved to them despite repeated failure on their side (cf. Mk 8:14-21, 9:17-19). Over and above he dealt with them tenderly (Jn 16:12; cf. Matt 12:20) and exhibited utter trust in God's further moulding of them (cf. Lk 22:32, Jn 14:12).

In the response to Thomas mentioned above Jesus went on to say, "I am the way and the truth . . . . " (Jn 14:6). He not merely told the truth (Jn 8:45), taught "the way of God in accordance with the truth" (Matt 22:16) and testified to the truth (cf. Jn 18:37), he <u>was</u> the truth. Jesus Christ embodied the absolute truth which saves, brings understanding, satisfaction and peace, which directs, corrects, liberates and sanctifies, which must not alone be perceived with the mind, but with the heart as well (cf. Jn 12:40). **By combining proclamation and personification the Lord Jesus gripped his trainees with the truth as both a concept calling for mental assent and an experience occasioning a life encounter.** The Twelve were impacted to the maximum as they witnessed the truth being taught and simultaneously evidenced through the Master's example in a broad variety of real life contexts.

Paul stressed the divine origin of the truth (cf. Rom 1:25, 15:8) and shared with the Corinthians the vital insight that "we cannot do anything against the truth, but only for the truth" (2 Cor 13:8). The truth can neither be changed nor abolished. Believers are not expected to fight for the truth but witness to it, so that its inherent power can make itself felt. Testifying for Christ amounts to pointing to him as the centre and manifestation of divine truth. And "the Spirit of truth" (Jn 15:26), who assists in the witnessing process (cf. Jn 15:26.27), makes the truth known and thus glorifies Jesus Christ (Jn 16:13.14).

Additionally Paul specified the truth needs to be acknowledged (cf. 2 Tim 2:25.26), believed (cf. 2 Thess 2:12.13) and obeyed (cf. Gal 5:7). He informed the Christians in Ephesus that it must be spoken in love (cf. 4:15) and reminded them of "the truth that is in Jesus" (4:21). The apostle made Jesus Christ the very core of his message; he preached him (1 Cor 1:23, 2 Cor 1:19), taught about him (Acts 28:31), portrayed him as the believers' wisdom, righteousness, holiness and redemption (1 Cor 1:30).

Christian leadership training endeavour today ought to be directed by an equal concentration on the person of Jesus Christ. **He must be focused upon as the sole model, central message and optimal method to guide our mentoring efforts, in the awareness that by means of the Holy Spirit's mediation and our humble co-operation the Lord Jesus himself will be the mentor.**

A third component of Jesus' reply to Thomas in Jn 14:6 was that he also designated himself as "the life". Several passages in the fourth Gospel named Jesus as the source of eternal life (cf. 5:40, 6:35.48, 20:31). Yet concurrently he exemplified temporal human existence at its very best. "In him was life, and that life was the light of men", the evangelist commented (1:4). Jesus himself announced his followers would possess "the light of life" (8:12) and underlined he had in fact come so that people might "have life, and have it to the full" (10:10). While he was in the world, Jesus exhibited by his life how men can best please, serve and glorify God, can fully materialize their God-given potential and lead the most satisfying form of existence at the same time.

"Jesus' leadership was not a style he adopted, but a reality he expressed," wrote L. Ford.[72] This observation tallies with Paul's pronouncement in Col 2:17 that "the reality, however, is found in Christ." The Lord Jesus did not introduce mentoring as a mere abstract system of thought but as a life-style reality. **Beyond leadership education he targeted and secured character formation.** He connected intellectual illumination with intimate association, thereby exposing his friends to **an intense and prolonged dual reality encounter** which led to a dramatic and permanent transformation of their lives. If we are occupied with spiritual leadership development, we need to honestly take up the question whether our training approach supplies the proper environment for our mentorees to powerfully experience this double encounter effect.

God's unique strategy for revealing his Son to mankind as the way, the truth and the life was the Incarnation. "The Word became flesh and made his dwelling among us . . .", we read in Jn 1:14. Through the Incarnation God entered history in unprecedented fashion, made himself available to be heard, seen, known and experienced as never before. In Jesus Christ as *Immanuel*, God manifested his with-ness among men in unparalleled measure, teaching and blessing people, defeating and triumphing over Satan. The apostle Paul explained relative to Jesus Christ's coming in the flesh:

> Who, being in very nature God, did not consider equality with God something to be grasped, but made himself nothing, taking the very nature of a servant, being made in human likeness. And being found in appearance as a man, he humbled himself and became obedient to death - even death on a cross! (Phil 2:6-8)

Jesus, "the Son of Man" (Mk 10:45), identified completely with the people whom he meant to serve, yet without losing his identity. He learned, worked, became hungry, thirsty and weary, was tempted, experienced loneliness and sorrow, was despised, criticized and rejected.

Important to realize, however, is that Jesus identified not only with such common aspects of humanity but also with his Jewish cultural environment in particular. "God in Jesus became so much a part of a specific human context," C.H. Kraft emphasized, "that many never even recognized that he had come from somewhere else."[73] A.H.M. Zahniser's remark, "The incarnation, as God's way of communicating, offers the model for mission across cultural boundaries",[74] opens our eyes to the fact that **Christ's Incarnation established the yardstick by which the effectiveness of all cross-cultural missionary undertakings has to be measured.**

Christ initiated God's global cause incarnationally and intended it to continue that way. This is evident from his repeated assertion that he sent his disciples into the world just as God sent him (Jn 17:18, 20.21). With respect to present-day endeavour to fulfill Christ's commission we should bear in mind Kraft's challenge: "Because Jesus identified with us, and because his life has been recorded for us, we are able to reciprocally identify with him in imitation of both his life and his approach to communicating God's message."[75] And Jesus' presence in his followers (cf. Jn 17:23), which enabled first the Eleven and later the Early Church to perpetuate his mission through their incarnational Christlike witness, is no less potent today.

One must be careful not to overlook in this connection that such ongoing incarnational witness to Jesus as the way, the truth and the life can only be undertaken and upheld in his authority. Relating G.S. Shogren's definition "Authority is the right to effect control over objects, individuals or events,"[76] to the sphere of Jesus' ministry, we observe he exercised extraordinary authority: over nature (e.g. Mk 4:39), men (e.g. Matt 4:18-22) and religious tradition (cf. Mk 2:28), over disease (e.g. Matt 12:15) and death (e.g. Lk 7:14.15), over Satan (e.g. Matt 4:10.11) and demons (e.g. Matt 8:16). He demonstrated authority in his teaching (Matt 7:29), by forgiving sin (Mk 2:10) and announcing judgement (cf. Matt 11:20-24).

This authority was at Jesus' disposal, because his heavenly Father had transferred it to him on the basis of their intimate relationship (cf. Jn 17:2, 5:19-22.27). The Master in turn delegated spiritual authority to his followers (Matt 10:1, Lk 10:19; cf. Mk 3:15, Matt 18:18, Jn 20:23). And even now the Lord Jesus, who wields all authority in heaven as well as on earth (Matt 28:18; cf. Col 2:10), makes his authority available to those who come to believe in him (cf. Mk 16:17.18).

Whoever engages in mentoring ought to be aware, as J.R. Clinton pointed out, "that spiritual authority is the primary authority base in leadership influence."[77] **Our qualification to move in divine authority is not due to expertise or academic achievement, to seniority or rank, instead it is a fruit of our relationship with God.** The foundation of Jesus' authority was neither positional nor functional, rather it was relational and 'unctional'.

Besides, the investiture with spiritual authority is conditional. Whether God will be able to entrust his authority to us will depend on various factors, like faith, prayerfulness, humility and integrity for instance. Yet **a special key is wholehearted submission** to him (cf. Jas 4:7). K. Phillips articulated an essential principle when he wrote, "The authority a person exercises is determined by the authority to which he submits."[78]

Evidently the centurion, whose servant Jesus healed, understood this truth very well (cf. Lk 7:7.8). As officer in the Roman army he new his authority to be backed by the might of the Roman Empire. Similarly, when we give ourselves to carrying out the Great Commission, we as Christ's witnesses can rest assured his divine authority will be there to cover us. It will be crucial though to remain under this shield, and our protection in this regard is going to be our willingness to be held accountable, firstly by God and then also by those leaders he has placed over and next to us. **Wanting in answerability opens the door to improper use of spiritual authority**, because, N.T. Anderson so rightly warned, "No one can survive his own unchallenged authority."[79]

While Jesus walked the earth, he incarnated his heavenly Father's loving concern for mankind as:
    the way for those ignorant of God's purposes
    the truth for those in error
    the life for those void of true satisfaction
    the light for those in darkness
    the teacher for the uninstructed
    the healer for the sick
    the shepherd for those who need to be led.

Likewise every Christian leader today is called upon to by his incarnational witness reflect Christ as God's answer to human wants. Through such activity he will show himself as a modern day member of the Way movement (cf. Acts 9:2, 24:14), which since Pentecost has incorporated all who decided to accept Jesus as the way by which to be saved and by which to live to God's glory. This movement will serve as salt of the earth and light of the world as long as it will remain focused on the person of the Lord Jesus Christ as its resource and measure.

4.6 Jesus Christ as the Measure

We do not have to read far in Paul's letters to discover that he was captivated by the person of Jesus Christ. One senses his ardent love for the Lord (cf. 1 Cor 16:22), his desire to see him exalted (cf. Phil 1:20), his longing to know Christ more intimately (cf. Phil 3:7-10) and his eagerness to proclaim him (cf. Rom 15:20). The apostle himself was committed to following Christ as his model (cf. 1 Cor 11:1), his readers he acquainted with the need to grow up into Jesus Christ in all respects (cf. Eph 4:15), to be "transformed into his likeness" (2 Cor 3:18), to develop towards perfection in the Lord (cf. Col 1:28) and to "become mature, attaining to the whole measure of the fullness of Christ" (Eph 4:13).

Mission history furnishes numerous instances where prominent Christian leaders conveyed a kindred perspective, making it their chief intent to aspire towards the measure of life-style and ministry exhibited by the Master. It was a lifelong prayer request of David Livingstone's that he would resemble Jesus Christ.[80] Robert Laws, who laboured as a pioneer missionary in Nyasaland, confessed, "I am far from what a Christian ought to be, but by the grace of God I desire to be more and more like what Christ Himself was and is."[81] "Blessed Jesus!", wrote J. Hudson Taylor, "how unworthy of Thee *I* am. Make *me* more like Thyself."[82] And Harold Schofield, who served with the China Inland Mission in Shan-si, asked of God, "Enable me to aim at nothing less than walking in this world as CHRIST Himself walked."[83] "Your supreme priority is not what you do for Jesus, but to be like Him." This directive for leaders given by W. L. Duewel[84] warns us against the danger of getting so busy for Christ that we neglect growing into his likeness. **The influence spiritual leaders exert on the lives of their followers is determined by the degree to which their attitudes and actions reflect the attributes of Christ.** Every leader, aware that he always models for good or bad, should identify with David's concern, "May those who hope in you not be disgraced because of me, O Lord, the LORD Almighty; may those who seek you not be put to shame because of me, O God of Israel" (Ps 69:6). Rather a leader's being and doing should bear the stamp of Christ, his words and deeds ought to reflect the Lord's likeness.

Jesus' incarnational model installed the final gauge for every mentor's mode of life and training approach. J. Haggai formulated so appropriately when he wrote, "The ultimate example of leadership is Jesus," and "The ultimate criterion is Christlike leadership."[85] This does not, of course, mean the leader's individual identity is eliminated; Simon Peter, for instance, certainly led differently from Barnabas or Paul. Yet it does mean **the underlying principles and overall characteristics of each Christian leader's activities must share the common denominator of Christlikeness.** In other words, the predominant Christlike features cover the leader's God-given individuality like a veneer.

While considering the aspect of Christlikeness we are actually dealing with the wider concept of holiness. "God is holy," A.W. Tozer stated, "and He has made holiness the moral condition necessary to the health of His universe."[86] Ever since God created man in his likeness (cf. Gen 1:26, 5:1), he intended humanity to live in conformity with his character. Accordingly the *Torah* contained the principal requirement to be holy, because God is holy (cf. Lev 11:45).

Through Christ's Incarnation God filled this demand with visible content, thus enabling us to define holiness in practical terms: **Holiness is to be and do what Jesus exemplified**.

Remarkable indeed is the discovery that the Gospels do not name a single instance in which the Master elaborated on holiness; rather than teaching it, he lived it. Demonstrating a life-style marked by total separation from sin and utter dedication to God, Jesus portrayed holiness in its practicality and beauty (cf. 1 Chr 16:29, AV). As a result of what he accomplished through his atonement and resurrection, the godlikeness lost through Adam's fall can be regained in Christ. Holiness is both imputed (cf. Heb 10:10) and imparted (cf. 1 Pet 1:2) to those who trust and follow him.

From a Biblical viewpoint our holiness is of greater concern than our happiness. The connection between the two can be compared to the correlation of light and heat,[87] which is to say when we are committed to leading a holy life in thought, word and deed, we will enter into a resulting happy life as well. Helpful, moreover, is the understanding that one must not equate holiness with sinless perfection, which can be attributed to the Trinity only. "Holiness or perfection as applied to the believer," clarified A. Murray, "does not mean we *can no longer sin*, but that we are *able not to sin*."[88] And Samuel L. Brengle provided the useful further characterization of holiness as "Christian perfection - such perfection and obedience of the heart as a poor, fallen creature, aided by Almighty power and boundless grace, can give."[89]

Once when the Master had healed a deaf and dumb man in the Decapolis, people present commented appreciatively, "He has done everything well" (Mk 7:37). This evaluation reveals that **in Jesus' case holiness of character was coupled with excellence of performance**. To substantiate this point from the realm of his mentoring, we can perceive in his association with the Twelve a perfect balance between:

availability and withdrawal
prayer and practical coaching involvement
servanthood and Lordship
gentleness and firmness
affirmation and exhortation
teaching by precept and training through application
attending to the Twelve as a group and as individuals
developing them in their personalities and their skills.

Spiritual leaders, similarly, ought to display excellence in their labours. God's work requires and deserves leaders of extraordinary moral fibre and task discharge. Their character should be unimpeachable in the face of scrutiny, their performance ought to honour the God of excellence they represent. Apt indeed is T.W. Engstrom's observation, "Striving for excellence in our work, whatever it is, is not only our Christian duty, but a basic form of Christian witness."[90] For spiritual leaders true excellence has to begin with their relationship to Christ but must then encompass all spheres of their lives. **Good leaders endeavour to not only model excellence themselves but to create an environment in which their followers can excel likewise.**

Why did God decree Christlikeness as the ultimate and only legitimate standard for spiritual leadership relative to both character and performance? **Christlikeness shows forth the fullness of consecrated living.** It is the realization of God's desires for man as originally created in his likeness, the fulfillment of what Christ lived and died for, the crown of the Holy Spirit's work in the believer. **To lead a Christlike life is the optimal mode to bless others.** The Lord wishes his followers to serve for the benefit of their fellow-men, as they sacrificially give of themselves to provide answers to the needs and problems surrounding them on all sides (cf. Matt 25:34-36.41-43). **Christlikeness procures effective witness.** Our world today discerns Christ by way of Christian testimony. Refashioned from a sinful past by the indwelling

Holy Spirit, true disciples establish an authentic and alternative witness. Displaying the fruit of the Spirit, e.g. love, joy and peace (cf. Gal 5:22.23), they radiate a supernatural attractiveness which challenges and guides towards holy living.

Besides, **Christlikeness furthers the extension of Jesus Christ's global movement.** "The quality and maturity of leadership determines the success or failure of an operation," C.S. Deir declared.[91] This perspective fits in with Jesus' practice of not sparing any effort to raise the Twelve up to his own standard (cf. Lk 6:40). It was a fundamental concern of his to see his followers shaped into proper replicas of himself before they in turn would spark a process of reproducing multiplying witnesses.

Christlikeness secures a vigorous personality impact. About John Hyde, outstanding missionary in India, a colleague said, "He was one of the holiest men I have ever known, and his life exerted a great influence."[92] Conversely the godly Scottish minister R.M. M'Cheyne once professed, "My people's greatest need is my personal holiness."[93] The power of a holy life is such that it directs, instructs, inspires yet also confronts and convicts; it serves as a most powerful weapon against all forces of evil, too. Finally, **Christlike living brings about the deepest satisfaction for man and the highest glorification for God.**

The secret to maintaining a Christlike life was disclosed by the Master when he told the Eleven:

> Remain in me, and I will remain in you. No branch can bear fruit by itself; it must remain in the vine. Neither can you bear fruit unless you remain in me.
> I am the vine; you are the branches. If a man remains in me and I in him, he will bear much fruit; apart from me you can do nothing. (Jn 15:4.5)

Remaining in Jesus is pivotal to a holy, Christlike way of life. The essence of holy living is not rigid adherence to a certain code of rules but consociation. It is the believer's vital union with Christ, a mutual abiding made possible through the Holy Spirit's indwelling; in other words, it is a relationship. The more intimately one associates with Christ, the more one will grow into his likeness. **Abiding in Jesus changes the aspiration after Christlikeness from striving into receiving.** Close consociation with Jesus as the model and source for consecrated living yields holiness as a fruit.

Paul reserved in his letters special attention for the notion of being in Christ. He outlined that in Christ there is salvation (2 Tim 2:10), hope (1 Thess 1:3), freedom (Gal 2:4), unity (cf. Gal 3:28), strength (cf. Eph 6:10), grace (1 Cor 1:4) and joy (Phil 1:26), - in fact "every good thing" (Phm 6). In Christ the believers are sanctified (cf. 1 Cor 1:2) and seated in heavenly places (Eph 2:6), can stand firm (cf. 2 Cor 1:21) and always triumph (cf. 2 Cor 2:14). Christ's followers are able to, in him, lead a godly life (cf. 2 Tim 3:12), he actually is their life (Col 3:4). Paul climaxed his teaching on being in Christ with a remarkable personal testimony to the exchange of life he experienced: "I have been crucified with Christ and I no longer live, but Christ lives in me. The life I live in the body, I live by faith in the Son of God, who loved me and gave himself for me" (Gal 2:20).

Rich as the believer's inheritance in Christ is (cf. Eph 1:3.14.18), it must be claimed by faith. When the apostle challenged the Philippians, "Only let us live up to what we have already attained" (3:16), he indicated the necessity of progressively appropriating what God has made available in Christ. This ongoing process of advancing conformation to the image of Jesus Christ constitutes sanctification. The latter requires a lifelong co-operation between the Trinity (cf. 1 Thess 5:23; 1 Cor 1:30, AV; 1 Pet 1:2) and the individual Christian (cf. Col 3:5-17).[94] He needs to realize that although sanctification on earth will always remain incomplete, he is to continue in Jesus (cf. 1 Jn 2:28), knowing the final consummation will come about only on Christ's return (cf. 1 Jn 3:2).

All this is of crucial relevance to the exercise of spiritual leadership, mentoring included, because **no leader will be able to make exploits for Christ unless he first sets up his operational basis in Christ.** Whatever a leader wants to undertake on Jesus' behalf, the supply-line must be intimate association with him. To experience and draw upon Christ's all-sufficiency, the leader has to first be in him and then abide in him. Jesus' followers today cannot be <u>with</u> him in the way the Twelve were, but through the Holy Spirit they are able to live <u>in</u> him. **In the final analysis the essence of Christianity and spiritual leadership can only be grasped from within,** that is, when supernatural revelation is received on the deeper significance of the affirmation which Jesus gave to his eleven friends, "On that day you will realize that I am in my Father, and you are in me, and I am in you" (Jn 14:20).

Before Moses was supposed to build the Tabernacle, God showed him its very pattern on Mount Sinai (Ex 25:9.40, Heb 8:5). Similarly, **God showed us the only viable pattern for spiritual leadership in his Son's example.** We would be well advised to acknowledge the principle M'Cheyne shared with a friend in 1840: "It is not great talents God blesses so much as great likeness to Jesus."[95] Time and again people have discerned that the power of Christian witness lies in the messenger's resemblance to Christ. An observer remarked about the distinguished Indian Christian Sádhu Sundar Singh, "To-day I have seen what man can become like, if he truly lives in Christ. For the Sadhu is very like Christ . . . ."[96] With respect to China missionary David Hill, somebody noticed, "Jesus Christ must have been like David Hill."[97]

Real competence for spiritual leadership can be achieved solely in Jesus Christ (cf. Jn 15:5; Phil 4:13). Do we possess godly ambition to become the best we can in him? The resources for living victoriously as Christ's witnesses are available in association with him. Aware of our own deficiencies and failures, let us remember that God's grace, which changed Paul from a fierce antagonist into a fervent protagonist of the Master's cause, is indeed sufficient for us too. **Effective spiritual leadership does not flow out of independence but out of deliberate dependence on Jesus Christ**, or - to use Murray's words - "Christ must be all to us every moment."[98]

*

In the ensuing chapter particular attention will be focused upon the implications of Jesus' consociational mentoring approach for leadership training across cultural boundaries. Evidence from mission history will be drawn upon to substantiate the view that faithful implementation of such principles as the Lord Jesus exemplified secures the powerful witnessing impact he desires and which our world so desperately needs.

5 Jesus Christ's With-ness Approach as Consummate Witness Strategy

Missiology, the study of mission, is concerned with questions pertaining to the global extension of God's kingdom, the spreading of the Christian witness to all the world. With some of these questions the focal point is predominantly theological, others are more centred on missionary practice. While the investigation into the missiological significance of Jesus' leadership development model was in the last chapter largely undertaken on the level of theological reflection, the chapter on hand will essentially concentrate on the ramifications for practical missionary involvement, especially when it reaches across cultural borderlines.

Full obedience to the Great Commission will lead Christians automatically into encounters with other cultures. According to S.G. Lingenfelter and M.K. Mayers **culture** can be understood as "the sum of the distinctive characteristics of a people's way of life."[1] It consists of the totality of ideas, beliefs, values, customs and behavioural patterns shared by certain individuals; in other words, culture comprises the specific ways in which a certain group of people thinks, believes, feels, communicates and acts.

The missionary who out on the field engages in the training of leaders, finds himself in a rather complex situation. Conditioned by his own cultural background, he seeks to influence members of a divergent host culture to adjust their lives to God's 'kingdom culture'. In the process of mentoring commensurate with the manner which the Lord Jesus exemplified, the missionary is in constant need to evaluate his own witness and the receptor culture in light of the absolute standards laid down in the Scriptures.

One can, as we have seen, derive a multiplicity of insights from Jesus' consociational discipling model, and in the preceding chapters numerous <u>general</u> guide-lines have already been pointed out. The ensuing sections will narrow the focus down to six <u>specific</u> principles which are **supracultural**, because their universal validity transcends any particular cultural fabric. Of these six dimensions, which must be understood as non-negotiables for all cross-cultural leadership training endeavour, the first to be considered is the fundamental aspect of relationship.

5.1 The Dimension of Affiliation

For every spiritual leader desirous of impacting the lives of others his relationship with God is vital. We read Abraham was called a friend of God (Jas 2:23), Job lived in close friendship with God (Job 29:4) and "Enoch walked with God . . . ." (Gen 5:24). The Scriptures leave no doubt that God regards his servants' intimate affiliation with himself as quintessential. Time and again we see him create special opportunities for his chosen leaders to develop further in this respect in seclusion, for instance Joseph in prison, Moses in Midian, John the Baptist in the desert and Paul in Arabia.

After Jesus' work on Calvary and the Holy Spirit's coming at Pentecost we are all the more able to live in close companionship and communion with God. Not only is this where matters of our identity, acceptance, self-worth and security are settled, it is also where our effectiveness has its source. There is a real need to continually remember the basic truth indicated by Moses, that it is no use embarking upon any enterprise if God's with-ness is not assured (cf. Ex 33:15).

Leaders must furthermore reserve primary attentiveness for cultivating vibrant fellowship with God, because **only out of a proper relationship with God can they properly relate** to people. This circumstance is of singular relevance for mentors. "Values, attitudes, and standards of conduct," J.S. Ellis stated, "are transmitted more through relationships than through precept."[2] To be productive, leadership development requires a relational context.

A mentoree is not a project but a person. Mentoring implies more than a lecturer-student connection, it is friendship. Conscious that relationship creates the environment conducive to efficient learning, Jesus, as we have seen, took great care to establish a deep friendship with the Twelve. Accordingly **our mentoring efforts, especially in cross-cultural settings, can only be successful if we take time to build meaningful relationships**. As we are with people and really get to know them, the more intimately we relate to them, the more profoundly we can influence them; **the closer the contact the stronger the impact**. Before we can claim attention, we must first gain credibility. Broad knowledge, great talents and subtle strategies on our part will not avail much if we fail to win people's trust.

Those who follow God's call to labour on foreign fields may soon realize striking differences between the host cultures and their own. Disparity in areas like language, food, dress and customs spring quickly to the eye. Yet beyond such more obvious features there are basic assumptions underlying the respective worldviews which vie for recognition and sensitivity. Western missionaries working in Two-Thirds World environments can discern a number of telling discrepancies between biases inherent in their home cultures on the one hand and the target cultures on the other: time- vs. event-orientation, result vs. process focus, status vs. achievement outlook, segmental vs. wholistic thinking, individualistic vs. group mentality.

Relative to our preoccupation at present with the dimension of affiliation there is one difference, however, which demands more detailed treatment, viz. **task- vs.**

relationship-orientation. Undoubtedly this is a point at which western missionaries are particularly vulnerable. Usually they are predominantly efficiency focused; their fulfillment stems largely from reaching their objectives, completing the tasks on hand well and fast. If they do not grasp the strong relationship-orientation of the host culture, whose representatives find their satisfaction primarily in association and interaction, they are in danger of becoming not merely disappointed with the people around but even critical of them. Lk 10:38-42, incidentally, provides us with a graphic illustration of how task-oriented Martha fell into this very trap during Jesus' visit to her home. Active Martha was "worried and upset about many things" (v. 41), whereas contemplative Mary sensed "only one thing is needed" (v. 42), fellowshipping with the Master and learning from him.

It is possible that a missionary, despite genuine dedication to his ministry, nevertheless experiences rejection from nationals, because they perceive his interest as directed chiefly towards the projects he undertakes and not towards them as individuals. Any cross-cultural missionary enterprise, including the development of leaders, should always be more personal than professional. What helps the nationals ought to be a higher concern than what serves our vision, plans or budget; from their viewpoint meeting people is more valuable than meeting deadlines.

Jesus desires us to be more committed to people than to programmes. If this truth is neglected in cross-cultural situations, the nationals may feel they as persons are merely of secondary importance and more accepted for their work contribution than for who they are. Instead we see in the Master's affiliation with the Twelve that with him task and relationship perspective were inseparably intertwined; actually one can say that he was relationally biased. L. Ford justly evaluated, "When he 'saw' a fisherman or a tax-collector, he did not see them as means to his ends. He saw they *were* his ends,"[3] and W. MacDonald went so far as to speak of the Lord's "leadership style of personal relationships."[4]

Wise leaders make sure that in their pursuit of goals and tasks they do not neglect those who are to benefit from their accomplishment. While moving along the road of work performance they do not bypass the legitimate needs of people. They are wary of running effective programmes while losing those who are to profit from them. All training geared for non-westerners must have a sound relational underpinning. **The more relationally-oriented the approach, the greater the potential for fruitful results.**

One major obstacle on the way to close affiliation across cultural boundaries is overbearing deportment. Without doubt missionary endeavour in the past yielded many valuable achievements in areas like proclamation of the Gospel, Bible translation, literature production, school education, vocational training, medical care and social reforms. Regrettably though it is also true that a lot of missionaries, especially in the days of colonialism, operated from a condescending stance. Superiority can express itself in a variety of ways, among them **cultural arrogance**. T.W. Dye articulated missionaries' particular susceptibility in this regard:

> Ethnocentricism, the idea that the customs, ideas, and values of one's own culture are right or natural or best, is a continual problem for every cross-cultural worker. Missionaries have a special problem with it because ideas about God's universal truth are first learned in terms of one's own cultural variation.[5]

Here it is helpful to remember that within the broad spectrum of cultures God created, each is different but none better than the other. Higher training, greater knowledge, more technology and funds at the missionary's command do not constitute the superiority of his culture, nor do they automatically earn him the right to lead.

Highlighting 'errors', despising beliefs, ridiculing customs or any other form of down-grading the target culture exert a detrimental effect on any attempt to intimately affiliate with nationals, who not infrequently possess an uncanny gift of accurately fathoming the missionary's character and motivation. Not without good reason did J. Hudson Taylor's successor Dixon E. Hoste pray for David H. Adeney, soon after the latter had joined him in China, that God would set him free from "national pride which would be as noticeable as a man who has been eating garlic."[6] For a missionary it is actually possible to go to another country, yet in his heart, never really go to its people.

Another fateful expression of superiority is what P. Wakatama called '**the director syndrome**' and explained in this way: "It seems as though a good number of missionaries do not feel their ministry is important unless they are director of something."[7] Insecurity in leadership may give rise to lack of trust in co-workers, to hankering after control over policies, procedures, finances and people; it may bring about a clinging to positions and a reluctance to hand over responsibility to locals. However, in our day missionaries bent on domineering are unwelcome anywhere in the Two-Thirds World. Wakatama underlined with reference to the African situation:

> We need only those missionaries who are qualified and willing to train Africans for responsibility. There is no longer room for missionaries who will come to work as directors without Timothys at their side who will eventually take over from them. Such missionaries will never be out of work because Africa has millions of Timothys waiting to be trained in order to train others.[8]

Misdirected dependence is a third manner in which close affiliation across cultural lines can be hindered. It seems only natural that those who become Christians through a certain missionary's efforts and then receive from him training as well as practical help, should initially develop considerable dependence upon him. Paternalism, however, may at best serve a temporary purpose, and Gospel messengers run the risk of keeping nationals reliant on themselves rather than on God. Moreover, by their example they can mislead local Christians into placing their trust in externals like finances, facilities, regulations, programmes or staff figures instead in God's with-ness and his Word. Both fallacies render the nationals a disservice as they stifle their growth towards spiritual autonomy.

The antidote against superiority in any shape is Christlike servanthood. We do well at this juncture to recall how emphatically the Lord Jesus accentuated servanthood as the indispensable attitudinal prerequisite for spiritual leadership (cf. Mk 10:42-45). Westerners may find it unusually difficult to adjust to this Biblical perspective, because in their culture leaders are commonly envisaged as being at the top, in charge, issuing orders to others. A true spiritual leader though, as a mere sub-leader following Christ, exercises authority not through commands but by his Christlike example.

When he finds himself on a foreign field, **a servant leader will pose as a learner.** Perceived cultural differences he meets with respect, at the same time conveying a humble and teachable spirit. Bruce Olson furnished an outstanding example along these lines by the manner in which he gradually made his entry into the unfamiliar world of the Motilone tribe in Colombia. It is fascinating to witness[9] how he comes into initial contact with the Indian Cobaydra, joins him in building a dam, spear-fishing and hunting, learns language items from him, becomes first his friend, then his blood brother and is finally accepted as his leader.

Besides, **a servant leader loves the nationals.** Knowledge, experience, communication skills, spiritual gifts and sacrifice are all beneficial, but if *agape* love is lacking, mission work will always be seriously hampered. The missionary's life and words should not leave any doubt that he unselfishly pursues the locals' highest good. Love will open his eyes to discern such traits in his hosts that will endear them to him. Love will induce the willingness to practise self-denial and to identify with their life-style, concerns and needs. William Carey, renowned missionary pioneer to India, claimed his heart was wedded to the land of his calling,[10] E. Stanley Jones testified, "I was born in the West and love it, but India has become my home; India's people have become my people; her problems, my problems; her future, my future...."[11] The secret to Donald Fraser's success amongst the Africans was "the people knew that he had given himself to them; they had his heart".[12]

"I look on foreign missionaries," J. Hudson Taylor explained, "as the scaffolding round a rising building; the sooner it can be dispensed with the better - or rather, the sooner it can be transferred to other places, to serve the same temporary purpose."[13] **A servant leader sees himself in a transitory role.** This was eminently true of the apostle Paul, who never settled anywhere for good, never allowed himself to get tied down by permanent local responsibilities, but instead maintained his temporary, itinerant, apostolic ministry approach throughout.

Cross-cultural acceptance is mainly determined in the realm of heart attitude. Both the centurion, whose servant Jesus healed, and Cornelius were, as Romans, respected and warmly received by their Jewish fellow-men, because they had won their hearts (cf. Lk 7:3-5, Acts 10:22.31). On Irian Jaya, Dani men told John Dekker:

> You have learned our talk quickly. You eat our potatoes. You sleep in our huts. You are now one of us here. You call yourself Ndeka, but that means nothing to us so we want to give you a name we understand. We want to name you after the Toli River. Your name shall be *Tolibaga*![14]

My personal experience among the Basotho in southern Africa was similar. Irrespective of my deficient competence to speak their Sesotho language, I was welcomed in their midst as 'one of them', adopted as 'son-in-law' into one of their families and honoured with the indigenous name "Pulamaliboho" ('the one who is opening river fords', i.e. pathfinder, pioneer).

More than anything else the people we desire to reach and influence must sense that we appreciate them, believe in them and are committed to serve them. They need to see us come alongside, willing to work with them hand in hand under the Holy Spirit's guidance to facilitate them into God's maximum for them. Our approach should be fraternal like Paul's,[15] that is to say **we must take our place as brothers in Christ and servant friends**. Loving affiliation and brotherly partnering of this kind were beautifully illustrated in the relation between ROBERT LAWS and WILLIAM KOYI.

The former was born at Aberdeen in 1851. After graduating from the local university, he joined a Central Africa expedition, arranged by the Free Church of Scotland, as medical missionary. The young doctor reached Lake Nyasa in 1875, helped build a station at Cape Maclear, worked temporarily at Blantyre and in 1881 moved to Bandawé, the newly established headquarters of the Livingstonia Mission.

A single-minded man of vision, faith and prayer, Robert Laws developed great confidence in the potential of African Christians. While regarding foreign missionaries as sheer "birds of passage, their object being to train up a native staff and develop a native church,"[16] he was convinced, "If Africa is to be won for Christ - only there is no *if* about it - it will be won by the Africans themselves."[17]

He longed for the evangelization of the bellicose Ngoni, descendants of warriors who had fled Zululand earlier in the century and subsequently settled in the highlands to the west of the Lake. The man to play the decisive role in turning Laws' desire into reality was William Koyi. Born in 1846 and by background a member of the Gaika tribe, a sub-group of the southern African Xhosa people, William became a Christian at twenty-three. In his yearning for better education he walked 240 kilometres to Lovedale. There, a few years later, he met James Stewart's endeavour to recruit African helpers for the work in Nyasaland with the humble response, "I have only a half talent, but I am willing to go and be a hewer of wood and drawer of water."[18] Koyi arrived at Cape Maclear in 1876.

In course of time Robert Laws sensed William was the one to pioneer amongst the Ngoni. The latter was uniquely fitted for this task not alone because he was African. Particularly, during his earlier years in southern Africa, he had become familiar with the Zulu way of life and language, therefore understood the customs of the Ngoni and was able to communicate with them freely. As interpreter, Gospel messenger and adviser, William proved invaluable to Laws. He in turn put absolute trust in Koyi and esteemed him highly: "In all those delicate negotiations he has been my right hand. He is doing true pioneer work of a very arduous kind and has his heart thoroughly in it."[19] 1882 saw William establish himself in the vicinity of the paramount chief's village.

His witness by life and word won Koyi the respect, affection and confidence of the Ngoni to such an extent that services he held would be attended by over 1500 people. Through loneliness, fatigue and frequent illness Laws supported William by way of counsel and encouragement, like when he wrote to him, "You are doing noble work, and God is blessing it and honouring you as His instrument. The angels in heaven might envy you your task."[20]

Koyi's devoted service among the Ngoni produced several disciples. Yet not until 1886 did the headmen's council decide to grant permission for unrestricted mission work and the setting up of schools in their midst. This piece of thrilling news, however, reached William Koyi, "the pioneer of the Gospel in Ngoniland,"[21] on his deathbed. He received it as an answer to prayer, echoing Simeon of old, "Lord, now You are letting Your servant depart in peace, . . . For my eyes have seen Your salvation" (Lk 2:29.30, NKJV).

5.2 The Dimension of Exemplification

At one time E. Stanley Jones had an opportunity to express to M. Gandhi his keen interest in seeing Christianity in India truly naturalized and divested of its foreignness so that it could powerfully conduce to the country's progress and salvation. When he went on to ask Gandhi what he would suggest in order to render that desire attainable, the latter pensively answered, "I would suggest, first, that all of you Christians, missionaries and all, must begin to live more like Jesus Christ."[22]

This immense challenge is before everyone who engages in cross-cultural mission work, markedly those who fulfill various leadership functions. "Nothing is more important in a leader's life and ministry," wrote W. L. Duewel, "than to lead an exemplary life in all things. His leadership can be no more effective than his life."[23] A spiritual leader is not alone expected to, for instance, impart vision, motivate and mobilize people, share valuable insights and experiences, but to be a model as well. In fact, C.S. Deir emphasized, "An exemplary leader knows the most valuable gift he can give is his godly example for others to follow."[24] It is beneficial at this point, moreover, to remind ourselves of Simon Peter's appeal that those exercising oversight should serve by "being examples to the flock" (1 Pet 5:3).

Spiritual leaders ought to be what they wish their followers to become. They are not only listened to but also watched. Their word witness is either established or discredited by their life witness. Legitimacy and authenticity of their message are judged against the backdrop of their example. Why is it that a leader's paradigm is such a potent tool in moulding the lives of his companions? P.J. Decker furnished the helpful explanation:

> Social learning theory specifically acknowledges that most human behaviour is learned observationally through modelling. Through the process of observing others, an individual forms an idea of how behaviours are performed and the effects they produce. This coded information serves as a guide for action.[25]

Whereas facts and principles can be quite aptly gathered from books and lectures, behavioural patterns are most appropriately assimilated from visible models. These influence us more than mere abstract concepts, what we actually see impacts us more strongly than what we solely hear. Observable actions test our personal views, values and conduct, make us aware of weaknesses and deficiencies, motivate us towards change and emulation; displayed attitudes exert a contagious effect. This circumstance was at one time stringently illustrated by J. Hudson Taylor. In his desire to introduce newly arrived missionaries to the Chinese culture, he invited them out to breakfast in Shanghai. One of those present recorded later:

> Our leader and director showed us how to do it by his own example, and stamped us at once, in all the freshness of our early zeal, with his own stamp. Hence we took to Chinese dress, Chinese food, Chinese ways as a duck to water . . . . the remembrance of his example has made things easy and silenced murmuring.[26]

It was K. Barth who observed that becoming a Christian signifies becoming a Christ to one's fellow-men.[27] This is both a great privilege and an awesome responsibility, singularly for spiritual leaders. As Gandhi's reply indicates, for a Christian leader it does not suffice to present just any model of his own choice or making, he needs to set a Christlike example. **Leadership influence, not least in cross-cultural contexts, is first and foremost determined by the measure in which the manner of Christ shines forth through his representative.**

Earlier sections centred considerable attention on the pivotal role which the dimension of exemplification played in the Lord Jesus' consociational approach to leadership development. We saw repeatedly how the Master, in his affiliation with the Twelve, utilized modelling to produce in them character formation. Their emulation in response to his exemplification was instrumental in preparing them to later on represent him and his cause authentically. Through his prototype the Master implanted into his disciples' lives what he purposed to reap through their future witness.

Similarly, Christian leaders in our day must seek to ensure the credibility and authority of their testimony through conscious patterning after Christ's prototype. Biblical leadership is meant to amount to more than just a certain degree of positive moral influence; when it is truly exercised within the parameters of his paradigm, it constitutes a powerful witness, guiding and stimulating others to holy living. **There is neither need nor hope to discover a better model for spiritual leadership than Jesus Christ's example.** From this perspective one understands why Paul refrained from comparing himself to other believers (cf. 2 Cor 10:12), Christians ought to rather focus on and gauge themselves against their Lord (cf. 1 Cor 11:1).

Leadership according to Biblical standards is a superhuman task and can be rightly accomplished solely by divine enabling, available through Jesus Christ's all-sufficiency and transmitted through the Holy Spirit's gracious working. Only as leaders yield to him so that he can perform God's purposes in and through them, they will be qualified to fruitfully serve their Lord. Admittedly, during his time on earth no leader will live a sinless life. Yet his followers should be able to notice that his face is set to emulate his Master, that in spite of vulnerability to temptation and occasional shortcoming he is progressing toward maturity in Christ. Under the shadow of permanent human proneness to failure, doubt may arise as to whether it is really possible to establish and uphold an exemplary witness for Christ that is authentic and powerful.

On 3 September 1889 a boy was born into the Hindu home of Sirdar Sher Singh, resident in the Indian village of Rampur. When the son, who was given the name of Sundar, reached the age of fourteen, he saw early one morning a vision of the Lord Jesus Christ.[28] This experience became the absolute turning-point in his life, because it rescued the restless adolescent from the abyss of suicidal thoughts into a life of deep peace and joy.

He was baptized on his sixteenth birthday and decided soon afterwards to become a Christian *sádhu* (a wandering devout man). Adopting the characteristic yellow robe and turban, bare-footed SADHU SUNDAR SINGH began to witness for Jesus Christ, first in Rampur and neighbouring villages, then farther afield in the Punjab, later he trekked to Kashmir, Baluchistan and Afghanistan. In 1908 he fulfilled for the first time the special commission he had received not long after his encounter with Christ - to go and proclaim him in Tibet. This charge he delivered faithfully under many hardships, undertaking numerous similar trips into the remote Himalayas.

Sundar ministered in Nepal and Sikkim, Ceylon, Burma, Malaya, China and Japan. 1920 found him in Great Britain, France, the United States and Australia, two years later he travelled again to Europe, from where he returned exhausted and sick. Living from 1923 onwards at Sabathu, he gave himself mainly to prayer, meditation and the writing of devotional literature. Nevertheless he did not lose sight of the spiritual neediness of Tibet. It was in fact another trip to the Himalayas, commenced in April 1929, from which he never returned.

The trait which marked Sádhu Sundar Singh's personality and ministry more than any other was Christlikeness. He, who confessed of himself, "I am not worthy to follow in the footsteps of my Lord....,"[29] was regarded by his biographer Mrs A. Parker as "a living copy of his Master."[30] She furthermore noted, "... many of us realize how by close fellowship with Jesus and complete obedience to His will he has become so approximated to his Lord that wherever he goes people say: "How like Christ he is!" "[31] A newspaper in Sydney commented in connection with Sundar Singh's visit, "It was the nearest conception one could form of what our Lord must have been like..., for the very presence of the Sádhu brought with it an atmosphere of things Christ-like ...."[32] Besides, it is reported that a certain servant on opening the door thought Jesus was standing in front of the house and that children wished 'Jesus would put them to bed'.[33]

Just like his Master the Sádhu was a man of love, faith, prayer, humility and courage, suffered hunger, heat, loneliness, persecution and imprisonment. He resembled him in his simple teaching style and the use of graphic illustrations like the following: "I found a stone in a pool among the Himalayas. It was hollow, and when I broke it I found the center completely dry. So it is here in the West. You have lain for centuries in the water of Christianity, but it has never penetrated your hearts."[34]

What made Sundar's witness, which led many to God, so powerful among his compatriots was on the one hand his Christlikeness, on the other the fact that he presented "a concrete example of what Christ means to India in an Indian way".[35] In his indigenous approach, Parker was convinced, the Sádhu possessed "a key to the hearts of his countrymen no foreigner can ever hope to have, however great his love for India and her people may be."[36] At the same time the truly Indian representation of Biblical Christianity evident in his life set a model for his fellow-men which greatly facilitated them in following the ways of Christ, too.

Resuming broader reflections on the dimension of exemplification, there is another facet of Jesus' mentoring method calling for closer attention. Our previous investigation unveiled that in his training of the Twelve the Master placed much stronger emphasis on their development in character than in skill. Paul obviously concurred with this orientation; for instance, most of the prerequisites for spiritual leaders listed in 1 Tim 3:2-7 pertain to the realm of character, only one refers to skill (the ability to teach, mentioned in v. 2). As the Lord Jesus intended his disciples to serve as witnesses not only of his deeds and thoughts but especially also of his character, their growth in this area had to be imperative. His choice technique to this end was modelling, and it is vital to understand that such **focalizing on exemplification shifts the centre of gravity in leadership influence from communicating to being.**

A person's character is of greater consequence than his words, because who he is bears upon how he shares. A godly personality constitutes a higher qualification for spiritual service than rich endowments. Samuel L. Brengle underlined this fact in the following manner:

> When God searches for a man to work in His vineyard, He does not ask, "Has he great natural abilities? Is he thoroughly educated? Is he a fine singer? Is he eloquent in prayer? Can he talk much?"
> But, rather, He asks, "Is his heart perfect toward Me? Is he holy? Does he love much? Is he willing to walk by faith, and not by sight? Does he love Me so much, and has he such childlike confidence in My love for him, that he can trust Me to use him when he doesn't see any sign that I *am* using him? Will he be weary and faint when 1 correct

him and try to fit him for greater usefulness? Or will he, like Job, cry out, 'Though He slay me, yet will I trust Him?' Does he search My Word, and 'meditate therein day and night, in order to do according to all that is written therein?' Does he wait on Me for My counsel, and seek in everything to be led by My Spirit?"[37]

Not all Christians are equally talented, but they can all mature unto godliness. Not every leader is gifted or trained as a good communicator, but every one is expected to live a Christlike witness. People tend to be more profoundly impacted by the messenger than the message. **In the last analysis, the fulfillment of the Great Commission will depend not so much on sophisticated proclamation strategies as on Christlike living on the field.** James Chalmers' last century experience in the Pacific clearly substantiates this view:

> It is not the preaching of a sermon so much as the living the life that tells on the native heart. It is by living a divine life, by striving to follow in the footsteps of Him who came to express the Father's love, that we win the heart of the savage, and raise him up to become a true man or woman in Jesus Christ.[38]

To assimilate the preponderance of character so prominent in Jesus' mentoring mode presents a special difficulty to westerners, because their cultural environment is attuned more to doing than being. This gives rise to the possibility of letting **a managerial fallacy** creep in to Christian leadership development.[39] That is to say, under the label of 'spiritual leadership training' one deals predominantly with subject areas - like for instance setting priorities, the effective use of time, decision-making procedures, circumspect planning, delegation principles - which are actually managerial issues.[40] Such sidetracking practice is misleading in several respects.

Firstly, it fades out the prominence of character which Christ's prototype established. There is the danger, secondly, of paying less attention to the spiritual infrastructure of individuals than to the organizational structure they operate in. It is a hazardous enterprise to position people beyond the orbit of their maturity, to entrust them with greater responsibility and power than they can handle. Different from a manager, a spiritual leader's influence does not stem primarily from his position, but from his personality. Thirdly, the erroneous notion may be entertained that it is possible to compensate lacking depth of character through greater breadth of knowledge and expertise. Yet the truth is that **followers are more inclined to put their trust in a leader's character than in his competence**. One must not overlook either, fourthly, that the fallacy alluded to above fosters the neglect of a genuine concern for the welfare of those being led, which is a dire necessity though and again was distinctly exemplified by the Lord Jesus.

Without doubt our concept of leadership will shape our practice. Whether we are more task- and efficiency-oriented or more people- and character-centred, will surface in the way we lead. Our safeguard will be to increasingly adjust to the well-balanced model of the Master who, while truly committed to shepherding those under his care, also displayed high proficiency in ministry performance.

Integrity is a cardinal ingredient of exemplary Christian living. In R.J. Clinton's estimation, "Integrity is the heart of character,"[41] and C.R. Padilla underscored, "Integrity in mission is not optional. It has to do with faithfulness to Jesus Christ, the Lord of the whole life."[42] Christ himself led a life of integrity (Matt 22:16, cf. also Jn 8:46, 14:30) and whoever claims to represent him as his witness has likewise to aspire towards it.

The Bible furnishes ample instruction on the subject. It teaches us principles (cf. e.g. Ps 25:21, 41:12, Pr 10:9, 11:3, Rom 2:17-23), mentions people who lacked integrity (e.g. Josh 7:20.21, 2 Kgs 5:20-27, 2 Sam 20:8-10), shows us how men were tested in this area (e.g. Gen 39:6-10, Job 2:3-6, Dan 1:8-16) and commends others for their integrity (e.g. 1 Sam 12:2-5, Jer 35:6-19, Ezek 14:14). The Scriptures highlight particularly David's example in this regard (e.g. 1 Kgs 9:4, Ps 78:72), and with Ps 101 the 'man after God's heart' (cf. Acts 13:22) gave us insight into how he consciously pursued a life of integrity:

> I will be careful to lead a blameless life - when will you come to me? I will walk in my house with blameless heart. I will set before my eyes no vile thing. The deeds of faithless men I hate; they will not cling to me.
> Men of perverse heart shall be far from me; I will have nothing to do with evil.
> Whoever slanders his neighbor in secret, him will I put to silence; whoever has haughty eyes and a proud heart, him will I not endure.
> My eyes will be on the faithful in the land, that they may dwell with me; he whose walk is blameless will minister to me.
> No one who practices deceit will dwell in my house; no one who speaks falsely will stand in my presence.
> Every morning I will put to silence all the wicked in the land; I will cut off every evildoer from the city of the LORD.
> (vv. 2-8)

We may describe integrity as oneness of inner and outer life, congruence between inward disposition and outward action. To its main components belong purity, truthfulness and consistency. Persons of integrity will shun hypocrisy, partiality and hidden agendas, scheming and shady financial dealings; they will not break promises or other commitments, neither rationalize personal failure and guilt nor take advantage of others. **Genuine integrity encompasses all spheres of life, radiates through attitudes, words and deeds at all times everywhere.** A true test of integrity is what we are and do when nobody sees us.

Unquestionably integrity is a summation of the type of

character needed to impact people for God. Powerful influence in witnessing and leadership is essentially contingent on credibility, yet credibility is established through integrity. On the other hand a lack of integrity in a Christian distorts this effect, just like a bell with a crack, he will not ring true.[43] As G. Hartis declared, "Ministry is what we leave in our wake as we follow Jesus."[44] Making it our primary concern to emulate the Master's paradigm (cf. Jn 21:19.22) is the best and in fact only way to secure a proper exemplary witness and leadership model for those around us.

5.3 The Dimension of Contextualization

For cross-cultural leadership development efforts to be crowned with success one must, next to affiliation and exemplification, take the dimension of contextualization into account. The term 'contextualization' was first introduced by S. Coe and A. Sapsezian in 1972[45] and has since then been filled with a wide range of content. Evidently the confines of this present study make it impossible to do justice to so extensive a subject area, but the attempt will be undertaken to sketch in broad strokes some salient aspects which have particular bearing on mentoring across cultural boundaries.

According to A.R. Tippett, "contextualisation includes not only the cultural forms of the past, but also political, sociological and acculturation realities of the present day and challenges proclamation to take them seriously."[46] **To contextualize, more specifically, denotes to render culturally relevant, meaningful and acceptable, to fit the message to the receptor culture.** Contextualization relative to leadership training implies the content in question is communicated in a culturally viable manner, is shared with the nationals on their terms, is clothed in an indigenous garb.

Because worldview and thought patterns are culturally conditioned, people comprehend and interpret newly received information within the framework of reference already established by their home culture. God created a multiplicity of cultures and in the Great Commission made each and every one of these the target for appropriate evangelistic witness. **Both the incomparable message of salvation and the dignity of the individuals to be reached require utmost diligence in contextualization.**

Failure in this regard would render our communication merely peripheral. Our witness would be unintelligible and hence not persuasive, neither would people's hearts be touched nor deeper changes in their lives accomplished. Biblical truth must be contextualized if its inherent power is to profoundly affect the receptors' whole existence. "The ultimate goal of contextualization," D.S. Mwakanandi wrote, "is a total incarnation of Christianity into the real life situation of the people."[47] Apt contextualization discerns and opens up ways so that Jesus Christ can impact the respective target culture. With all endeavour along these lines **the key question therefore is, "What would the Lord Jesus do, if he were in this specific cultural context?"**[48]

Indisputably contextual reflection can have its danger zones. One treacherous tendency is to consider contextualization as terminable, but it has always to be looked upon as an ongoing process, because culture as such is subject to continual change. A.F. Glasser indicated another problem when he warned, "The tragedy today is that some of the ardent enthusiasts for contextualization are virtually ignoring the text because of their preoccupation with the context."[49] Further dangers arise when contextualization is over-estimated. Admittedly it is vital, yet by itself it is insufficient. For a message to be truly heard, it has to be not only suited to the local culture but also shared on a sound relational basis. Otherwise the addressees will not receive the message into their very hearts. Besides, human shortcoming in contextualization will never neutralize God's divine resources for communicating with people; he can - and did, as we saw in Sádhu Sundar Singh's case - sovereignly surmount man's limitations and expectations to reveal himself.

To facilitate a process of circumspect contextualization, gathering as much relevant cultural data as possible cannot be dispensed with. A humble attitude, which approaches the new culture with respect and embraces it from a teachable disposition, is likewise imperative. We need to sit where the people sit, listen to them often and carefully, pick up language items from them eagerly and ask them stimulating questions. **We must tap resourceful information channels** like their traditions, customs and ceremonies, their art, music, dances and plays, their stories, legends, riddles and proverbs. We should research their history, study their beliefs, analyze the political and social conditions they are living under and find out what they enjoy and dislike, are familiar with and afraid of.

When embarking upon fact-finding of this sort, we do well to remember the relativity of all cultures as well as our own conditioning which works against our adopting the other culture readily. Building solid relationships with nationals, who uncover for us the deeper dimensions of their home culture, seems therefore all the more important. Their insider information is greatly needed to complement and correct our outsider observation. Only in this way will we be enabled to on the one hand grasp better and better how the locals perceive, think, evaluate and feel, and on the other detect wrong assumptions and misconceptions on our part. Such a **relational bridge-head**, founded on mutual openness, can also protect us against imposing our foreign cultural patterns and offering answers for issues which presented no problems to the nationals to start with.

Notwithstanding all dedicated personal efforts our adjustment to the new culture can never be more than an approximation, even if we cultivate a bicultural personality.

Hence securing the willing and competent co-operation of nationals will always be a cardinal factor in effectually 'acclimatizing' the message we bring. This horizontal linkage needs to be coupled, however, with a vertical perspective, that is with prayer to God for his wisdom and assistance. The missionary depends on God's granting the sensitivity to discern ways in which he has already been at work in the local setting, to spot key individuals he has prepared to serve as cross-cultural bridge-builders, to discover cultural elements whose utilization will enhance fruitful communication. **Contextualization of Biblical content consists of more than mere intellectual activity, it amounts to fabricating with God's help the very key that will unlock people's hearts for the reception of divine truth.** "In the final analysis", C.R. Padilla epitomized, "the contextualization of the Gospel is not man's work, but God's."[50]

Missionaries with a heart for cross-cultural mentoring face the challenge of exercising their ministry in a fashion compatible with the receptor culture. As they labour in true servanthood to accommodate their mode of operation to the targeted environment, they will find that structures and training patterns already present in the local context provide - as long as they are not sinful - the most fertile soil for Christian leadership training. Taking advantage of these indigenous hinges furthers the intended transmission process, kindles the addressees' natural interest and paves the way for them to respond authentically to the Holy Spirit's working in their midst.

Proper fulfillment of such a catalytic function, exhibited by Philip in Acts 8:31-35, necessitates a willingness to die to one's own cultural leanings and preferences. The threatening prospect of levelling the rich cultural diversity God generated by a uniform training approach can only be averted through **a conscious de-westernizing effort**. For instance, programmes intended for a Two-Thirds World setting have to be re-designed as less task- and more relationship-centred, less managerially preoccupied and less academic than their western counterparts.

Two sources in particular provide the observant leadership trainer in his search for cultural clues with valuable insight, firstly **the existing social structure**. Obviously an urban context will vary considerably from a rural one. Subdivisions like tribes, clans, castes or extended families play a significant role, too. From a mentoring perspective especially, those indicators prove priceless which reveal the ways in which leaders traditionally emerge and function among their own people:

What does the community expect of a leader?
Which leadership qualifications are regarded as desirable or even indispensable?
Are there special selection procedures?
Does a certain leadership style prevail?
How are potential leaders groomed?
Is the community directed by single or plural leadership?
Are decisions taken by one leader or through group consent?

In parts of Africa, for instance, a basic requirement for recognition as a leader is that one has a household and runs it well. Thai society relates leadership acceptance to mature age. Within both settings it would be counter-productive to concentrate the thrust of leadership training chiefly on young people. Furthermore, western individualism may cause serious conflict for those from the Two-Thirds World who grew up with a communal outlook, expect guidance to come from their superiors and are accustomed to group decisions. Do we hesitate to attribute validity to a village chief's announcement that all his people are willing to become Christians?[51] Did not, after all, the turning of whole households to Christ feature as a rather common phenomenon in Early Church times (cf. Acts 11:14, 16:15,

16:31-34, 1 Cor 1:16)?

We can assure that the nationals will deem our cross-cultural mentoring endeavours neither irrelevant nor irritating by integrating our labours with indigenous leadership patterns, by **flowing with and not against the tide of the local leadership idiom,** which to them is familiar, authentic and therefore credible. Great benefit, moreover, can be derived from **targeting primarily individuals who already enjoy the respect and confidence of their people** (cf. Deut 1:15, Jer 30:21). A striking illustration in this respect was furnished by John Dekker's work among the Dani.[52] When John, who had arrived on New Guinea in 1960, sensed the time had come to start raising up leaders, he opted for a strategy which had been successfully applied before by other missionaries on Irian Jaya.

He told a group of Danis who had come to see him, "You go home to your villages and appoint representatives to come for teaching four days each week in a witness school. You choose leaders who show a desire to listen to God's words and to follow them."[53] So the Danis selected fifteen representatives, some in their teens, the oldest one over forty. What John taught at the school the witness men repeated, memorized and discussed. On Fridays they went back to their villages and in turn instructed their families and friends. To prevent misunderstandings from creeping in, John undertook occasional visits to the witness men's villages. Thus in due course the teaching originally shared in the witness school reached hundreds of other lives.

The other source from which profitable clues can be gathered is the range of **indigenous teaching modes** operational within the local culture. Whereas in the western hemisphere strong emphasis is placed on formal (institutional) education, many Two-Thirds World societies still show a strong adherence to **informal (relational) training.** The latter was common in Old Testament times (cf. e.g. Deut 32:7,

1 Chr 25:6-8, Ps 78:2-6) and - as we saw earlier on - of eminent importance in Jesus' day. Likewise in Africa, items such as trades, handicrafts, customs and folklore are frequently passed on informally, be it on professional level through vocational apprenticing, on communal level through initiation rites,[54] or on family level through the older generation teaching the younger.

Availing ourselves of **authentic communicative devices** like legends, stories, parables, proverbs and songs can further enhance our contextualizing attempts. The traditional Basotho saying, "A good prince lights the fire for his people,"[55] for example, lends itself ideally as starting-point for sharing on humility and servanthood. Songs in particular are of great value for disseminating and preserving Scriptural truth, as among others, Dekker and the Colombian church planter Victor Landero experienced.[56] We must not allow a common western leaning toward instruction through literary means to blind us to the fact that the Lord Jesus gave clear preference to oral instruction. Settings where illiteracy prevails, of course, demand this approach anyhow. Over and above it seems timely to recall that the decisive influence in leadership development stems from a chiefly non-verbal source altogether, viz. modelling.

At this juncture some further practical hints can help those actively involved in training non-westerners. They will do well to employ plain language; to refrain from lecturing and stimulate questions, dialogue and discussion instead; to frequently draw illustrations from everyday experiences and nature; to use visual aids; to elaborate on cardinal truths repeatedly; to encourage memorization; if appropriate, to distribute simple follow-up material; to challenge the listeners to apply what they learned and to pass it on to others.

God himself saw fit to reach out to man in contextualized fashion. Through the Incarnation his Son identified with the human race. At the same time Jesus adopted the Jewish culture so thoroughly that for most of his contemporaries his divinity was veiled behind perceptions of him such as carpenter (Mk 6:3), teacher (Jn 3:2), prophet (Jn 4:19), gardener (Jn 20:15) and casual travel companion (cf. Lk 24:13-18). While sharing with individuals, he consciously built a bridge to their respective ways of thinking, as instanced in the cases of Nicodemus (Jn 3:1-21) and the Samaritan woman (Jn 4:4-26). He took on the conventional role of a rabbi, who could be found teaching in synagogues and on the Temple precincts, and surrounded himself with a select group of disciples. For their mentoring into spiritual leaders he applied the common Hebrew with-ness approach. To accomplish his coaching intentions he did not practise extraction but rather located their training close to the hub of ordinary Jewish existence.

Jesus accommodated his life-style and ministry to his environment, became a Jew to the Jews, thus demonstrating consummately how his witnesses are **to incarnate the truth in a way that does not erect cultural obstacles but instead with credibility reach peoples' hearts for God.** The apostle Paul followed the Master's precedent closely in his commitment to contextualization, evident both from his testimony (cf. 1 Cor 9:19-23) and his missionary practice (cf. e.g. Acts 13:14-41, 17:22-31).

To further fathom the significance of contextualization for cross-cultural leadership development it seems advantageous to consider the concept of **dynamic equivalence** originally developed in the field of translation theory. By translating Bible passages literally on the basis of formal correspondence, one may actually misrepresent the true meaning. "In such cases," advised the Willowbank Report,[57] "the better way is to find in the other language an expression which makes an equivalent impact on the hearers now as did the original. This may involve changing the form in order to preserve the meaning. This is called "dynamic equivalence"." A translation geared to dynamic equivalence attributes lower priority to form than to function; while guarding the content, it takes liberty to select culturally appropriate expressions in order to achieve equivalence of response in the receptor.

Working on a Gahuku translation of 1 Cor 5:6, "... Don't you know that a little yeast works through the whole batch of dough?," Ellis Deibler, missionary on Papua New Guinea, discovered through his translation helper that the locals knew of neither leaven nor bread-making. Consequently, to render the scripture meaningful for them, he had to use "gall" instead of "yeast".[58] Larry Clark, serving the Barasano in Colombia, was in reference to Lk 11:11 confronted with the necessity of replacing "snake" with "eel", because in the nationals' eyes providing your son with a snake to eat in fact makes a good gift.[59]

As with Bible translation so in cross-cultural evangelism one may miss the mark of dynamic equivalence. Missionaries of the past often, unconsciously or consciously, propagated formal correspondence. For instance, the church architecture was of European origin, no less were the imported musical instruments, the service order and liturgy, the hymns translated into the vernacular; people were expected to dress up European-style when coming to church. Thus the impression evolved that outward conformity was quintessential to Christianity, an erroneous notion which was already unequivocally refuted by the apostles' council in Jerusalem (Acts 15:1-31, esp. vv. 10.19.28). The fateful tendency to burden nationals with non-essentials causing cultural dissonance still casts its shadow today. "The mental identification of Christianity with a Western culture," David H. Adeney rightly analyzed, "is one of the biggest obstacles to building up an indigenous witness."[60] And what about dynamic equivalence applied to cross-cultural mentoring?

The reason why many well-intended training attempts initiated by westerners have proved ineffective is that in reality they produced formal correspondence and fell short

of dynamic equivalence. Unfortunately, programmes were more often institutionalized than suitably contextualized. Where only minor attention was reserved for indigenizing the approach chosen, the nationals were partially affected with a western mindset and mode of operation, yet substantially left ill prepared to cope with the specific challenges arising from spiritual leadership responsibilities shouldered within their culturally divergent environment.

Viable contextualization on the other hand facilitates dynamic equivalence. **It so engrafts the supracultural aspects of Jesus Christ's mentoring prototype into the respective indigenous cultural idiom that a measure of leadership influence on the nationals is secured which is comparable to the impact Jesus exerted on his disciples.** A high goal? - yes indeed, but Jesus procured the model and the Holy Spirit the enabling for its wholehearted pursuit. The Master's permanent with-ness through the Paraclete is the inexhaustible divine resource for the fulfillment of the commission to disciple all people groups (cf. Matt 28:19). If the Lord entrusted this mandate to us, dare we question its practicality?

V.K. Samuel once pointed out that Jesus Christ's Incarnation was both authentically cultural and profoundly supracultural.[61] Identifying with the Jewish culture, he at the same time modelled and shared the supracultural values of the kingdom of God. Cross-cultural witness meets with a similar duality, "though Christianity is supracultural in its origin and truth, it is cultural in its application," D.J. Hesselgrave declared.[62] Hence a missionary faces **the task of differentiating between absolute Biblical values and norms on the one hand and relative cultural values and forms on the other**, between non-negotiable elements of content and flexible courses of communication as well as implementation.

Leadership development according to Christ's example is essentially a matter of content which is ready to be transmitted in a multiplicity of culturally acceptable forms.

With the target of dynamic equivalence in mind, however, various supracultural non-negotiables have to be allowed for. Among these, I would suggest, one should include four categories comprising at least the following items:

1. <u>Axioms</u>

   affiliation
   exemplification
   contextualization
   integration
   multiplication
   impartation

2. <u>Attitudes</u>

   love
   faith
   obedience
   humility
   servanthood
   commitment

3. <u>Attributes</u>

   accountability
   integrity
   anointing
   holiness
   spiritual authority
   vision

4. <u>Actions</u>

   following Jesus
   abiding in Christ
   appropriating God's Word
   praying
   witnessing
   making disciples

While the first category is comprehensively dealt with in the chapter on hand, the majority of the other features have already come into view in the course of our preceding investigations. May it be sufficient at this point to briefly touch on one trait to further elucidate the supracultural nature of such elements as listed above.

No matter whether a given culture shows preference for a more supportive, directive or even authoritarian leadership style for instance, those taking on spiritual leadership responsibilities are expected to exemplify servanthood, a quality which the Lord Jesus established as a non-negotiable in Mk 10:42-45. That he at one time demonstrated it through washing his disciples' feet (Jn 13:4.5) was, culturally speaking, incidental. A Christian leader among the Basotho may manifest servanthood by providing his friends with straw to thatch their huts, a Motilone through making arrows for his companions, a Dani by clearing a piece of ground for other members of his tribe to start a sweet potato garden. **The culturally determined form in which servanthood finds its expression is secondary. Of primary importance is that the modelling brings about an impact on the followers similar to the one Jesus' demonstration had on the Twelve.**

The validity of Jesus' mentoring method transcends all cultural boundaries. Paul employed it diligently in the culturally diversified Mediterranean setting. For us today the issue cannot be whether we favour a western model or one from the Two-Thirds World, the question is whether we are willing to truly follow Jesus' consummate prototype in the awareness that "the most outstanding thing about a Christian should not be his culture, but his Christlikeness."[63] **Matters of culture need to be tested in the light of absolute Scriptural standards and judged against the backdrop of Christ's exemplary life and ministry in particular.** D.S. Gilliland indicated the major part contextualization plays 'in this evaluation process when he stated, "Contextualization utilizes cultural factors that are compatible with the Word; it transforms what can be changed under the authority of the Word, and it confronts, even rejects, what is antithetical to the Word."[64]

A sensitive cross-cultural missionary is only too conscious of his own conditioning. He is also mindful of the possibility that some of his values and behavioural patterns may in fact differ more from Jesus' model than such discernible in the native culture. So, wherever possible, he strives to prevent his ethnocentric biases from polluting the purity, simplicity and power of Jesus' prototype which he seeks to emulate under the Holy Spirit's enabling.

At one stage a Hindu told E. Stanley Jones, "I have hated Christianity, but if Christianity is Christ, I do not see how we Indians can hate it."[65] The essence of true Christianity cannot be defined in cultural, only in supracultural Biblical terms; it consists in following Christ. Man's need is Christ, God's answer is Christ. Cultural values and expressions may change, Jesus Christ remains unchanged. **When labouring cross-culturally, we must not train people into our culture but into Christ; our contextualization efforts are to facilitate their increasing conformation to his likeness.** The Lord Jesus did not commission us to hand down a certain system of thought but to witness of him as a person. Irrespective of the given cultural context, his person contains and displays all the pertinent lessons ever to be learned about spiritual growth and leadership.

Our considerations would be incomplete if mention were not made afresh of the Holy Spirit's decisive role. Firstly, **in order to be productive in cross-cultural mentoring, we cannot do without a Spirit-enlightened working knowledge of Jesus Christ's consummate paradigm.** The Holy Spirit, moreover, is the one who has already taken influence on the target culture even before we commence our witness (cf. Eccl 3:11). Accordingly, contextualization efforts can link up with the cultural beach-heads he has prepared. Thirdly, the Holy Spirit guides all participants of the communication process into divine truth. Finally, as we model and impart supracultural principles in submission to his specific guidance, he furthers dynamically equivalent results.

5.4 The Dimension of Integration

Within the framework of our current inquiry integration is understood as the bringing together of information and implementation, theory and practice, knowledge and experience. Luke, on introducing the Book of Acts, alluded to the Lord Jesus' integrated ministry style by reminding Theophilus that in his earlier Gospel he "wrote about all that Jesus began to do and to teach . . . ." (1:1). The Master's mentoring of the Twelve in particular displayed the same combined mode of operation, in K. Phillips' words, "He perfectly balanced His disciples' theological input with their practical participation."[66] Not satisfied with instructing his followers to solely know certain theoretical concepts, **Jesus made his coaching immensely practical, trained his friends through action for action.**

At this point it is helpful to notice that the word *manthano*, from which *mathetes* (disciple) is derived, denotes "to increase one's knowledge" but also "to learn by use and practice."[67] Jesus evidently took special care to provide his disciples with opportunities to put their knowledge to practical use. He started off by delegating to them simple tasks, like baptizing (Jn 4:2), buying food (Jn 4:8) and getting a boat ready for him (Mk 3:9). In due course he exposed them to more complex and demanding 'field practice', entrusting them with the responsibility to preach the message of the kingdom (Matt 10:7) as well as, "Heal the sick, raise the dead, cleanse those who have leprosy, drive out demons . . . ." (Matt 10:8). Added menial assignments (cf. Jn 6:10.12, Matt 21:1.2, Mk 14:12-15) were conducive to further develop their capacity to serve.

We must not lose sight of the fact either that Jesus interspersed his public and private instruction time and again with challenges urging his disciples to application (cf. e.g. Matt 5:16, 11:28.29, 22:37-39; Mk 11:22, 16:15, Lk 17:3.4, 21:34-36, Jn 13:15, 15:12). When the apostle Paul engaged in leadership development, he followed the Master's integration precedent. His coaching of Timothy, for instance, affords us with insight as to how he sought to mould his trainee by way of practical ministry exposure and frequent calls to action (cf. Acts 19:22, 2 Cor 1:19, Phil 2:22; 1 Tim 4:6-16, 6:11-14, 2 Tim 1:6-8, 2:1-7, 4:1.2.5).

Repeatedly the Lord Jesus drew attention to blessings connected with implementation of known truth:

> Therefore everyone who hears these words of mine and puts them into practice is like a wise man who built his house on the rock. (Matt 7:24)
> But everyone who hears these words of mine and does not put them into practice is like a foolish man who built his house on sand. (Matt 7:26)
> My mother and brothers are those who hear God's word and put it into practice. (Lk 8:21)
> Now that you know these things, you will be blessed if you do them. (Jn 13:17)

Obedience is a vital link between knowing and doing. It is prerequisite for entering the kingdom of God (Matt 7:21), proves genuine love for Jesus (cf. Jn 14:21), releases divine favour (cf. Lk 11:28) and understanding (cf. Jn 7:17). **Jesus' training of his disciples was from beginning to end obedience-centred**. Consequently it was only natural that on commissioning the Eleven to make disciples on their part, he obligated them to pursue this task essentially through teaching their understudies full obedience to his commands (cf. Matt 28:20).

Numerous Christians are familiar with Psalm 119 as a celebration of God's Word. Fewer though are aware that it emphatically commends obedience to this Word at the same time. In fact, either by overt reference or by implication, the psalm spotlights obedience more than forty times. We learn, while approaching God's Word from a heart disposition of awe (cf. v. 120), love (cf. v. 159) and trust (cf. v. 42), one ought to make it the subject of thorough meditation (cf. v. 97). Besides, the obedience which the Word of God deserves and claims should be earnest (cf. v. 106), determined (cf. v. 112), wholehearted (cf. v. 69), prompt (cf. v. 60) and constant (cf. v. 44).

If our leadership training is to meet Biblical standards, we need to first assure its obedience-orientation and then work for an allegiance response from our mentorees of the quality just outlined. Such obedience goes beyond sporadic efforts, it is habitual. In other words, we must aim at leading our trainees into a life-style marked by their "walking in the truth" (2 Jn 4).

Obedient application of Christ's commands and Scriptural truth in general yields twofold benefits. On the one side integration fosters individual growth, on the other it serves the overall good. **God expects his servants to be concerned for their personal spiritual progress, yet to produce rich blessing for their fellow-men too.** As we invest ourselves under his direction for the welfare of those around us, the principle inherent in Lk 6:38 comes into effect, that God will return and even increase what was made available to his cause at the outset. This enables us all the more to respond to his wish that his people should provide balm for the festering wounds of hurting mankind and be enriched themselves in this process:

> Is not this the kind of fasting I have chosen: to loose the chains of injustice and untie the cords of the yoke, to set the oppressed free and break every yoke? Is it not to share your food with the hungry and to provide the poor wanderer with shelter - when you see the naked, to clothe him, and not to turn away from your own flesh and blood? Then your light will break forth like the dawn, and your healing will quickly appear; then your righteousness will go before you, and the glory of the LORD will be your rear guard. Then you will call, and the LORD will answer; you will cry for help, and he will say: Here am I . . . . (Isa 58:6-9)

One man who took the implications of this passage seriously in exemplary fashion was WILLIAM BOOTH.

During his childhood already, William, who was born at Nottingham on 10 April 1829, became acquainted with poverty. His father was a petty builder, and at the age of thirteen William had to discontinue school training in order to contribute to family earnings as apprentice at a pawnbroker's shop. In 1844 he turned to Christ, disclosing years later in retrospect the secret of his usefulness for God had been that as a fifteen year old he had made the total commitment, "God shall have all there is of William Booth."[68] While still a teenager he engaged in evangelism among the poor of his hometown. Later he transferred his activities to London, and at the age of twenty-three took up work as a Methodist circuit minister. He married Catherine Mumford in 1855 and was ordained three years later.

However, in 1861 Booth resigned from the Methodist Connexion. His ensuing ministry as itinerant evangelist met with distinct divine confirmation; an eighteen-month campaign in Cornwall alone brought no less than 7, 000 people into a new relationship with God. From 1865 onwards William and Catherine concentrated their service on East London and there founded "The Christian Mission". William felt a special burden to share the Gospel with those outsiders of society who were not being reached through established churches. For Bramwell, Booth's eldest son, it remained an unforgettable experience how his father took him for the first time to an East End pub and told the shocked then thirteen year old, "These are our people. These are the people I want you to live for and bring to Christ."[69]

The work grew quickly, by 1878 about forty-five stations had been established. During the same year the Mission's name was changed to "The Salvation Army". At the beginning of 1879 William Booth as 'the General' was in charge of 127 full-time staff on eighty-one stations; the Army's gazette "The War Cry" appeared for the first time in December. The following year saw the Army 'open fire' in the United States, Ireland and Australia, to be followed by France a few months later. Between 1881 and 1885 the Salvationists' witness[70] won 250,000 people to Christ. By 1890 the Army had 2,874 corps in thirty-four countries and colonies with 9,416 officers, the annual distribution of Army literature amounting to 37,400,000 pieces. When the General died in

1912, the Army's activities had spread to fifty-eight countries through 16,000 officers who had identified with his vision.

Actually this vision had undergone a major modification in 1887. Up to that time Booth's overwhelming concern had been to reach souls for Christ. But now, sparked through the heart-rending sight of homeless men squatting in the niches of London Bridge, he was gripped with an increasing burden for people's temporal plight as well. In one of the introductory paragraphs of his book *In Darkest England and the Way Out* Booth explained:

> My only hope for the permanent deliverance of mankind from misery, either in this world or the next, is the regeneration or remaking of the individual by the power of the Holy Ghost through Jesus Christ. But in providing for the relief of temporal misery I reckon that I am only making it easy where it is now difficult, and possible where it is now all but impossible, for men and women to find their way to the Cross of our Lord Jesus Christ.[71]

In its war against destitution, unemployment and homelessness, hunger and disease, drunkenness, vice, prostitution and crime, the Army utilized a broad array of strategies. For example, during the General's lifetime Salvationists in different parts of the world created work opportunities, provided shelter, helped widows as well as deserted and orphaned children, opened crèches, ran soup kitchens and cheap food depots, visited the sick, cared for lepers and blind people, established rescue homes for women and girls, ministered to prisoners and assisted those who had been discharged. Booth's passion for supplying answers to the totality of human neediness surfaced once again powerfully in his last public speech when he affirmed, "While women weep as they do now, I'll fight; while little children go hungry as they do now, I'll fight; while men go to prison, in and out, in and out, I'll fight; while there yet remains one dark soul without the light of God, I'll fight - I'll fight to the very end!"[72]

Undoubtedly the Salvation Army would never have won its many early victories without the dedication, zeal and maturity of its officers. The discipline and essentially practical training which cadets experienced, moulded them into leaders of stature who, under the empowering of the Holy Spirit, were not only equipped to overcome contempt and ridicule, opposition and persecution, but also to achieve exploits for God. Particularly impressive in the latter respect were the 'invasion' of America[73] under George Scott Railton and the pioneering work in India[74] with Frederick Booth-Tucker in charge.

Integrated leadership training, like the six-month programme introduced in 1886, offered definite advantages. It connected learning of theoretical content (i.e. Bible truths as well as the Army's orders, regulations and doctrine) with learning through practical experience (e.g. attending to chores at the training centre, looking after sick people, witnessing in pubs, holding open air meetings), engulfing the cadets in conditions highly favourable to **the concurrent development of knowledge, ministry skills and character.**

"The purpose of application," L.O. Richards pointed out, "is to make truth usable, to get it into the experience, into the life, of the learner."[75] As we provide mentorees with frequent hands-on opportunities, theoretical insight becomes personal and functional. **Repeated implementation transforms perceived truths into habits and personality traits. Real life, with all its complexities, is the best workshop for the manufacturing of competent spiritual leadership.** Certain lessons cannot be gathered from study alone but have to be learned by doing, those arising from one's own failures for example.

On-the-job training reveals the presence or absence of needed talents, and brings one face to face with individual strengths or weaknesses; it shows us, among other things, whether we lack in diligence, patience, humility, obedience, self-denial or faith. Besides, **direct involvement serves to increase motivation and to promote a sense of responsibility and ownership.** Joint action has the potential of furthering a team spirit amidst the co-trainees and of strengthening their relationship with the mentor.

Jesus Christ embedded his development of the Twelve into an active ministry context. He coupled initial teaching with practical follow-up assignments. His focus was on learning by doing, because he was not interested in raising up academicians but missionaries and did not want to prepare his men to pass exams or earn degrees but to function as skilful witnesses. **So he made sure they both observed and served.** Put differently, he did not offer them mere leadership education, he subjected them to leadership training.

Effective Christian mentors will do the same. They estimate theoretical classroom instruction as insufficient and therefore seek to lead their trainees to consistent implementation of discerned truth.[76] They are conscious that "leadership maturing comes from having hands-on opportunity in leadership situations, not just from watching a model over a period of years," as K.O. Gangel remarked.[77] That is to say exemplification, indispensable as it is, nevertheless has its limitation, for no follower will ever emerge as a leader just because of inactively observing his mentor; rather he will have to assiduously apply what he has seen and heard.

Furthermore, to have mentorees serve as witnesses with integrity calls for their cognition and life practice to match. Any activity a Christian undertakes can be a channel for glorifying God and testifying to his fellow-men. His full witness comprises what he is, says and does. **For a follower of Christ to fail in obedient application of the truth he has come to understand dismantles his integrity and weakens his testimony.**

M. Friedeman made mention of the fact that, according

to contemporary educators, "We remember ... 10% of what we hear, 50% of what we say, 70% of what we see, 90% of what we do."[78] The conclusion suggests itself that in leadership development programmes we should seek to avoid artificial lecture settings aimed at hearing and a constricted, intellectual response. Instead **we ought to as much as possible incorporate real life situations requiring practical implementation and a broad, behavioural reaction.**

A bias towards the theoretical, so typical of many westerners, can have far-reaching ramifications for both theological outlook and missionary practice. J.H. Kane declared, "We in the West equate religion with truth, forgetting that in the Third World the people equate religion with power. We ask, Is it true? They ask, Does it work? If it works, they want it; if it doesn't, they don't."[79] People in the Two-Thirds World are less precept- than power-oriented, are looking for evident proof of the predominance of the power they are encouraged to believe in. They "give their allegiance to Christ when they see that his power is superior to magic and voodoo, the curses and blessings of witch doctors, and the malevolence of evil spirits, and that his salvation is a real liberation from the power of evil and death."[80]

To non-westerners destructive satanic forces are often very tangible and threatening. The Danis, for example, were convinced all diseases in their midst were caused by evil spirits, their term for 'sickness' in fact signified "evil spirit pain".[81] In a South East Asian village at some stage the mortality rate among tribal children up to the age of seven was eighty per cent. There as well the locals attributed the root of the problem to evil spirits.[82] For the Christian witness to be credible and compelling in such surroundings, it has to reach beyond the sphere of the intellectual and touch the current existential needs, the nationals must see God's omnipotence in operation.

God is a God of holiness and love, yet of power, too (cf. e.g. Ex 9:16, 1 Chr 29:11.12, Job 37:23, Ps 66:3.7, 106:8, 147:5). As witnesses we should join the psalmist in his desire to make God's power known (cf. 71:18, AV). **If the message we share is accompanied by a demonstration of divine power, we glorify God by directing attention to this important facet of his nature.** This is singularly the case when the testimony takes place within the framework of a 'power encounter',[83] that is, a visible supremacy confrontation between divine and satanic power. Several incidents of this kind can be found in the Old Testament, e.g. Moses vs. Pharaoh's magicians (Ex 7:14-8:19), David vs. Goliath (1 Sam 17:4-54), Elijah vs. Baal's prophets (1 Kgs 18:16-40). Power encounters were also experienced by the Lord Jesus (e.g. Matt 4:1-11, Mk 1:21-28, Lk 8:26-39) and the apostle Paul (Acts 13:6-12, 16:16-18). Again and again mission history has illustrated[84] how the public triumph of divine might over evil power proved instrumental in expanding the Gospel witness.

Those exercising authority on behalf of God's kingdom ought to manifest its power in their lives and ministries, "For the kingdom of God is not a matter of talk but of power" (1 Cor 4:20). Without this ingredient we can meet neither the challenge of a Christlike witness nor the totality of human need around us. However, **Christ's wholistic model and the Holy Spirit's wholistic enduement are geared to encourage and enable us to present a wholistic witness**, including a powerful demonstration of God's confirming withness.

With respect to missionaries and local Christians on the field C.H. Kraft underlined, "The missing element for them and for us is . . . genuine New Testament power, the continual experience of the presence of God, who every day does things the world calls miracles."[85] In the light of this assessment the question arises: Wherever God has placed us to promote his cause, are we sufficiently endued by the

Holy Spirit to overcome opposing evil forces through God's more than commensurate power? May it be so that we will be privileged to conspicuously evidence by our witness how the ascended Lord Jesus Christ, through his with-ness in his followers, is powerfully continuing his work on earth today.

5.5 The Dimension of Multiplication

The Chinese proverb, "Anyone can count the seeds in an apple but who can count the apples in a single seed,"[86] vividly highlights reproductive multiplication. This correlation occupied a central place in God's plan for the development of his original creation (cf. Gen 1:11.12.22.28) and is also of fundamental relevance for the dispensation of the new creation through the Holy Spirit. Those who experience regeneration, the Lord Jesus desires to embrace his charge to reach all the world for God by way of multiplication, as they establish a Christlike witness in the lives of numerous disciples.

Leadership development in Christ's name ought to be undertaken with keen awareness of this dimension of multiplication so recognizable in Christ's ministry. He selected a core group of men, associated with them closely and coached them intensely. Rather than aiming at popularity with the masses, he devoted himself to produce maturity in his followers. The overarching intention was that they would be trained into his likeness (cf. Lk 6:40) to both exhibit his character and continue his work.

Apart from transmitting his prototype, the Master purposed his mentorees to become instrumental in the rise of a dynamic witness movement. On announcing his imminent departure he assured them they would nevertheless not be forsaken, because his permanent with-ness, mediated through the Holy Spirit, would enfold them. The versatile mentoring his with-ness had provided came to full fruition when the

Holy Spirit empowered them on Pentecost. Directed and energized by the Spirit they moved into various leadership functions, extending their authentic Christian testimony and leadership influence.

One of the multiplying leaders who emerged in the days of the Early Church was Joseph, by background a Levite from Cyprus, whom the apostles renamed 'Barnabas' (i.e. 'son of exhortation, encouragement, comfort'). He, who manifested his total commitment to God by selling a field and putting the proceeds at the apostles' disposal, was of high moral standing, filled with the Spirit and a man of faith (Acts 11:24). As such he received Saul, at a time when the young Pharisee was still unpopular due to his earlier persecution of followers of the Way, and introduced him to the apostles (Acts 9:26.27).

Later he searched for Paul in Tarsus and took him to the cosmopolitan city of Antioch, ranked third in importance within the Roman Empire. In the aftermath of persecution disciples had gone to Antioch and through their witness had established a congregation. As Acts 11:22-29 and 13:1-3 let us know, it was not only a growing, giving, worshipping and praying church but one that evidenced mature leadership and mission-mindedness as well. Here Saul found the ideal environment for investing his talents into God's work (cf. Acts 11:26) and for learning valuable leadership lessons under Barnabas' tutelage, which lasted as long as they linked hands in ministry. After their ways parted (Acts 15:37-40), Paul's ministry entered a new phase marked by extraordinary fruitfulness in evangelism and utmost efficiency in mentoring.

There are several features of his leadership training practice which seem particularly noteworthy at this point. Corresponding to the Master's precedent he operated from a global perspective (cf. e.g. Rom 16:26), coaching his understudies essentially on-the-job and on-the-move. Yet, while the Lord Jesus selected a homogeneous group of twelve

Palestinian Jews as his close associates, **Paul brought the Master's mentoring prototype to bear upon changing entourages of considerable cultural diversity.** Among his co-workers were both Jews and Greeks, men hailing from Palestine as well as Macedonia, Pontus, Lycaonia and the province of Asia.

Paul, therefore, was the first to apply the supracultural principles of Jesus Christ's mentoring mode on a large scale in cross-cultural context. His success in this endeavour can be attributed to the fact that he pursued his calling "as an expert builder" (1 Cor 3:10). Close affiliation, modelling, teaching, hands-on learning experiences and follow-up letters were among the means he utilized. Of special significance, however, were his abundant confidence in God's ongoing work in the trainees (cf. Phil 1:6, 2:13, 1 Thess 5:23.24) and his dedicated intercession for them (cf. 2 Tim 1:3, Ph'm 4-6).[87]

With the apostle, as with his Master, all mentoring was mentoring for mission. The paramount goal in raising individuals up to maturity in Christ was not so much their personal spiritual welfare but their being equipped to spread the Gospel message, to multiply a Christlike testimony (cf. 1 Thess 1:6-8). Since Paul sowed generously through his labours he also reaped bountifully. Wherever his activities served to spark off reproduction according to the 2 Tim 2:2 formula, a network of meaningful relationships, authentic Christian witness and godly leadership impact evolved, which fostered a powerful movement of the Spirit and hence the expansion of the kingdom of God.

This expansion will one day culminate in the grand sight disclosed by the apostle John in Rev 7:9: "After this I looked and there before me was a great multitude that no one could count, from every nation, tribe, people and language, standing before the throne and in front of the Lamb. . . ." The path leading the multitude to this heavenly destination is the multiplication of true Christian witness here on earth. From this angle we can easily understand why Jesus placed the making of disciples right at the core of the Great Commission (cf. Matt 28:19). Regrettably, missionary practice of the past not infrequently overlooked the crucial need for multiplication of reproducing disciples; as a result the Lord's initial intention was frustrated.

"Disciple making creates a quality product and an effective work force," B. Hull aptly observed.[88] When we engage in building disciples, our focus must be more on the quality than the quantity of the people we train. Those who have been with us ought to show the will and skill to reproduce and multiply themselves in the lives of others. They should exemplify and teach what it means to live with and for Jesus Christ. **In an age of much religious activity we are well advised to time and again honestly assess our productivity for God in the light of the criteria of his Word.** It would seem misleading to be preoccupied with externals like the size of the budget, the amount of programmes run, or the number of staff employed, yet neglect a real concern for progress in Christlikeness with those entrusted to us.

Spearheading multiplication is not the only task expected of Christian leaders, but, in M. Rush's words, "There is no greater leadership challenge than the challenge to help our followers become leaders capable of training their followers to be leaders also."[89] Do we concede it is less commendable to totally immerse ourselves in one sector of God's work than to equip leaders to tackle additional areas? Are we convinced we are less effectively employed in merely attracting followers than in raising up leaders who will win such on a larger scale? Can we somewhat sense why Dawson Trotman, outstanding discipler and founder of the Navigators, repeatedly enjoined the probing reproduction-oriented question, "Where is your man?"[90] **It ought to be an integral part of our mentoring strategy to pass on the vision, dedication, character qualities and skills we possess**

to men who in turn can and will do the same with others.

The multiplication of leaders presents a special challenge to the cross-cultural missionary. He may find that in his ministry situation on the foreign field various factors work in his favour, for instance his often wider knowledge and broader experience as well as his neutral position relative to existing social strata, tribal rivalries, cultural biases or bondages. On the other side the nationals are the ones accustomed to climate, food and living conditions, familiar with language, customs and modes of thinking and already possess credibility among their own people. Their close affinity to the local cultural context enables them to witness to their fellow-men with an efficiency aliens can only seldom, if ever, hope to match.

William Carey's wise perception, "I think it becomes us to make the most of every one whom the Lord gives us,"[91] reminds cross-cultural missionaries of the task of releasing nationals into their full potential in God. Their individual lives are meant to count for the fulfillment of the Great Commission, they have been endowed by the Holy Spirit with gifts to further God's cause. Missionary domination, however, will stunt leadership development in native Christians. It stifles their initiative and creativity, weakens their commitment and willingness to sacrifice, withholds from them opportunities to shoulder responsibility and exercise faith, robs them of full satisfaction in serving God. **Undue paternalism and over-protectiveness may allow for willing followers but will not produce strong leaders.** A vital key for unleashing people's dormant potential for competent leadership is the relational element of trust.

To invest confidence in someone else involves a conscious choice and at the same time a risk, because trust may be disappointed, betrayed or broken. By way of contrast, mutual trust can be cultivated through openness, integrity and loyalty. While trust generates trust, mistrust breeds mistrust. Genuine trust approaches others on the basis of equality, sees them as partners. To select leadership trainees carefully and - within established confines of accountability - to then entrust them with enough space to be in charge of their lives and ministries, tends to draw the best out of them.[92] This space must include the freedom to fail repeatedly and to gather valuable lessons from such incidents.

In 2 Thess 3:4 Paul assured the recipients of his letter, "We have confidence in the Lord that you are doing and will continue to do the things we command." From this remark one may derive the basic principle that **in spiritual leadership development it is not enough to simply trust the trainees' natural abilities, the secret is to put one's confidence in the Holy Spirit in them.**[93] Paul laid a foundation by modelling and instruction, then exercised implicit trust in the Spirit to further groom the believers. "He set them an example according to the mind of Christ," wrote Roland Allen, "and he was persuaded that the Spirit of Christ in them would teach them to approve that example and inspire them to follow it."[94] If we really trust the Holy Spirit's presence and power in our mentorees, are thoroughly convinced that he will lead them into all truth (cf. Jn 16:13), then it will not be problematic for us to see them take initiative, assume responsibility, utilize their spiritual gifts and even make mistakes. After all, it is God's work they are engaged in, not ours.

Perplexing indeed seems the observation made by D.S. Gilliland, "One of the ironies of mission history is that missionaries who profess to know the most about the Holy Spirit find it very difficult to foster an environment in cross-cultural situations where inexperienced Christians can really discover the Holy Spirit for themselves."[95] **Should it not be natural for missionaries to have faith in the Holy Spirit to achieve in the nationals what they have known him to accomplish in their own lives?** When they personally experience how the Spirit guides, teaches, convicts, corrects, cleanses and empowers, can he not be trusted to minister to the locals in the same way?

Such trust thrives most readily in servant leaders, who place the nationals' concerns first, long for their optimal progress, rejoice in their growth and success.[96] Conscious of being not more than tools in the hands of the Holy Spirit as the actual mentor, servant leaders put their trust in him to bring about what they know they cannot do. Perceiving themselves in the temporary roles of guides and facilitators, they give their all to further a process whereby he can build the trainees up to maturity in Christ. With the nationals' sole and total dependence on God targeted right from the start, they look forward to the day when they will be redundant and free to embark upon a new challenge in God's global work. **Whenever mentorees on their part notice that they are honoured and loved, served, encouraged and trusted to reach their maximum in God, they will gain confidence in their own potential for his purposes.**

Uncommonly efficient mentoring and leadership multiplication occurred in conjunction with the preparation of RAROTONGANS for missionary endeavour in the Pacific during the last century. Rarotonga, situated approximately 600 miles to the south-west of Tahiti, belongs to the Hervey group of the Cook Islands.

John Williams, the great South Seas pioneer of the London Missionary Society, rediscovered Rarotonga in 1823 and initially left one Polynesian evangelist there. Christianity took root so powerfully that eleven years later Williams could observe family prayer being conducted mornings and evenings in every home on the island. As he desired to have trained Rarotongans accompany him to Samoa and Melanesia, the idea of a college was born. It was realized at Takamoa in 1839, and in the first year eleven young men attended the institution; by 1857 sixty-one graduates were employed on various mission fields.

Ten years later James Chalmers, also affiliated with the London Missionary Society, arrived on the island. "He came to know the Rarotongans intimately", his biographer R. Lovett recorded. "He could speak their language as well as a native. Many of them became his closest personal friends. . . ."[97] His main activities consisted of strengthening the existent churches and preparing nationals at Takamoa for pastoral and missionary service. When Chalmers, a true pioneer at heart, found out that the London Missionary Society had decided to extend its labours to New Guinea, then regarded as the 'darkest' spot in Melanesia, he wished to go there. But, unable to do so, he gave himself wholeheartedly to the priming of Rarotongans for this dangerous undertaking. His integrated approach combined theoretical classroom education with practical apprenticing, e.g. for building furniture and houses; outdoor chores and visitation work were also included.

After a season of spiritual refreshing the first group of five native missionaries and their wives set out for New Guinea in July 1872. Chalmers' trust in the Rarotongans' capacity for leadership surfaced in a comment he made two years later:

> I fail to see why some new field should not be taken up every year, neither can I see why these churches in the Hervey group require foreign pastors. Well-trained native pastors under the supervision of one foreign missionary ought to do the work. Such men will keep the natives together better than any foreigner can. Again I assert that there is no mission in the South Pacific under the control of a white missionary which surpasses the stations that are under native pastors superintended by a European missionary.[98]

His Rarotongan friends on New Guinea - joyful, determined and sacrificial in their witness, men of one book, the Bible - more than justified confidence of this kind. In the course of 1877 Chalmers joined up with them and from then on laboured alongside his former students, arranging their placement, spending time with them on the field, overseeing their activities. Ever since the first detachment had left Rarotonga, the island connection provided a steady flow of reinforcements to establish new stations but also to replace those islanders who had fallen ill, succumbed to the climate or suffered violent death. Chalmers himself was murdered at Dopima on Goaribari Island in April 1901.

William G. Lawes in retrospect underlined concerning the Rarotongans' relationship to Chalmers, his former colleague, that "they revered and obeyed him as their own father in Christ.... His example was their inspiration and his approval their stimulus."[99] Nearly twenty years before his death Chalmers had challenged, "Let the church give her very best in heart, mind, and body, for Christ's world work. The best and greatest of all works requires the best and greatest men."[100] It appears he was privileged to help shape some of them. When his long-term Rarotongan associate Ruatoka received word that Chalmers had lost his life, he volunteered to live and share the Word of God in the village where his friend had met his end.

A more recent as well as highly instructive strategy for the multiplication of leaders is the GREAT COMMISSION INSTITUTE concept developed by Asian Outreach.[101] Its overall purpose is the following:

1. In a life-sharing situation, equip, train and motivate Asian leadership and missionary personnel for effective, indigenous and cross-cultural ministry.
2. To sharpen their skills, gifts and talents in areas of ministry, whether it be evangelism and church planting in the cities or in the villages.
3. To develop culturally appropriate ministries to meet the needs of the people.

4. To further develop discipleship training among the Body of Christ in Asia.
5. To ensure that each GCI participant develops a strategy to fulfil the specific call God has placed on his or her heart.
6. To develop a network of indigenous ministries throughout the entire continent of Asia. . . . [102]

The integrated programme of the <u>international GCI</u>, which is arranged in a different Asian country every year, is made up of ten core courses, various workshops, field exposure and a personalized project. While the courses address topics like the Biblical foundations of missions and evangelism, cross-cultural communications, church planting, spiritual gifts and power theology, the personalized project is meant to assist the participants in devising specific strategies to facilitate their respective ministry visions. On the whole the scheme aims at not only information and inspiration but also impartation in the realms of attitude and skill.

In 1986 the first international GCI was launched in Jakarta, Indonesia. The eight-week event conjoined twenty-five students from nine countries who were motivated, taught and enabled to pursue their God-given vision for their personal contribution to seeing the Great Commission fulfilled. So one graduate, for instance, started Wheels Fellowship, an evangelistic ministry to pedicab drivers in Ozamiz, Philippines. Another founded a "Tribal Discipleship Center" in Chiang Rai, northern Thailand, to train leaders for evangelism, church planting and discipling among the tribal population of the area.

Participants of the annual GCI are encouraged to run <u>national GCIs</u> in their home countries. Such programmes for the training of grassroots leadership are usually held in the vernacular, they are contextualized and their curricula to a large extent determined by the existing local situation. Furthermore there is room for <u>mini GCIs</u>, individual courses geared to meet specific needs in given settings. However, national GCIs form the gist of the entire GCI pattern, with the final goal that outside assistance will become dispensable as national GCI co-ordinators organize self-supporting programmes amidst their own people.

Within a few years only the outstanding GCI concept has provided Asia with a broad spectrum of trained ethnic leaders and an expanding network of indigenous ministries. No doubt an increasing number of effective multiplication strategies[103] in different parts of the world will be crucial in procuring and equipping more and more labourers for the kingdom harvest force Jesus already envisaged when he told his disciples, "The harvest is plentiful but the workers are few. Ask the Lord of the harvest, therefore, to send out workers into his harvest field" (Matt 9:37.38).

5.6 The Dimension of Impartation

The prime purpose of the preceding investigation has been to characterize Jesus Christ's mentoring strategy of with-ness for witness and to outline essential implications of his prototype for leadership development in missionary contexts.

Analyzing the manner in which the Master trained the Twelve has opened our eyes to a wealth of principles which can and should direct our coaching efforts today. We have become more keenly aware that permeating the Gospel records there is, as G. Smith summarized so well, "the personality of Christ, Himself the subject as well as the teacher, the message as well as the trainer of the messengers, the model and the moulder in His own type of all whom He calls to witness, to preach, to live His life and death for sinners."[104] Yet we have also come to understand that Jesus' physical with-ness alone does not fully explain the matchless success of his mentoring. Rather, one must further recognize the decisive role of God's special with-ness, which was imparted to Jesus at the time of his baptism through the Holy Spirit's anointing.

Jesus formed his men through paradigm, precept, prayer and "power from on high" (Lk 24:49). His confession that he could do nothing by himself (Jn 5:19.30) revealed that he was utterly conscious of his need for divine enablement to carry out his ministry. But by offering himself as open channel for the Holy Spirit's mediation of God's power, he facilitated the impartation of divine truth (cf. Jn 17:17, 1:14) and divine life (cf. Jn 6:63, 14:6), which proved quintessential in the disciples' grooming for their subsequent witness and leadership functions. The acute realization that the Spirit's enabling presence was indispensable to his own ministry, led the Master to impress upon his friends their total dependence on supernatural qualification for the accomplishment of their designated mission.

During the Last Supper discourse he told them categorically, "apart from me you can do nothing" (Jn 15:5). On the same occasion he assured them even after his departure he would not leave them orphaned but come to them again (cf. Jn 14:18) by sending them the Holy Spirit (cf. Jn 16:7), thus indicating that his leadership covering would continue through the Third Person of the Trinity. Later on he added the promise, his permanent with-ness would accompany them in the fulfillment of the Great Commission (Matt 28:20).

As only the abundant enduement with the Holy Spirit would make all this a powerful reality in their lives and ministries, they were not to embark upon their worldwide witness assignment yet. Instead Jesus commanded them to remain in Jerusalem until they had been sufficiently equipped from above (cf. Acts 1:4, Lk 24:49). **The Master did not want his trainees to go at all until they could go with divine power.** He regarded it as absolutely necessary that the preparation which he had provided through their association-based mentoring, would be complemented as the Holy Spirit supernaturally fitted them for their forthcoming labours.

Eventually the Lord Jesus' promise of the Holy Spirit was fulfilled on the day of Pentecost. Luke recorded in Acts 2:2-4:

> Suddenly a sound like the blowing of a violent wind came from heaven and filled the whole house where they were sitting. They saw what seemed to be tongues of fire that separated and came to rest on each of them. All of them were filled with the Holy Spirit and began to speak in other tongues as the Spirit enabled them.

The arrival of the Holy Spirit was a revolutionizing experience for those gathered, because **it furnished them with the multifaceted and inexhaustible divine adequacy which they needed to pursue their calling according to the will of God.** Specifically, they received power to radiate the presence of their Lord, follow his example and glorify him. They were qualified to lead holy lives, testify effectively, preach and teach with authority, move in spiritual gifts and perform miracles. The Holy Spirit equipped them to win and train disciples as well as give competent leadership to the Way movement soon to emerge. He enabled them to be courageous in ministry and bold in prayer, to exercise radical faith, overcome in the hour of temptation and defeat the forces of darkness.

Through the Holy Spirit as mediator, on Pentecost the Lord Jesus' abiding presence and active power was imparted to his followers. **The secret of their outstanding fruitfulness from that day on was no other than that "Christ the power of God" (1 Cor 1:24) was mightily at work in and through them.** Nor was the unction granted from above primarily for their own benefit. True, it served their personal spiritual welfare and progress. More than their happiness, however, it was to facilitate their usefulness; it was meant above all to turn them into potent and productive witnesses of their risen and reigning Lord.

Profitable to note is also that Acts 2:3 mentions fire in connection with the Spirit's coming. This may remind us of John the Baptist's announcement that Jesus would baptize them with the Holy Spirit and with fire (cf. Matt. 3:11, Lk 3:16). Just as fire burns away dross and refines, the Holy Spirit consumes unholy traits and sanctifies. Fire illumines and directs, the Spirit gives revelation and guidance. As fire penetrates, so the Holy Spirit ignites hearts with love and zeal, disseminates truth and expands God's work. With this perspective in mind, our earlier reference to Lk 12:49, where Jesus expressed his desire that the fire he had come to bring to earth were already kindled, takes on deeper significance.

Obviously in Early Church days the empowering with the Holy Spirit was regarded as an imperative ingredient of Christian living. Acts 8:14-17 tells us when news reached the leaders at Jerusalem that Samaritans had accepted God's word, they sent Peter and John to them. As the apostles prayed, the Holy Spirit was imparted to those who had come to Christ. Ananias was directed by the Lord Jesus to the newly converted Paul so that he would receive the Spirit's fullness (Acts 9:17). When later on the apostle met believers in Ephesus who had become acquainted with John's baptism of repentance only, he led them to be baptized into Christ's name and to be endued with the Holy Spirit (Acts 19:1-6).

In this way the Spirit's fire was in a chain reaction passed on from one place to another and from one generation of disciples to the next. **Neither was the equipping with the Spirit's fullness meant to be a one-time experience.** We know, for instance, that Simon Peter was repeatedly filled (Acts 2:4, 4:31, cf. also 10:44), and the Greek text of Eph 5:18 allows us to interpret Paul's words as the charge to be continually filled with the Holy Spirit.

Our considerations up to this point suggest a number of conclusions that have momentous bearing on Christian leadership training. There is great need to heed R.E.

Coleman's warning, "Make no mistake, God's work, whatever the form, is accomplished only through the Holy Spirit,"[105] and to subscribe to J.O. Sanders' conviction, "Spiritual leadership can be exercised only by Spirit-filled men. Other qualifications for spiritual leadership are desirable. This is indispensable."[106] Competence for Christian ministry comes from God (cf. 2 Cor 3:5.6). We may learn leadership principles, communication skills and behavioural patterns, for example, yet anointing as the chief prerequisite has to be received supernaturally. Hence for those aspiring to lead in God's work, to be filled with the Spirit is no optional extra but a dire necessity. **It is self-evident that we cannot do without what the Lord Jesus himself was in need of.** Does not the mere fact that we view ourselves as followers and witnesses of Christ, the Anointed One, already challenge us to ensure that our lives carry the stamp of divine anointing, too?

Moreover, it should go without saying that mentoring according to the Lord Jesus' prototype can be carried out effectively only under the Holy Spirit's assistance. **In the final analysis, all true spiritual leadership is Spirit-leadership.** We can neither do without his initiative, enlightenment and guidance, nor without his convicting, transforming and sanctifying influence. We need him as advocate, comforter and exhorter, we depend on his enabling and equipping and would be ineffective without his wisdom, fruit and gifts. Both in our witnessing and practice of leadership the addressees will be spiritually impacted and helped only to the extent that God can use us to impart to them "the Spirit of Jesus" (Acts 16:7). The truth is, people do not need us so much as the life of Christ flowing from us.

The accomplishment of the Great Commission has time and again been jeopardized by various hindrances. Lack of vision, zeal, prayer, personnel and funds could be named. One may also think of unclear priorities, goals and strategies, of communication barriers, of economic, social and cultural obstacles. However, it would seem **the supreme concern in mission circles ought to be a deficit in divine unction.**

"I cannot go on like a mere machine," the missionary pioneer Dan Crawford of Luanza confessed, "I must get fresh enduement from on high."[107] Charles T. Studd wrote from the heart of Africa about his longing for a "Holy Ghost storm and atmosphere."[108] And James Calvert, trailblazer on Fiji, underscored, "The one special need is power from on high, and this we may have in its fulness and richness."[109] The apostle Peter clarified that the gift of the Holy Spirit is a privilege valid and attainable for Christians of all times, by pointing out in his sermon on Pentecost, "The promise is for you and your children and for all who are far off - for all whom the Lord our God will call" (Acts 2:39).

As we engage in God's work, we have to make room for the Holy Spirit to recover the paramount position he occupied in New Testament times. "We must take God at His word and return to the rapture and fire of the first apostleship . . . .", A. Murray summoned. "God will put no difference between the Church of that time and ours in the results that He will give us to reap."[110] The truth of this assertion is born out by J.H. Kane's notable observation, "In our own day we have ample evidence that the groups that emphasize the presence and power of the Holy Spirit are the ones that, year after year, are showing the greatest growth at home and overseas. And the growth is not simply quantitative, it is qualitative as well."[111]

Attempting to bring about spiritual results through sheer energy of the flesh is a futile enterprise. Like a sailing-vessel, although fully rigged, cannot put to sea without wind, we cannot achieve maturity in our own spiritual development and our mentoring of others without being filled with the Holy Spirit. In no way can any believer procure this divine endowment through his own striving, yet he can qualify to obtain and retain it by meeting certain requirements under which God has committed himself to pour out his blessing. At least four such conditions are laid down in the Scriptures.

There is, to begin with, the prerequisite of **thirst**, which the Lord Jesus recurrently touched upon (Matt 5:6, Jn 4:13.14, 6:35, 7:37),[112] The question arises whether we are as ambitious for God's best today as were Jacob (cf. Gen 32:26), Jabez (cf. 1 Chr 4:10) and Elisha of old (cf. 2 Kgs 2:1-15). It is not the number but the calibre of people that will determine the influence Christian witness will exert on the world. "Give me one hundred preachers," J. Wesley claimed, "who fear nothing but sin and desire nothing but God, and I care not a straw whether they be clergymen or laymen, such alone will shake the gates of hell and set up the kingdom of heaven on earth."[113]

Simon Peter referred to **obedience** as another condition for receiving the Holy Spirit (cf. Acts 5:32). William Borden, who dedicated his life to taking the Gospel to Muslims in China, explained, "Obedience, absolute and unqualified, which is made a daily principle of living, carried even into little things, this is the price of power."[114] Wholehearted consecration, a total surrender of ourselves, of all we are, have and desire, is the gateway to increased usefulness for God. In a time when believers yearn for a revitalizing of the Body of Christ through a powerful spiritual awakening, they do well to remember C.G. Finney's esteemed definition, "A revival is nothing else than a new beginning of obedience to God,"[115] and to avoid anything that would grieve the Holy Spirit (cf. Eph 4:30).

Through **prayer**, in the third place, one lays hold of God's gracious provision, of his Spirit as the answer to every spiritual need. Jesus encouraged his disciples, "If you then, though you are evil, know how to give good things to your children, how much more will your Father in heaven give the Holy Spirit to those who ask him!" (Lk 11:13). Christian leaders in particular face the ever-present danger of prioritizing more on work than on prayer.[116] They can benefit greatly from taking the advice, voiced by Murray, that "our true aim must not be to work much, and have prayer enough to keep the work right, but to pray much and then to work enough for the power and blessing obtained in prayer to find its way through us to men."[117] Actually, W.L. Duewel contended that to learn how to receive power and guidance through prayer is the most relevant aspect of leadership preparation.[118] Prayer secures divine with-ness and sustains the fire of the Holy Spirit.[119] Therefore it is a matter of supreme consequence for all servants of God to keep this life-line intact at all times.

Finally, to be effective, prayer has to be coupled with **faith**. The Letter to the Hebrews informs us that "without faith it is impossible to please God, because anyone who comes to him must believe that he exists and that he rewards those who earnestly seek him" (11:6). Biblical faith rests in the evidence of God's character and God's Word. Claiming his promises, it draws on divine resources and channels them into human existence. Exercising such trust, we shall unleash God's power and see his glory (cf. Jn 11:40), and thus live as powerful witnesses to his glory.

The crowning experience of the Spirit-filled Christian is the exchanged life.[120] While he appropriates by faith the fullness of the indwelling Christ (cf. Col 2:10), the latter virtually lives out his life in and through him (cf. Gal 2:20). On this basis following Christ, in the last regard, is not a trying hard in the flesh to copy Jesus but a drawing on his active with-ness, a participating in his divine nature (cf. 2 Pet 1:4). **In order to be a proper witness and efficient leader on Christ's behalf, it is not enough to merely learn from him, one must live in him.**[121] Only in this way can Christ's intention be realized to see a worldwide movement of Spirit-filled followers through whom he continues to impact mankind for God.

This exchanged life is an **exemplary** life, because it models authentically the wonderful features of Christlikeness. Besides, it is a **reproductive** life, as it imparts the vision and resources for Christlike living to others. It is also a **victorious** life, for while we can do nothing apart from Christ, we can do all things through him (cf. Phil 4:13). Such a life is within reach of every believer, if he remains in Jesus and avails himself through the Holy Spirit of everything there is for him in Christ. All this is only possible because of the unmerited favour which God has extended in Jesus Christ (cf. Eph 1:6), and because the risen and ruling Lord Jesus upholds his followers in this life by his faithful intercession (cf. Heb 7:25).

A man who in singular fashion illustrated the nature and blessings of the Spirit-filled life was JAMES HUDSON TAYLOR. Directed and equipped by the Holy Spirit, his missionary career evidenced a powerful witness which touched thousands of lives, and his Christlike example marked him as one of the most distinguished leaders in mission history.

Born into a Christian home on 21 May 1832 at Barnsley, England, Hudson Taylor as a child already expressed the wish to one day be a missionary in China. After he had found peace with God at seventeen years of age, this intention matured into a clear call. In preparation Hudson studied medicine in Hull and eventually, in September 1853, set out as a representative of the Chinese Evangelisation Society.

Following in the footsteps of the missionary pioneers Matteo Ricci, Robert Morrison and Karl Gützlaff,[122] Taylor decided about a year and a half after his arrival at Shanghai to become a Chinese to the Chinese, adjusting his dress and hair-style accordingly. His radical dedication to cultural adaptation was to prove a real key in reaching the hearts of the people he had come to serve.

On 25 June 1865 he felt led to pray for twenty-four co-workers, and two days later deposited £10 on behalf of the

'China Inland Mission'. The C.I.M., which he had thus founded, was an interdenominational faith mission from the start and later on became international, too.

An appeal for eighteen further workers was issued in 1875, six years afterwards the call for seventy additional missionaries went out. Among those who responded were the famous Cambridge Seven, including Charles T. Studd and Dixon E. Hoste. When in 1886 the need for another one hundred labourers was made a matter of prayer, actually 600 volunteered yet only 102 were selected. At the end of thirty years of ministry the C.I.M. employed 550 missionaries on 110 stations in fourteen provinces. It was in May 1890 during a missionary conference in Shanghai that Hudson Taylor shared the vision for a reinforcement of 1,000 workers over the next five years. His clarion call was echoed by other societies, as a result in due time 1,153 new China missionaries were active under the auspices of various organizations.

By 1900 the witness of C.I.M. missionaries, then numbering 700, had introduced 13,000 Chinese to a new life in Christ. Two years later Taylor appointed Hoste to take over the directorship. After eminent achievements as medical doctor, translator, administrator, Bible teacher and exemplary spiritual leader, Hudson Taylor, one of the greatest missionary pioneers of all time, died on 3 June 1905.

As a servant of God, Taylor was marked by deep humility. Once, when asked by a leading clergyman whether he was not tempted towards pride because God had used him so remarkably, the missionary responded, "I often think that God must have been looking for someone small enough and weak enough for Him to use, and that He found me."[123] Taylor, moreover, was such a man of prayer that he was able to testify the sun had never risen upon China without finding him at prayer.[124] His biographer M. Broomhall pointed to the strong faith characteristic of the C.I.M.'s founder when he emphasized that from beginning to end Taylor's life was dominated by his conviction of God's utter faithfulness.[125]

Besides, Hudson Taylor was divinely gifted with exceptional strategic insight. As far as working for God is concerned, for example, he outlined three possible approaches:

> One is to make the best plans we can, and carry them out to the best of our ability . . . . Or, having carefully laid our plans and determined to carry them through, we may ask God to help us, and to prosper us in connection with them. Yet another way of working is to begin with God; to ask His plans, and to offer ourselves to Him to carry out His purposes.[126]

Among other shrewd observations reflecting his penetrating grasp of principles crucial to fruitful missionary endeavour are the following:

> Missionary intelligence is essential to missionary effort.[127]
> Depend upon it, God's work done in God's way will never lack God's supplies.[128]
> How can we secure the development of strong, healthy, Christlike native Christians unless we are living strong, healthy, Christlike lives ourselves? . . . . What the spiritual children will be depends on what the spiritual father is . . . .[129]
> We have given too much attention to method, and to machinery, and to resources, and too little to the source of power.[130]
> The supreme want of all missions in the present day is the manifested presence of the Holy Ghost.[131]

The decisive turning-point in Hudson Taylor's missionary career came about on 4 September 1869. Over the preceding months he had been burdened with a deep longing for more holiness and power both in his personal life and in the C.I.M. at large. The utilization of various means of grace like reading God's Word, prayer and fasting, had not brought the desired result. He came to understand that the key to the problem was faith, but that he did not possess the quality of faith necessary. Then, one day, he found the answer he had been looking for in a letter from his friend John McCarthy which furnished the explanation, "How then to have our faith increased? Only by thinking of all that Jesus *is*, and all He is *for us* .... *Not* a striving to have faith, or to increase our faith, *but* a looking off to the Faithful One seems *all* we need."[132] All of a sudden his spiritual eyes were opened. Shortly afterwards he shared his newly received understanding in these words:

> Here, I feel, is the secret: not asking how I am to get sap *out* of the vine *into* myself, but remembering that Jesus *is* the Vine - the root, stem, branches, twigs, leaves, flowers, fruit, all indeed .... Let us not then want to get anything out of Him, but rejoice in being *ourselves in Him* - one with Him, and, consequently, with *all* his fulness. Not seeking for faith to bring holiness, but rejoicing in the *fact* of perfect holiness in Christ, let us realize that - inseparably one with Him - this holiness *is* ours, and accepting the fact, find it so indeed.[133]

Such fresh revelation of his oneness with and richness in Jesus Christ impacted Hudson Taylor so profoundly that he declared God had made him a new man.[134] Fanning the Holy Spirit's fire through increased prayer and appropriating Christ's all-sufficiency by faith, he experienced the blessedness of the exchanged life. New power, peace and joy filled his life as human striving was replaced by divine grace, being burdened by resting in Jesus Christ's with-ness. Henceforth Hudson Taylor's witness abundantly evidenced the truth of Jesus Christ's promise, "If anyone is thirsty, let him come to me and drink. Whoever believes in me, as the Scripture has said, streams of living water will flow from within him" (Jn 7:37.38).

*

". . . surely I am with you always . . . ." (Matt 28:20)

"All God's giants have been weak men, who did great things for God because they reckoned on His being with them . . . ."

J. Hudson Taylor[135]

Appendix:
Essentials of Jesus Christ's Discipling Model. A Survey

He studied the Hebrew culture thoroughly before launching his training efforts.

He proceeded according to a clear plan of action.

He operated under the Holy Spirit's anointing.

He contextualized his discipling approach.

He adapted the indigenous training format of rabbinic tutoring to his specific purposes.

He took the initiative in calling a nucleus of men to follow him.

He selected them prayerfully.

He chose a culturally homogeneous group.

He opted for unsophisticated, teachable, dedicated and zealous candidates.

He gave preference to a team setting which brought advantageous group dynamics into play.

He called the Twelve into a close personal relationship, not just to a programme.

He made association the cornerstone of his mentoring strategy.

He shared his life with his companions in transparency.

He communicated intimately with them.

He first made them his friends and only later his representatives.

He practised discipling as dynamic life-transference through the channel of relationship.

He never spoke of the abstract concept of 'discipleship'.

He made himself readily available to his associates.

He spent a lot of time with them.

He watched over the quality and quantity of time needed to coach them sufficiently.

He utilized the power of personality.

He created through his consociational discipling technique the very atmosphere in which his character and life-style could and would 'rub off' on the Twelve.

He reached a measure of closeness with them where his spirit touched their spirits, his heart impacted their hearts.

He induced into them his vision, mindset and mode of operation.

He provided not only intellectual information but produced actual character formation.

He ensured that beyond truth taught attitude was caught.

He supplied a model by what he was, did and said.

He lived what he taught.

He exemplified all he intended his followers to learn and become.

He impacted them to the maximum as they saw the principles he shared simultaneously evidenced in his life and ministry.

He coupled in his example holiness of character with excellence of performance.

He went about rebuilding the disciples' outlook and behaviour so that they would come to reflect increasingly the way he thought, felt and acted.

He aimed their training at moulding them into replicas of himself, in order to qualify them to serve as his authentic witnesses.

He made his personal experience of God's love the standard for the manner in which he expressed his benevolent concern for his protégés.

He was considerate in dealing with them.

He displayed an utterly positive mentoring stance.

He in faith focused less on the disciples' apparent deficiencies than on their latent potential.

He promoted their strengths and worked on their weaknesses.

He trusted them.

He encouraged them.

He corrected them when necessary.

He attended to the Twelve as a group and as individuals.

He attached special importance to the grooming of John and James, invested himself most of all, however, in Simon Peter.

He placed a higher priority on character development than on task performance.

He facilitated his understudies' growth in the realms of personality, knowledge, experience and skill.

He exercised authority over them which was not positional but spiritual and relational in origin.

He expected their total commitment to him as a person.

He designed his training as obedience-centred from beginning to end.

He exposed his associates to faith challenges.

- He interceded for them.
- He taught them how to pray.
- He did not practise extraction but located their mentoring close to the hub of ordinary existence.
- He turned the totality of shared life experiences into one big class-room.
- He wove the threads of his teaching most naturally into the overall fabric of everyday events.
- He gave clear preference to oral instruction.
- He clothed his utterances in memorable form to help his friends remember the gist of his teaching.
- He used parables as imaginary case studies to bring home relevant precepts and behavioural patterns.
- He reiterated vital truths.
- He emphasized the exemplary nature of his life and ministry.
- He rejected the secular practice of rulership as a viable design for the exercise of spiritual leadership.
- He advocated servanthood instead.
- He pointed to the need for leaders to exhibit integrity.
- He embedded his coaching of the Twelve into an active ministry context.
- He combined initial instruction with opportunities for practical application.
- He entrusted his followers with responsibility.
- He delegated authority to them.
- He subjected them to leadership training, not mere leadership education.
- He produced excellent leaders by developing good followers.
- He shunned any tendencey to formalize, structuralize or institutionalize his dynamic discipling approach.
- He mentored through prototype, precept, prayer and power from on high.
- He exerted distinctive effort to lead the disciples to an understanding of the person and ministry of the Holy Spirit as the one to equip them adequately for their future responsibilities.
- He made them aware that, to complete their grooming for effective witness and fruitful leadership, they needed the impartation of the Spirit's empowering.
- He prepared his companions all along with the perspective that they were to take over, continue and expand the work he started.
- He mentored them for mission.
- He geared their training at rendering them fit to serve as his powerful

emissaries to different people groups.
He instilled in them a strategic grasp of the necessity to promote his cause among the nations through the reproduction of multiplying disciples.
He raised them up so that they, under the directing and energizing influence of the Holy Spirit, would give competent leadership to the worldwide movement he envisaged.

Endnotes

† Quoted from Beach, H.P. *Princely Men in the Heavenly Kingdom*, New York, 1907, p. 107.

Introduction

1. Wagner, C.P. *On the Crest of the Wave*, Ventura, 1983, p. 159.
2. Chandapilla, P.T. *The Master-Trainer*, Bombay, 1974, p. x.

PART ONE

* Taylor, J.H. *Hudson Taylor's 'Retrospect'*, [18]1974, pp. 16f.

Chapter 1

1. Vermes, G. *Jesus and the World of Judaism*, London, 1983, p. 4.
2. There has been on-going discussion among scholars as to the exact year of Jesus Christ's birth. According to Ward, K. (ed.). *Jesus and His Times*, Pleasantville, 1987, p. 24, the majority prefer to place the birthdate into the period of 6 or 7 BCE. However, all we know with certainty is that Jesus was alive during the lifetime of Herod the Great (cf. Matt 2:1-20), whose death is recorded for the year 4 BCE.
3. In the course of this publication, the term 'Law' and its Hebrew counterpart *Torah* (lit. 'instruction') are used interchangeably to denote God's Law as laid down in the first five books of the Bible.
4. *Jesus* is the Greek form of *Yeshua* which in turn is a contraction of *Yehoshua* (Gk. *Joshua*), meaning 'Yahweh saves'.
5. Scripture states that Jesus was conceived of the Holy Spirit (cf. Matt 1:20). Although, strictly speaking, Joseph merely functioned as Jesus' earthly foster-parent, I follow Luke's example in speaking of him as Jesus' "father" (Lk 2:33.48).
6. See Mk 3:17, 5:41, 7:11, 7:34, 15:34; consider also Acts 26:14.15.
7. *Shema*, Hebrew for 'hear, listen', is taken from the opening of Deut 6:4 ("Hear, O Israel . . .").
8. On these occasions, the *Shema* was followed by the *Tefillah*, whose eighteen benedictions comprise elements of praise, petitioning and thanksgiving, whereas in the afternoons only the *Tefillah* was prayed.
9. For a more detailed description of how a synagogue service proceeded, see A.W. Morton's article "Education in Biblical Times", in Tenney, M.C. (ed.). *The Zondervan Pictorial Encyclopedia of the Bible*, 5 vols., Grand Rapids, 1975/76, vol. 2, p. 210.
10. His development illustrates the effectiveness of their training approach and proves the validity of Lam 3:27 and Prov 22:6.
11. Cf. the extensive "List of Old Testament Quotations in the Gospels"

provided by Robertson, A.T. *A Harmony of the Gospels for Students of the Life of Christ,* New York, 1922, pp. 295-301; see also Coleman, R.E. *The Mind of the Master,* Old Tappan, 1977, p. 54.

12 "The Life of Flavius Josephus" 45, in Josephus, F. *Complete Works,* Grand Rapids, 1978, p. 12.
13 Headlam, A.C. *The Life and Teaching of Jesus Christ,* London, ²1927, p. 98.
14 It is interesting to note that the Old Testament Scriptures contain various mnemotechnic devices, e.g. in Ps 136 (refrain), Ps 150 (anaphora) and Eccl 3:2-8 (parallelism); the Hebrew texts of Ps 119 and Prov 31:10-31 make use of acrostics.
15 Barclay, W. *The Mind of Jesus,* London, 1988, p. 15.
16 Packer, J.I. s.v. "Carpenter" in Brown, C. (ed.). *The New International Dictionary of New Testament Theology* (abbr. NIDNTT), 4 vols., Grand Rapids, 1986, vol. 1, p. 279.
17 The statement in question can be found in R. Riesner's book *Jesus als Lehrer,* Tübingen, ³1988, p. 220.
18 Matt 7:3-5, 11:29.30, Lk 6:48.49, 23:31; cf. also Lk 23:31.
19 From Joseph's conspicuous absence in the Gospel records of Jesus' later life has been inferred that Joseph had already died before Jesus began to minister in public; cf. e.g. Barclay, *Mind,* p. 20.
20 The literal translation of the Hebrew *rabbi* is 'my great one, my master'. This courteous title of respect was given to learned men.
21 Schlatter, A. *Geschichte Israels von Alexander dem Großen bis Hadrian,* Stuttgart, ³(1925)1977, p. 261.
22 Edersheim, A. *The Life and Times of Jesus the Messiah,* 2 vols, McLean, ³1886, vol. 1, pp. 117, 119.
23 So the Jewish scholar J. Klausner in his work *Jesus of Nazareth,* New York, 1927, p. 223.
24 This definition was furnished by K. H. Rengstorf in his contribution "mathetes" in Kittel, G. & Friedrich, G. (eds.). *Theological Dictionary of the New Testament* (abbr. TDNT), 9 vols., Grand Rapids, 1964-1974, vol. 4, pp. 431f.
25 A large number of such rabbinic thoughts and teachings has been preserved in the *Mishnah* as well as the *Babylonian Talmud* and *Jerusalem Talmud.* In the running text, quotes from the *Mishnah* will be introduced with 'M', those from the *Babylonian Talmud* by 'BT'. The respective editions used are *The Mishnah,* transl. by H. Danby, London, 1933, and *The Babylonian Talmud,* ed. by I. Epstein, 18 vols., London, 1935-1952.
26 See Gerhardsson, B. *Memory and Manuscript,* Lund & Copenhagen, 1961, pp. 160f.
27 Ibid., p. 127.
28 Quoted ibid., p. 137.
29 Friedeman, M. *The Master Plan of Teaching,* Wheaton, 1990, p. 48.
30 This citation is mentioned ibid., p. 110.
31 *Messiah* is the Hebrew equivalent of the Greek *Christ,* both signifying 'the anointed one'.
32 Thus explained by J. Denney, s.v. "Holy Spirit" in Hastings, J. (ed.). *A Dictionary of Christ and the Gospels* (abbr. DCG), 2 vols., Edinburgh & New York, 1906/09, vol. 1, p. 735.
33 Notice the kindred perception voiced by the Jewish theology teacher Nicodemus during his conversation with Jesus (Jn 3:2).
34 Consider also the way in which Jesus announced and characterized the

	Holy Spirit's anointing which the disciples were to receive (Jn 14:16.17).
35	The special with-ness of God is also indicated through expressions like: 'the Spirit came upon' Othniel (Judg 3:10), Gideon (Judg 6:34), Jephthah (Judg 11:29), Samson (Judg 14:6.19), Amasai (1 Chr 12:18), Azariah (2 Chr 15:1), Jahaziel (2 Chr 20:14) and Zechariah (2 Chr 24:20); 'God's hand was on' Ezra (Ezra 7:6, 8:31), Nehemiah (Neh 2:8.18) and Ezekiel (Ezek 3:22); Bezalel was 'filled with the Spirit of God' (Ex 31:3).
36	See 1 Sam 16:18, 18:12.14.28, 2 Sam 5:10, 7:3.9, 1 Kgs 1:37, 1 Chr 11:9, 17:2.8; Ps 23:4; cf. also 2 Sam 23:1.
37	Denney, art. cit., p. 735.
38	J.S. Stewart encapsulated the distinct thrusts of the three temptations as. "The Spiritual Versus the Material", "The Lure of the Spectacular" and "The Way of Compromise" in his book *The Life and Teaching of Jesus Christ*, Nashville, 1978, pp. 45-49.

Chapter 2

1	God showed himself as a God of strategy in his creation of the world (cf. Gen 1:1-31); furthermore his strategizing is indicated in passages like Job 42:2, Isa 25:1, 46:11, 55:11, Jer 29:11, Mic 4:12, Eph 1:11 and can be seen time and again in his dealings with the people of Israel (cf. e.g. Gen 50:20, Ezek 20:5-44, 36:22-32, 1 Kgs 8:44, 2 Sam 5:17-25, 2 Chr 20:15-17.22.23).
2	Over the years, much attention and scholarly effort has been devoted to Jesus as a teacher. Apart from the books by Riesner, Headlam and Friedeman already referred to, the following works will provide valuable additional insights: Wendt, H.H. *The Teaching of Jesus*, 2 vols., Edinburgh, 1892/93; Ross, D.M. *The Teaching of Jesus*, Edinburgh, 1904; Deane, A.C. *Rabboni*, London, s.a.; Manson, T.W. *The Teaching of Jesus*, Cambridge, England, ²1935.
3	Cf. Schlatter, A. *Die Geschichte des Christus*, Stuttgart, ⁴1984, p. 34; Klausner, *Jesus*, pp. 384-389; Ronai, A. & Wahle, H. *Das Evangelium - ein jüdisches Buch?*, Freiburg im Breisgau, 1986, pp. 80f., 124, 152f.; Flusser, D. *Jesus*, New York, 1969, p. 72.
4	For a comprehensive analysis of Jesus' teaching technique see: Griffith-Jones, E. *The Master and His Method*, London, 1902, pp. 66-83; Horne, H.H. *Teaching Techniques of Jesus*, Grand Rapids, (1920)1978, pp. 1-176, 204-206.
5	Schlatter, *Geschichte des Christus*, p. 228.
6	Klausner, *Jesus*, p. 263.
7	A supportive perspective is given by Schlatter, *Geschichte des Christus*, p. 34.
8	Cf. Vermes, *Jesus*, p. 31.
9	Pointed out by W.M. Christie, s.v. "Sea of Galilee" *DCG* , vol. 2, p. 594.
10	"Life" 17, in Josephus, *Complete Works*, p. 5.
11	So Klausner, *Jesus*, p. 285; see also Tasker, J.G. s.v. "Judas Iscariot" *DCG*, vol. 1, p. 908.
12	This perception was derived from the subdividing of Jesus' association with the Twelve into several distinct phases, as undertaken in Bruce, A.B. *The Training of the Twelve*, Grand Rapids, ⁴(1894)1971, pp. 11f. and in Hull, B. *The Disciple Making Pastor*, Old Tappan, 1988, pp.

216, 221.
13. Coleman, R.E. *The Master Plan of Evangelism*, Old Tappan, ²1964, p. 83.
14. Notice Prov. 24:32 which says: "I applied my heart to what I observed and learned a lesson from what I saw".
15. The central task of a spiritual leader was summarized in this very way by J.R. Clinton in his publication *The Making of a Leader*, Colorado Springs, 1988, p. 222.
16. Here Jesus made use of a familiar Old Testament image; see Num 27:17, 1 Kgs 22:17, Isa 13:14, Ezek 34:5.8, Zec 10:2.
17. Cf. Rengstorf, art. cit., pp. 444-447, and D. Müller, s.v. "mathetes" *NIDNTT*, vol.1, p. 488.
18. Stewart, *Life and Teaching*, p. 65.
19. Once more I am following the reasoning of Hull, *Disciple Making Pastor*, pp. 200, 238.
20. *Webster's New Universal Unabridged Dictionary*, New York, ²(copyright 1983), p. 390.
21. Watson, D. *Discipleship*, London, 1983, p. 80.
22. Coleman, R.E. *The Master Plan of Discipleship*, Old Tappan, 1987, p. 146.
23. Coleman, *Evangelism*, pp. 42f.
24. Manson, *Teaching*, pp. 320-323.
25. Riesner, *Jesus*, p. 408.
26. Vine, W.E. *Vine's Expository Dictionary of Old and New Testament Words* (abbr. VED), Old Tappan, 1981, vol. 2, p. 132.
27. Consider the example of the friendship between Jonathan and David (particularly 1 Sam 18:1).
28. On this point see Hengel, M. *The Charismatic Leader and His Followers*, Edinburgh, 1981, p. 32; Rengstorf, art. cit., pp. 436, 447; Riesner, *Jesus*, p. 417; Betz, H.D. *Nachfolge und Nachahmung Jesu Christi im Neuen Testament*, Tübingen, 1967, p. 12.
29. Within this context, Jesus' theology of leadership is seen as the convictions, values, goals and principles which governed his understanding and exercise of spiritual leadership. The succeeding chapters will unfold various aspects of this leadership concept.
30. Gilbert, G.H. s.v. "Father, Fatherhood" *DCG*, vol. 1, p. 581; cf. also Manson, *Teaching*, p. 102. - According to Jeremias, J. *Neutestamentliche Theologie* I, Gütersloh, ⁴1988, p. 20, Jesus addressed God as 'Father' over 150 times in the four Gospels, of which 109 instances are found in John.
31. See ibid., pp. 68-73.
32. Rengstorf, art. cit., p. 441.
33. Ibid., p. 445.
34. Ibid., p. 447.
35. For this very reason wherever possible the term will also be relinquished for the course of the publication on hand.
36. Kittel, G. s.v. "akoloutheo" *TDNT*, vol. 1, p. 214 (footnote 31).
37. Bruce, *Training*, p. 30.
38. Griffith-Jones, *The Master*, p. 43.
39. Jones, E.S. *Growing Spiritually*, New York, 1953, p. 316.
40. Duewel, W.L. *Ablaze for God*, Grand Rapids, 1989, p. 22.
41. See Barclay, W. *Begriffe des Neuen Testaments*, Wuppertal, 1979, p. 34.
42. Schlatter, *Geschichte des Christus*, p. 285.
43. Stalker, J. *The Life of Jesus Christ*, Grand Rapids, 1983, p. 75.

44 Eims, L. *Laboring in the Harvest*, Colorado Springs, 1985, p. 86.
45 Bruce, *Training*, p. 201.
46 Passages disclosing Jesus Christ's humility are e.g. Jn 8:50, Matt 20:28, 9:10.11; Isa 53:7.12; Phil 2:5-8.
47 For further insight in this respect one may turn to the thorough investigations contained in Riesner, *Jesus*, pp. 359-379, 394-406, 440, 447, 491, 511f. and in Jeremias, *Neutestamentliche Theologie* I, pp. 19-40. - See also endnotes 2 and 4 to chapter 2.
48 Finkel, A. *The Pharisees and the Teacher of Nazareth*, Leiden, 1964, p. 134.
49 On the practice of rabbinic ordination see Ward, *Jesus*, p. 160 and Lohse, E. *Umwelt des Neuen Testaments*, Göttingen, ³1977, p. 84.
50 W.B. Moore cited this statement by J.M. Price in his book *Multiplying Disciples*, Colorado Springs, 1981, p. 91.
51 Flusser, *Jesus*, p. 91.
52 Charlesworth, J.H. *Jesus within Judaism*, New York, 1988, p. 167.
53 Bruce, *Training*, p. 100.
54 Ibid., p. 99.
55 Coleman, *Evangelism*, p. 27.
56 For the most part, Jesus' communication on the Holy Spirit occurred in privacy with his chosen disciples. This subject area evidently fell similarly into the category of his esoteric teaching as the topic of the Fatherhood of God; on the latter aspect see Manson, *Teaching*, pp. 96-113.
57 *VED*, vol. 1, p. 208.
58 Moss, R.W. s.v. "Paraclete" *DCG*, vol. 2, p. 317.
59 On the understanding of *parakletos* as 'exhorter' see C.K. Barrett in Boice, J.M. *Witness and Revelation in the Gospel of John*, Exeter, 1970, p. 156.
60 Thayer, J.H. *A Greek-English Lexicon of the New Testament*, Grand Rapids, 1977, p. 29.
61 Coleman, *Evangelism*, p. 68.
62 Denney, art. cit., p. 742.
63 Bruce, F.F. *The Hard Sayings of Jesus*, Downers Grove, 1983, p. 124.
64 So suggested by the expert on Aramaic G.M. Lamsa in his book *Idioms in the Bible Explained and A Key to the Original Gospels*, San Francisco, 1985, p. 58.

Chapter 3

1 Coenen, L. s.v. "Witness" *NIDNTT*, vol. 3, p. 1041. - It is of interest to note that - according to Coleman, *Mind*, p. 100 - a difference in meaning between 'witness' and 'martyr' only surfaced in the course of the second century.
2 Scriptures like Acts 1:22, 2:32, 3:15, 4:33, 5:30-32, 10:39-41 direct attention to the resurrection as the focal point of the apostles' witness.
3 Kilpatrick, T.B. s.v. "Character of Christ" *DCG*, vol. 1, p. 290.
4 Notice how this perspective is also communicated by the apostle John in Rev 1:2.9, 17:6, 19:10; furthermore cf. Acts 23:11, 26:16 and 2 Tim 1:8.
5 Griffiths, M. *The Example of Jesus*, London, 1985, p. 23.
6 Coenen, art. cit., p. 1039.
7 Guder, D.L. *Be My Witnesses*, Grand Rapids, 1985, p. 27.

8   Coenen, art. cit., p. 1042.
9   Van Pelt, J.R. s.v. "Witness" *DCG*, vol. 2, p. 832.
10 Boice, *Witness*, p. 28.
11 Consider e.g. the accounts in Jn 6:15, Matt 16:22.23, Jn 12:27, Matt 26:53.54, 27:39-43.
12 According to Lohse, *Umwelt*, p. 108.
13 So Briscoe, S. *Everyday Discipleship for Ordinary People*, Bromley, 1989, p. 140.
14 See Ward, *Jesus*, p. 233.
15 Cf. Matt 11:25, Lk 12:21, Jn 9:39, 12:25, Matt 18:3.4, 23:11.12, 19:30.
16 The apostle Paul enumerated the fruit of the Spirit in Gal 5:22.23.
17 C.R. Swindoll quoted R.V.G. Tasker in his book *Improving Your Serve*, Toronto, 1986, p. 119.
18 This dualism was one of the governing concepts of Essenic thinking. More comprehensive insight into the Essenic movement can be gained from: Charlesworth, *Jesus*, pp. 54-76; Maier, J. & Schubert, K. *Die Qumran-Essener*, München, 1982, esp. pp. 41-141; Lohse, *Umwelt*, pp. 64-82; Pileggi, D. "Who Were the Essenes?" *Jerusalem Perspective* July/August 1990, pp. 9f., 15; Ward, *Jesus*, pp. 216-222; Barclay, *Mind*, pp. 24-28; Flusser, D. "Jesus and the Essenes" *Jerusalem Perspective* July/August 1990, pp. 6-8.
19 Briscoe, *Discipleship*, p. 144.
20 Barclay, W. *The Daily Study Bible. The Gospel of Matthew Volume 1*, Edinburgh, ²1958, p. 118.
21 Bosch, D.J. *Witness to the World*, Atlanta, 1980, p. 239.
22 See e.g. Gen 26:4, Ex 9:16, Deut 4:6, Josh 4:24, 1 Kgs 8:43, 1 Chr 16:24.31, Ps 2:8, 57:9, 82:8, 117:1, Isa 49:6.22, 51:4.5, 66:18-20, Jer 31:10, Joel 3:2, Mal 3:12; notice also Ezek 38:23, Mic 4:2, Zech 2:11, 8:22.
23 Scroggie, W.G. *Eight Things That Matter*, London, s.a., p. 41.
24 Furthermore, Jn 6:29.38.39.44.57, 7:16.28.29.33, 8:16.18.26.29.42, 9:4, 11:42, 12:44.45.49, 13:20, 14:24, 15:21, 16:5, 17:3.18.21.23.25, 20:21; cf. also Matt 15:24, Mk 12:6.
25 Neusner, J. *First-Century Judaism in Crisis*, Nashville, 1975, pp. 58-62: cf. Hengel, *Charismatic Leader*, p. 55.
26 Sanders, J.O. *The World's Greatest Sermon*, London, 1972, p. 41.
27 Anderson, R.S. *Minding God's Business*, Grand Rapids, 1986, p. 127.
28 The term "As" (Gk. *kathos*) can be more expressively translated with "in what manner", "in the manner that", or "according as, just as, even as"; see *The Analytical Greek Lexicon*, Grand Rapids, 1975, p. 208 and Thayer, *Greek-English Lexicon*, p. 314 respectively.
29 Referring to A. Schlatter's investigation into Matthew's style, Bosch pointed out that *poreuthentes* has only unaccented significance and can even be looked upon as redundant; see Bosch, *Witness*, p. 69.
30 Richardson, D. *Eternity in Their Hearts*, Ventura, 1984, p. 187.
31 Rush, M. *The New Leader*, Wheaton, 1987, p. 56.
32 Taylor, J.V. *The Go-Between God*, London, 1972, p. 111.
33 Bruce, A.B. *Training*, p. 536.
34 *Analytical Greek Lexicon*, p. 47. - According to Strong, J. *The Exhaustive Concordance of the Bible*, Iowa Falls, s.a., p. 73, in the Gospels the word 'apostles' is used by Luke not more than six times (6:13, 9:10, 11:49, 17:5, 22:14, 24:10), in Matthew and Mark only once (Matt 10:2, Mk 6:30), by John not at all.
35 Sanders, J.O. *Men from God's School*, London, 1974, p. 186.

36 Stalker, J. *Imago Christi*, London, 1907, p. 237.
37 Cf. Acts 9:2, 19:9.23, 22:4, 24:14.22.
38 To further characterize the phenomenon of being filled with the Holy Spirit, Luke employed in Acts varying terminology; he also spoke of being 'anointed' (4:27, 10:38) or 'baptized with the Holy Spirit' (1:5, 11:16), of the Spirit being 'received' (2:38), 'given' (5:32, 8:18), 'poured out' (2:17.18.33, 10:45) or 'coming upon' individuals (8:16, 11:15).

PART TWO

* Broomhall, M. (ed.). *Hudson Taylor's Legacy*, London, 1974, p. 31 is the source of this quotation.

Chapter 4

1 Cited ibid., p. 30.
2 Kane, J.H. *Christian Missions in Biblical Perspective*, Grand Rapids, 1976, p. 73.
3 Bosch, D.J. *Transforming Mission*, Maryknoll, 1991, p. 67.
4 Notice also the close connection between loving and following Jesus as indicated in the intimate dialogue between the Master and Simon Peter towards the end of John's Gospel (21:15-22).
5 Günther, W. & Link, H.-G. s.v. "Love" *NIDNTT*, vol. 2, p. 539.
6 Campolo, T. & Campolo, B. *Things We Wish We Had Said*, Milton Keynes, 1989, p. 197.
7 Blaikie, W.G. *The Life of David Livingstone*, London, [6]1910, p. 397.
8 The quote is furnished in Taylor, Dr & Taylor, Mrs H. *Hudson Taylor and the China Inland Mission*, London, 1918, p. 227.
9 With this view I am following E.G. Hoffmann's and H. v. Siebenthal's interpretation that the fullness of what Paul sought to communicate in 2 Cor 5:14 can be more adequately grasped if one considers the possibility that in *agape tou Christou* the categories of both *genitivus subiectivus* and *genitivus obiectivus* are present; see Hoffmann, E.G. & v. Siebenthal, H. *Griechische Grammatik zum Neuen Testament*, Riehen, 1985, pp. 233f.
10 O.J. Smith made reference to this dictum in his book *The Challenge of Missions*, Bromley, 1983, p. 125.
11 Quoted in Lovett, R. *James Chalmers*, London, [4]1903, p. 98.
12 Axling, W. *Kagawa*, London, [6]1937, p. 57.
13 R.H. Glover cited Zinzendorf with these words in *The Bible Basis of Missions*, Chicago, 1946, p. 95.
14 Lovett, R. (ed.). *James Gilmour of Mongolia*, London, 1892, p. 32.
15 Mentioned in Taylor, Dr & Taylor, Mrs H. *Hudson Taylor in Early Years*, London, 1911, p. 503.
16 McGinnis, A.L. *Bringing out the Best in People*, Minneapolis, 1985, p. 170.
17 Duewel, *Ablaze*, p. 95.
18 Twice we also find the Palestinian Aramaic form of *"rabboni"* (Mk 10:51, Jn 20:16).

19 See Riesner, *Jesus*, p. 263.
20 Clark, D. s.v. "Master" *DCG*, vol. 2, p. 142.
21 Barclay, *Mind*, p. 141.
22 Bietenhard, H. s.v. "Lord, Master" *NIDNTT*, vol. 2, p. 510.
23 Ibid., p. 514.
24 A similar example is Mk 9:5 / Lk 9:33 / Matt 17:4.
25 From this perspective it is not difficult to understand Paul's concern for communicating "all the counsel of God" (Acts 20:27, AV); cf. also Col 1:25, 2 Tim 4:17, Tit 1:9, 1 Tim 1:10.11.
26 Observe the apostle's numerous challenges to relate and minister to 'one another': e.g. Rom 12:10, 15:7.14, Gal 5:13, 6:2, Eph 4:2.32, 5:21, Col 3:16, 1 Thess 4:18, 5:11. - In the Old Testament the book of Proverbs highlighted various benefits of holding one another accountable; see e.g. 9:8, 12:1, 13:10.18, 15:31, 25:12.
27 F. Smith presented his useful perception, "The measurement of success is simply *the ratio of talents used to talents received*", in the article "Giving People Permission to Succeed" *Leadership* 9, no. 3, 1988, p. 52.
28 The yoke metaphor is quite common in the Old Testament; see e.g. Gen 27:40, Lev 26:13, Deut 28:48, 1 Kgs 12:4, Isa 9:4, Jer 2:20, Lam 3:27, Ezek 34:27, Nahum 1:13.
29 Maher, M. "'Take My Yoke upon You' (Matt xi. 29)" *NTS* 22, 1975-76, p. 103.
30 Barclay, W. *Crucified and Crowned*, London, 1988, p. 184.
31 Taken from Taylor, *H. Taylor and the C.I.M.*, p. 484.
32 The source for this quote is Padwick, C.E. *Henry Martyn*, Chicago, 1980, p. 149.
33 So according to Ellis, J.J. *John Williams*, London, s.a., p. 52.
34 These words were recorded by his brother J. Paton (ed.). in *John G. Paton*, vol. 2. London, 1890, p. 382.
35 Quoted in Moore, *Multiplying Disciples*, p. 21.
36 *Hypodeigma*, the Gk. word used for "example" in Jn 13:15, also denotes "model" and "proof", whereas "image" (Gk. *eikon*) in 2 Cor 4:4 (cf. Col 1:15) can be translated with "replica" or "likeness" as well; see W. Mundle s.v. "Image, Idol, Imprint, Example" *NIDNTT*, vol. 2, p. 284.
37 Eims, *Laboring*, p. 63.
38 This term stemming from leadership model theory, J.R. Clinton gave to understand, "usually refers to informal training models in which the person learns primarily by observing a role model and imitating skills, values, and attitudes"; see *The Making*, p. 217.
39 Ford, L. *Jesus: The Transforming Leader*, London, 1991, p. 43.
40 According to Moffat, J.S. *The Lives of Robert & Mary Moffat*, London, s.a., p. 124.
41 Hull, *Disciple Making Pastor*, p. 65.
42 Cited in Borthwick, P. *A Mind for Missions*, Colorado Springs, 1987, p. 11.
43 Elliston, E.J. "Designing Leadership Education" *Missiology* 16, no. 2, 1988, p. 209.
44 Stott, J.R.W. "What Makes Leadership Christian?" *CT*, August 9, 1985, p. 26.
45 Ibid.
46 Among those Scripture instances which mention Jesus Christ's servanthood are Isa 49:1-7, 50:4-11, 52:13-53:12, Matt 12:17-21, Lk

22:27, Rom 15:8, Phil 2:7, cf. also Jn 13:4-11, 21:9-13, 1 Jn 3:16.
47 Glover, *Bible Basis*, p. 101.
48 Richards, L.O. & Hoeldtke, C. *A Theology of Church Leadership*, Grand Rapids, 1980, p. 117.
49 Mentioned in Blaikie, *Livingstone*, p. 185.
50 As quoted in Lovett, *Gilmour*, p. 218.
51 This information is contained in Wells, J. *Stewart of Lovedale*, London, 1908, p. 99.
52 I owe the citation to Engstrom, T.W. with Rohrer, N.B. *The Fine Art of Mentoring*, Brentwood, 1989, p. 102.
53 L. Ford passed on this definition in *Jesus*, p. 155.
54 Cf. 2 Tim 1:3; 1:6-8; 1:2.4; 1:3; 1:14, 2:7; 3:10.11; 1 Tim 4:7.8, 6:11.
55 Wong, M.-D. *A Stone Made Smooth*, Southampton, ²1984, p. 131.
56 Jernigan, J. "Not According to Plan" *Discipleship Journal*, issue 67, vol. 12, no. 1, 1992, p. 39.
57 Manz, C.C. & Sims, Jr., H.P. *Superleadership*, New York, 1990, p. 86.
58 A parable can be defined as an instructive narrative which by way of comparison express abstract truth in concrete terms. - Parables occurred in the Old Testament (Judg 9:7-15, 2 Sam 12:1-6, Ezek 17:2-10, 24:3-12) and were an integral part of rabbinic teaching practice. Worth mentioning, incidentally, is the surprising resemblance between Jesus' parable of the wedding feast (Matt 22:2-14) and the story of the royal banquet as recounted by his contemporary Rabbi Johanan b. Zakkai (BT Shabbath 153a).
59 This Arabian proverb is cited in Friedeman, *Master Plan*, p. 170.
60 Stalker, *Imago*, pp. 275f.
61 Keller, P. *A Shepherd Looks at the Good Shepherd and His Sheep*, London, 1979, p. 64.
62 The leader as a shepherd was a familiar concept in the Old Testament; see e.g. Isa 40:10.11, Jer 23:1-4, Ezek 34, Ps 23, 78:70-72.
63 As a matter of fact the not unusual western custom of the shepherd's walking behind his flock can be a misleading picture, because in spiritual leadership the followers should neither be pushed ahead nor left to determine on their own the direction to be taken.
64 Chua, W.H. *Learning to Lead*, Leicester, 1987, p. 38.
65 Rush, *New Leader*, pp. 84f.
66 Manz & Sims, Jr., *Superleadership*, p. 224.
67 Thus quoted in A.R. Fraser's biography *Donald Fraser of Livingstonia*, London, 1934, p. 166.
68 Wells, *Stewart*, p. 123 is the source for this citation.
69 Jeremiah the prophet recorded an instance where leaders in Israel failed to seek divine directive, to their own and their followers' detriment (Jer 10:21).
70 Coleman, *Evangelism*, p. 78.
71 Taken from McGinnis, *Bringing Out the Best*, p. 32. - Notice also the perspective of B.E. Goodwin II, "People have a tendency to try to live up to the genuine expectations of persons whom they admire and respect," expressed in his booklet *The Effective Leader*, Downers Grove, 1981, p. 41.
72 Ford, *Jesus*, p. 62.
73 Kraft, C.H. *Christianity in Culture*, Maryknoll, 1979, p. 175; italics omitted.
74 Zahniser, A.H.M. "The Trinity: Paradigm for Mission in the Spirit" *Missiology* 17, no. 1, 1989, p. 69.

75 Kraft, *Christianity*, p. 178.
76 Shogren, G.S. s.v. "Authority and Power" in Green, J.B., McKnight, S. & Marshall, I.H. (eds.). *Dictionary of Jesus and the Gospels*, Downers Grove, 1992, p. 50.
77 Clinton, *The Making*, p. 103.
78 Phillips, K. *The Making of a Disciple*, Eastbourne, 1982, p. 52.
79 Anderson, N.T. *The Bondage Breaker*, Eugene, 1990, p. 164.
80 Blaikie, *Livingstone*, p. 397.
81 Cited in Livingstone, W.P. *Laws of Livingstonia*, London, s.a., p. 23.
82 The quotation stems from Taylor, *H. Taylor and the C.I.M.*, p. 364.
83 According to Guinness, M.G. *The Story of the China Inland Mission*, vol. 2, London, 1894, p. 419.
84 Duewel, *Ablaze*, p. 281.
85 Haggai, J. *Lead On!*, Milton Keynes, 1987, pp. xii and 6.
86 Tozer, A.W. *The Knowledge of the Holy*, New York, 1961, p. 113.
87 This comparison was used by R.M. M'Cheyne and recorded in Bonar, A.A. (ed.). *Memoir and Remains of Robert Murray M'Cheyne*, Edinburgh, (1892)1966, p. 154.
88 Contained in Choy, L.F. *Andrew Murray*, Fort Washington, 1978, p. 174.
89 Brengle, S.L. *Helps to Holiness*, London & Glasgow, 1896, p. 2.
90 Engstrom, T.W. *The Pursuit of Excellence*, Grand Rapids, 1982, p. 22.
91 Deir, C.S. *The Potential Leader*, Columbia, 1989, p. 22.
92 The source for the quote is Carré, E.G. *Praying Hyde*, South Plainfield, s.a., p. 58.
93 Mentioned in Inrig, G. *A Call to Excellence*, Wheaton, 1985, p. 44.
94 On the human side importance must be attached to the utilization of various means of grace, especially faith, prayer, the study of God's Word, obedience, repentance and confession.
95 Taken from Bonar, *Memoir*, p. 282.
96 C.F. Andrews included this statement in his publication *Sadhu Sundar Singh*, London, 1934, p. 235.
97 Quoted in Rattenbury, H.B. *David Hill, Friend of China*, London, 1949, p. 55.
98 Murray, A. *In Search of Spiritual Excellence*, Springdale, 1984, p. 89.

Chapter 5

1 Lingenfelter, S.G. & Mayers, M.K. *Ministering Cross-Culturally*, Grand Rapids, 1986, p. 17.
2 Ellis, J.S. *The Church on Purpose*, Cincinnati, 1982, p. 70.
3 Ford, *Jesus*, pp. 198f.
4 As found in Boehme, R. *Leadership for the 21st Century*, Seattle, 1989, p. 223.
5 Dye, T.W. "An Experiment in Indigeneity" in Kraft, C.H. & Wisley, T.N. (eds.). *Readings in Dynamic Indigeneity*, Pasadena, 1979, pp. 204f.
6 Recorded by D.H. Adeney in *The Unchanging Commission*, London, 1961, p. 55.
7 Wakatama, P. *Independence for the Third World Church*, Downers Grove, 1976, p. 41.
8 Ibid., p. 42.
9 See B. Olson's book *For This Cross I'll Kill You*, Basingstoke, 1983, pp. 103-108.

10 Adopted from Smith, G. *The Life of William Carey*, London & New York, 1909, p. 287.
11 Jones, E.S. *The Christ of the Indian Road*, London, 1925, p. 122.
12 Fraser, *Fraser*, p. 268.
13 I owe the quote to Taylor, *H. Taylor and the C.I.M.*, p. 232.
14 Thus in Dekker, J. with Neely, L. *Torches of Joy*, Westchester, 1985, pp. 63f.
15 Obviously the apostle had a remarkable capacity for friendship. Various instances in Acts and references in his letters document the cordial affiliation which linked him with his converts and mentorees. See e.g. Acts 15:36, 16:40, 20:31.38, Rom 16:1-16, 2 Cor 7:1-3, Phil 4:1, 1 Thess 2:8.11.17; Col 1:7, 2 Tim 1:2, Ph'm 1:12.16.
16 Livingstone, *Laws*, p. 260.
17 The source of the quotation is ibid., p. 259.
18 Cited ibid., p. 104.
19 G.H. Campbell reprinted these words in the booklet *Lonely Warrior*, Blantyre, Malawi, 1975, p. 36.
20 Quoted ibid., p. 40.
21 So W.A. Elmslie in his *Among the Wild Ngoni*, Edinburgh, 1899, p. 208.
22 Documented in Jones, *Christ*, p. 146.
23 Duewel, *Ablaze*, p. 169.
24 Deir, *Potential Leader*, p. 15.
25 Decker, P. J. "Social Learning Theory and Leadership" *The Journal of Management Development* 5, no. 3, 1986, p. 46.
26 This report was preserved in Taylor, *H. Taylor and the C.I.M.*, p. 248.
27 Barth, K. "An Exegetical Study of Matthew 28:16-20" in DuBose, F.M. (ed.). *Classics of Christian Missions*, Nashville, 1979, p. 50.
28 Andrews, *Singh*, pp. 22, 70-72; Heiler, F. *Sadhu Sundar Singh*, Bietigheim, 1987, pp. 25f.; Parker, Mrs A. *Sadhu Sundar Singh*, London, ⁶1927, pp. 20f.
29 The Sádhu's words were taken from Davey, C.J. *Sadhu Sundar Singh*, Bromley, 1980, p.50.
30 Parker, *Singh*, p. 67.
31 Ibid., p. xv.
32 Cited ibid., p. 136.
33 See Davey, *Singh*, p. 143.
34 The analogy can be found ibid., p. 141.
35 Parker, *Singh*, p. x.
36 E.J. Sharpe included this observation by Mrs A. Parker in "The Legacy of Sadhu Sundar Singh" *IntBulMissR* 14, no. 4, 1990, p. 166. - Sharpe's article also addresses the controversy which arose around the Sadhu's person in 1923; see especially p. 163.
37 Brengle, *Helps*, p. 45.
38 Quoted in Lovett, *Chalmers*, p. 274. - Notice furthermore Robert Laws' echoing remarks, "Africa takes far more out of a man - just as it can put more into a man, probably more than better civilized fields. It needs also the finest character. Here, if anywhere, one has to do Christ's work in a Christ-like way. You see, we are all under the microscope on the Station, and it is not one's preaching that tells on the native, but one's life", in Livingstone, *Laws*, p. 371.
39 S. Escobar pointed to a similarly disturbing phenomenon in the field of missiology; see his article "The Elements of Style in Crafting New International Mission Leaders" *EMQ* 28, no. 1, 1992, pp. 13f.

40 Managing, stated simply, is concerned with directing resources and manpower effectively towards certain predetermined goals.
41 Clinton, *The Making*, p. 58.
42 Padilla, C.R. "Toward the Globalization and Integrity of Mission" in Anderson, G.H. et al. (eds.). *Mission in the Nineteen 90s*, Grand Rapids & New Haven, 1991, p. 32.
43 This striking comparison I found in Stiles, A.R. *Samuel Logan Brengle*, London ²1980, p. 12.
44 Mentioned in Ford, *Jesus*, p. 129.
45 See Tippett, A. R. *Introduction to Missiology*, Pasadena, 1987, p. 112.
46 Ibid.
47 Mwakanandi, D.S. *The Role of African Traditional Religion in the Promotion of the Christian Faith in Malawi*, Stellenbosch, 1990, p. 173.
48 Cf. also Luzbetak, L.J. *The Church and Cultures*, Maryknoll, 1988, p. 133.
49 Glasser, A.F. "Training to Go Now!" *Mission Frontiers*, 12, no. 12, 1990, p. 33.
50 Padilla, C.R. "The Contextualization of the Gospel" in Kraft & Wisley, *Readings*, p. 306.
51 In his book *Communicating Christ Cross-Culturally*, Grand Rapids, 1978, pp. 445f., D. Hesselgrave outlined an impressive experience in this regard which G. Linwood Barney had among the Meo of northern Laos.
52 See Dekker, *Torches*, pp. 56-62.
53 Ibid., p. 56.
54 Personal acquaintance with the Basotho culture opened my eyes to remarkable parallels between such traditional instruction and Jesus' discipling method. There also the teacher's character was of high relevance, he was expected to mould the trainees into his likeness, for the training period he was continually with them, all instruction was exclusively oral and committed to memory. - For additional information on various African initiation rites see Mbiti, J.S. *African Religions & Philosophy*, London, 1969, pp. 121-131.
55 Included in a list of Basotho proverbs contained in Casalis, E. *The Basutos*, London, 1861, p. 310.
56 See Dekker, *Torches*, p. 71 and Owen, B. with Howard, D.M. *The Victor*, Old Tappan, 1979, p. 135. - Along a similar vein notice the vital part which songs played in the work of the Moravians, early Methodists and Salvation Army.
57 The Willowbank Report was the outcome of a consultation on the relation between the Gospel and culture which took place at Willowbank, Somerset Bridge, Bermuda in 1978; cited from "The Willowbank Report" in Winter, R.D. & Hawthorne, S.C. (eds). *Perspectives on the World Christian Movement*, Pasadena, 1981, p. 510.
58 This example stems from E. Deibler's article "Yeast or Gall?" *In Other Words* 11, no. 4, 1985, p. 6.
59 According to Clark, L. "But We Like Snake Meat!" *In Other Words* 10, no. 4, 1984, p. 6.
60 Adeney, *Unchanging Commission*, p. 32.
61 Samuel, V.K. "Gospel and Culture" in Samuel, V.K. & Hauser, A. (eds.). *Proclaiming Christ in Christ's Way*, Oxford, 1989, p. 76.
62 Hesselgrave, D.J. "Christ and Culture" in Winter & Hawthorne, *Perspectives*, p. 366.
63 "The Willowbank Report", ibid., p. 535.

64 Gilliland, D.S. "Contextual Theology as Incarnational Mission" in *The Word Among Us*, ed. by D.S. Gilliland, Dallas, 1989, pp. 28f.
65 Quoted in Jones, *Christ*, p. 22.
66 Phillips, *The Making*, p. 152.
67 Thayer, *Greek-English Lexicon*, pp. 388f.
68 Contained in N.H. Murdoch's compilation "Sayings of William Booth" reprinted in Miller, K.E. (ed.). *William & Catherine Booth*, Carol Stream, 1990, p. 7.
69 Taken from Collier, R. *The General Next to God*, London, 1965, p. 53.
70 William Booth's personal witness was powerful indeed. At an early stage he introduced his widowed mother and three sisters to Christ. Of the time when he and Catherine were raising a family of their own, one of their daughters remembered, "My parents did not have to say a word to me about Christianity. I saw it in action" (quoted in Collier, *General*, p. 57). Seven of their eight children became prominent Army officers. Bramwell succeeded his father as General (1912-1929), his sister Evangeline also served in this capacity (1934-1939).
71 Booth, General. *In Darkest England and the Way Out*, London, 1890, Preface. - This publication of Booth's scheme for social reformation, especially relative to unemployment and poverty, received a phenomenal response. The initial edition of 10,000 was sold out on the first day, within a year 200,000 copies were in print.
72 Cited in Collier, *General*, p. 244.
73 See the overview given ibid., pp. 80-86.
74 Detailed information is furnished by Williams, H. *Booth-Tucker*, London, 1980, pp. 56-134; cf. also Collier, *General*, pp. 90-101.
75 Richards, L.O. *Creative Bible Teaching*, Chicago, 1970, p. 116.
76 In his book, *Spiritual Power and Church Growth*, Altamonte Springs, 1986, pp. 88-93, C.P. Wagner commended 'street seminaries' he became acquainted with in Latin America. There Christian leaders felt "the best place to learn how to be a pastor is with pastor and people, not so much with theologians and scholars" (p. 89). Wagner noted, "Theoretical training or knowledge for its own sake has no place there. All training is functional, geared for effectiveness in the ministry" (p. 92), later adding the thought-provoking observation, "institutionalizing pastoral training can be one of the sure signs that a vital grassroots Christian movement is running out of steam" (p. 93).
77 Gangel, K.O. "Developing New Leaders for the Global Task" *EMQ* 25, no. 2, 1989, p. 170.
78 Friedeman, *Master Plan*, p. 74; slightly edited. - Cf. also Hull, B. *Jesus Christ, Disciplemaker*, Colorado Springs, 1984, p. 134 and de Bono, E. *Tactics*, London, 1991, p. 219.
79 Kane, J.H. *Wanted: World Christians*, Grand Rapids, 1986, p. 215.
80 "The Willowbank Report" in Winter & Hawthorne, *Perspectives*, p. 525.
81 Dekker, *Torches*, p. 39.
82 See Morse, E. *Exodus to a Hidden Valley*, London, 1975, p. 127.
83 According to Kraft, C.H. "What Kind of Encounters Do We Need in Our Christian Witness?" *EMQ* 27, no. 3, 1991, p. 258, A.R. Tippett was the first to use this term in his work *People Movements in Southern Polynesia*, Chicago, 1971.
84 For specific instances the more widely interested reader may turn to: Kane, J.H. *A Concise History of the Christian World Mission*, Grand Rapids, 1978, pp. 41f.; Tippett, *People Movements*, pp. 21-23, 80-82; Tucker, R.A. *From Jerusalem to Irian Jaya*, Grand Rapids, 1983, p.

205; Paton, *Paton*, vol. 2, pp. 176-192; Landgrebe, W. *I. Ludwig Nommensen*, Gießen, ³1986, pp. 33-37; Fugmann, W. (Hrsg.). *Christian Keyßer*, Neuhausen-Stuttgart, 1985, pp. 35f.; Anderson, A.E. *Pelendo*, Wetzlar, 1978, pp. 46-52, 67-71.
85 Kraft, "What Kind of Encounters?", op. cit., p. 265.
86 P.E. Kauffman mentioned the saying in "When the Plowman Overtakes the Reaper" *Asian Report*, issue 191, vol. 24, no. 4, 1991, p. 5.
87 Passages granting us insight into how Paul interceded for spiritual progress are e.g. Eph 1:16-19, 3:16-19, Phil 1:9-11, Col 1:9-12, 2 Thess 1:11.12.
88 Hull, *Disciple Making Pastor*, p. 52.
89 Rush, *New Leader*, p. 57.
90 See Trotman, D.E. *Born to Reproduce*, Colorado Springs, s.a., pp. 37, 39; cf. also pp. 32f.
91 Source of the citation is Smith, *Carey*, p. 101.
92 It appears that genuine trust in the nationals' God-given potential has characterized outstanding missionary pioneers all along. See e.g. Oussoren, A.H. *William Carey*, Leiden, 1945, pp. 279-281; Moffat, R. & M. *Moffat*, p. 133; Casalis, E. *My Life in Basuto Land*, Cape Town, (1889)1971, pp. 292f.; Taylor, *H. Taylor and the C.I.M.*, p. 227; Livingstone, *Laws*, p. 166.
93 Cf. also 2 Thess 2:13; Rom 8:26; 8:11, Eph 3:20; Gal 5:22.23; 1 Cor 12:4.7.11.
94 Allen, R. *Missionary Methods: St. Paul's or Ours?*, Grand Rapids, 1962, p. 149.
95 Gilliland, "Contextual Theology", op. cit., p. 16.
96 One of the spectacular success stories in mission history is the expansion of Christianity in Fiji. In connection with a renewed visit to Fiji for the 1885 Jubilee of Christianity James Calvert wrote: "The latest statistics to hand show extraordinary results of Christian work; and it is remarkable that where there was not a single Christian in Fiji in 1835, when the mission commenced, in 1885, when the Jubilee was celebrated, there was not an avowed heathen left in all the large group of eighty inhabited islands. The returns show that in 1885 there were 1,322 churches and other preaching-places, 10 white missionaries, 65 native ministers, 41 catechists, 1,016 head teachers and preachers, 1889 local preachers . . . and 104,585 attendants on public worship, out of a population of 110,000." - According to Vernon, R. *James Calvert*, London, s.a., p. 143.
97 Lovett, R. *Tamate*, London, s.a., p. 87.
98 R. Lovett documented these considerations in *Chalmers*, p. 110.
99 Quoted ibid., p. 488.
100 Noted ibid., p. 214.
101 The following description is primarily based on *The Great Commission Institute*, an unofficial manual composed by Asian Outreach International, Hong Kong, s.a.. Additional light was drawn from personal correspondence with Jean Harper, GCI registrar, and various articles from *Asian Report* magazine, especially "GCI: A Launching Pad for Asia Mission", issue 163, vol. 19, no. 6, 1986, pp. 12-14; "Pilot GCI a Success", issue 164, vol. 20, no. 1, 1987, pp. 14-16; "This Is a G.C.I. Baby!", issue 166, vol. 20, no. 3, 1987, pp. 12-15; "18 More GCI Graduates Set Out to Change Asia", issue 170, vol. 21, no. 1, 1988, pp. 12f.; Konrad, M.S. "GCI: An Asian Power Force", issue 180, vol. 22, no. 5, 1989, pp. 20-22; Konrad, M.S. "Lifeboat to Palawan Island",

issue 185, vol. 23, no. 4, 1990, pp. 15f.; Harper, J. "Fulfilling the Vision", issue 189, vol. 24, no. 2, 1991, pp. 17-20; Harper, J. "Church Planting with GCI Graduates", issue 194, vol. 25, no. 2, 1992, pp. 16-18.

102 *The Great Commission Institute*, p. 1; cited by permission from the GCI registrar.
103 For another remarkable example see R. Rosedale's article "Mobile Training Centers: Key to Growth in Thailand" *EMQ* 25, no. 4, 1989, pp. 402-406.
104 Smith, G. *Short History of Christian Missions from Abraham and Paul to Carey, Livingstone, and Duff*, Edinburgh, ⁸s.a., p. 27.
105 Coleman, *Discipleship*, p. 121.
106 Sanders, J.O. *Spiritual Leadership*, London & Bromley, 1981, p. 70.
107 Ellis, J.J. *Dan Crawford of Luanza*, Kilmarnock & London, s.a., p. 94, is the source of this quote.
108 Mentioned in Grubb, N. *C.T. Studd*, London, 1933, p. 208.
109 So according to Vernon, Calvert, p. 149.
110 As found in Choy, *Murray*, pp. 227f.
111 Kane, *Wanted*, p. 213.
112 Cf. also Ps 42:2, 63:1, 143:6, Isa 44:3(AV), 55:1.
113 This statement of the founder of the Methodist Church was used in Coleman, *Mind*, p. 84.
114 Mrs Howard Taylor recorded these words in her biography *William Borden*, Chicago, 1980, p. 184.
115 The great North American revivalist furnished this succinct characterization of the essence of a spiritual quickening in his work *Revivals of Religion*, Old Tappan, s.a., p. 7.
116 P. Borthwick inferred that because of lacking belief in the power of prayer and the neglect to give prayer the place it deserves, "we face a spiritual power failure in our efforts to fulfill the Great Commission"; see his *Mind for Missions*, p. 55.
117 Murray, A. *With Christ in the School of Prayer*, Old Tappan, 1965, p. 176.
118 Adopted from Duewel, *Ablaze*, p. 213.
119 It was William Booth who sounded the sobering exhortation, "Take time to pray God's blessing down on your own soul every day. If you do not, you will lose God. God is leaving men every day. They once had power. They walked in the glory and strength of God, but they ceased to wait on Him and earnestly seek His face, and He left them." Brengle quoted the utterance in *Helps*, p. 49.
120 Cf. in this connection my earlier explanations concerning being and abiding in Christ; see section 4.6, pp. 142-144.
121 With this perspective before us William G. Lawes' testimony of James Chalmers appears of particular interest: "But that which characterized our beloved Tamate most as a missionary, and as a leader among his brethren, was spiritual power . . . . A man of great faith, mighty in prayer, and full of the love of Christ. He realized to a greater degree than most men what it is to live *in* Christ, and to him His presence was very real, and true, and constant. And this spiritual power was the secret of his wonderful influence over men, and of his great success as a missionary . . . ."; thus in Lovett, *Chalmers*, pp. 489f.
122 See Hoffmann-Herreros, J. *Matteo Ricci*, Mainz, 1990, p. 66; Hayes, E.H. *Robert Morrison*, Wallington, ⁵1942, pp. 46f.; Oehler, W. *Geschichte der deutschen evangelischen Mission* I, Baden-Baden, 1949, pp. 147, 149.

123 According to Lyall, L.T. *A Passion for the Impossible*, London, 1965, p. 56.
124 Recorded in Taylor, *H. Taylor and the C.I.M.*, p. 624.
125 Broomhall, M. *Hudson Taylor*, Sheffield, 1929, p. x.
126 Advice given by H. Taylor to a group of co-workers in 1881; see Taylor, *H. Taylor and the C.I.M.*, p. 355.
127 Taken from Broomhall, *Taylor*, pp. 204f.
128 Quoted ibid., p. 109.
129 Shared by the founder of the C.I.M. in 1886 during a conference, as pointed out in Taylor, *H. Taylor and the C.I.M.*, p. 404.
130 So in Broomhall, *H. Taylor's Legacy*, p. 42.
131 Communicated in a circular to the C.I.M. missionaries in March 1892; see Taylor, *H. Taylor and the C.I.M.*, p. 512.
132 This passage, documented in a letter dated from 6 September 1869, is referred to ibid., p. 172.
133 Cited ibid.
134 Thus reported by a colleague; noted ibid.
135 Taylor included the memorable observation, reprinted ibid. p. 279, in an article for the magazine "China's Millions" during November 1875.

Bibliography

Apart from the titles already referred to I offer a selection of additional resources I consulted and which I trust will prove helpful to those who share a broader interest in the issues considered.

1. Texts and Reference Works

The Analytical Greek Lexicon, 12th printing, Zondervan, Grand Rapids, 1975.
The Babylonian Talmud, transl. into English with notes, glossary and indices, ed. by Isidore Epstein, 18 vols., Soncino Press, London, 1935-1952.
Barclay, William. *Begriffe des Neuen Testaments,* Aussaat, Wuppertal, 1979.
Brown, Colin (ed.). *The New International Dictionary of New Testament Theology,* 4 vols., Regency Reference Library, Grand Rapids, 1986.
Encyclopaedia Judaica, 16 vols., Keter, Jerusalem, 1971/72.
Green, Joel B., McKnight, Scott and Marshall, I. Howard (eds.). *Dictionary of Jesus and the Gospels,* InterVarsity, Downers Grove, 1992.
Hastings, James (ed.). *A Dictionary of Christ and the Gospels,* 2 vols., T. & T. Clark, Edinburgh, and Charles Scribner's Sons, New York, 1906/09.
Hoffmann, Ernst G. and von Siebenthal, Heinrich. *Griechische Grammatik zum Neuen Testament,* Immanuel, Riehen, 1985.
Huey, Jr., F.B. and Corley, Bruce. *A Student's Dictionary for Biblical and Theological Studies,* Academie Books, Grand Rapids, 1983.
Kittel, Gerhard and Friedrich, Gerhard (eds.). *Theological Dictionary of the New Testament,* transl. and ed. by Geoffrey W. Bromiley, 9 vols., Eerdmans, Grand Rapids, 1964-1974.
Lamsa, George M. *Idioms in the Bible Explained and A Key to the Original Gospels,* Harper & Row, San Francisco, 1985.
— *New Testament Light. More Light on the Gospels, Acts, the Epistles and Revelation,* Harper & Row, San Francisco, 1968.
The Mishnah, transl. from the Hebrew with introduction and brief explanatory notes, by Herbert Danby, Oxford University Press, London, 1933.
Robertson, A.T. *A Harmony of the Gospels for Students of the Life of Christ,* Harper & Brothers, New York, 1922.
Strecker, Georg und Maier, Johann. *Neues Testament - Antikes Judentum,* Grundkurs Theologie Bd. 2, Urban-Taschenbücher Bd. 422, Kohlhammer, Stuttgart, 1989.
Strong, James. *The Exhaustive Concordance of the Bible,* Riverside Book and Bible House, Iowa Falls, s.a.
Der Talmud, ausgew., übers. und erkl. von Reinhold Mayer, 3. Aufl., Goldmann, München, 1963/80.
Tenney, Merril C. (ed.). *The Zondervan Pictorial Encyclopedia of the Bible,* 5 vols., Regency Reference Library, Grand Rapids, 1975/76.

Thayer, Joseph Henry. *A Greek-English Lexicon of the New Testament,* Baker, Grand Rapids, 1977.
Vine, W.E. *Vine's Expository Dictionary of Old and New Testament Words,* Old Testament ed. by F.F. Bruce, 4 vols. bound in one, Revell, Old Tappan, 1981.
Webster's New Universal Unabridged Dictionary, 2nd ed., extensively revised, Dorset & Baber, copyright 1955-1983 by Simon and Schuster, New York.
Wigram, George V. and Green, Jay P. *The New Englishman's Greek Concordance and Lexicon,* Hendrickson, Peabody, 1982.
Young, Robert. *Analytical Concordance to the Bible,* Mac Donald, McLean, s.a.

2. The Life, Times and Ministry of Jesus Christ

Barclay, William. *Crucified and Crowned,* Arthur James, London, 1988.
— *The Mind of Jesus,* Arthur James, London, 1988.
Betz, Hans Dieter. *Nachfolge und Nachahmung Jesu Christi im Neuen Testament,* Beiträge zur historischen Theologie 37, J.C.B. Mohr, Tübingen, 1967.
Bruce, F.F. *The Hard Sayings of Jesus,* The Jesus Library, InterVarsity, Downers Grove, 1983.
Charlesworth, James H. *Jesus within Judaism. New Light from Exciting Archaeological Discoveries,* The Anchor Bible Reference Library, Doubleday, New York, 1988.
Coleman, Robert E. *The Mind of the Master,* Revell, Old Tappan, 1977.
Conzelmann, Hans. *Geschichte des Urchristentums,* Grundrisse zum Neuen Testament, NTD Ergänzungsreihe 5, 2. durchges. Aufl., Vandenhoeck & Ruprecht, Göttingen, 1971.
Deane, Anthony C. *Rabboni. A Study of Jesus Christ the Teacher,* The People's Library, Hodder and Stoughton, London, s.a.
Edersheim, Alfred. *The Life and Times of Jesus the Messiah,* 2 vols. bound in one, 3rd ed., Mac Donald, McLean, originally published 1886.
Farrar, Frederic W. *The Life of Christ,* Cassell, London, 1904.
Finkel, Asher. *The Pharisees and the Teacher of Nazareth. A Study of Their Background, Their Halachic and Midrashic Teachings, the Similarities and Differences,* Arbeiten zur Geschichte des Spätjudentums und Urchristentums Bd. 4, E.J. Brill, Leiden, 1964.
Flusser, David. *Jesus,* transl. by Ronald Walls, Herder and Herder, New York, 1969.
— "Jesus and the Essenes" *Jerusalem Perspective,* July/August 1990, pp. 6-8.
Flynn, Leslie B. *Dare to Care Like Jesus,* Victor Books, Wheaton, 1982.
— *Holy Contradictions,* Victor Books, Wheaton, 1987.
Friedeman, Matt. *The Master Plan of Teaching,* Victor Books, Wheaton, 1990.

Friedrich, Gerhard. "Die formale Struktur von Mt 28, 18-20" *Zeitschrift für Theologie und Kirche*, vol. 80, 1983, pp. 137-183.

Gerhardsson, Birger. *Memory and Manuscript. Oral Tradition Written Transmission in Rabbinic Judaism and Early Christianity*, Acta Seminarii Neotestamentici Upsaliensis 22, C.W.K. Gleerup, Lund, and Ejnar Munksgaard, Copenhagen, 1961.

Goodman, George. *Seventy Lessons in Teaching and Preaching Christ*, Marshall Pickering, Basingstoke, (1939) 1986.

Goppelt, Leonhard. *Theologie des Neuen Testaments*, hrsg. von Jürgen Roloff, 3. Aufl., Neudr., UTB 850, Vandenhoeck & Ruprecht, Göttingen, 1985.

Griffith-Jones, E. *The Master and His Method*, Christian Study Manuals, Hodder and Stoughton, London, 1902.

Headlam, Arthur C. *The Life and Teaching of Jesus Christ*, 2nd ed., John Murray, London, 1927.

Hengel, Martin. *The Charismatic Leader and His Followers*, transl. by James C.G. Greig, ed. by John Riches, Studies of the New Testament and Its World, T. & T. Clark, Edinburgh, 1981.

Horne, Herman Harrel. *Teaching Techniques of Jesus*, Kregel, Grand Rapids, (1920) 1978.

Jeremias, Joachim. *Neutestamentliche Theologie. Erster Teil: Die Verkündigung Jesu*, 4. Aufl., Gütersloher Verlagshaus Gerd Mohn, Gütersloh, 1988.

Josephus, Flavius. *Complete Works*, transl. by William Whiston, Kregel, Grand Rapids, 1978.

Kirschner, Robert. "Imitatio Rabbini" *Journal for the Study of Judaism in the Persian, Hellenistic and Roman Period*, vol. 17, no.1, 1986, pp. 70-79.

Klausner, Joseph. *Jesus of Nazareth. His Life, Times and Teaching*, transl. from the original Hebrew by Herbert Danby, Macmillan, New York, 1927.

Lohse, Eduard. *Umwelt des Neuen Testaments*, Grundrisse zum Neuen Testament, NTD Ergänzungsreihe 1, 3., durchges. und erg. Aufl., Vandenhoeck & Ruprecht, Göttingen, 1977.

Maher, Michael. "'Take My Yoke upon You' (Matt. xi. 29)" *New Testament Studies*, vol. 22, 1975-76, pp. 97-103.

Maier, Johann und Schubert, Kurt. *Die Qumran-Essener. Texte der Schriftrollen und Lebensstil der Gemeinde*, UTB 224, Ernst Reinhardt, München, 1982.

Malina, Bruce J. "Jesus as Charismatic Leader?" *Biblical Theology Bulletin*, vol. 14, no. 2, 1984, pp. 55-62.

Manson, Thomas Walter. *The Teaching of Jesus. Studies of Its Form and Content*, 2nd ed., Cambridge University Press, Cambridge, England, 1935.

Neusner, Jacob. *First-Century Judaism in Crisis. Yohanan ben Zakkai and the Renaissance of Torah*, Abingdon, Nashville, 1975.

Pileggi, David. "Who Were the Essenes?" *Jerusalem Perspective*, July/August 1990, pp. 9f., 15.

Riesner, Rainer. *Jesus als Lehrer. Eine Untersuchung zum Ursprung der Evangelien-Überlieferung*, Wissenschaftliche Untersuchungen zum Neuen Testament, 2. Reihe 7, 3., erw. Aufl., J.C.B. Mohr, Tübingen, 1988.

Ronai, Alexander und Wahle, Hedwig. *Das Evangelium - ein jüdisches Buch?*

Eine Einführung in die jüdischen Wurzeln des Neuen Testaments, Herderbücherei Bd. 1298, Herderbücherei, Freiburg im Breisgau, 1986.
Ross, D.M. *The Teaching of Jesus*, T. & T. Clark, Edinburgh, 1904.
Sanders, E.P. *Jesus and Judaism*, Fortress Press, Philadelphia, 1985.
Sanders, J. Oswald. *The World's Greatest Sermon. A Devotional Exposition of the Sermon on the Mount*, Marshall, Morgan & Scott, London, 1972.
Schlatter, Adolf. *Die Geschichte der ersten Christenheit*, 6. Aufl., Calwer Verlag, Stuttgart, 1983.
— *Die Geschichte des Christus*, 4. Aufl., Calwer Verlag, Stuttgart, 1984.
— *Geschichte Israels von Alexander dem Großen bis Hadrian*, unveränd. reprografischer Nachdr. der 3., neubearb. Ausg., Stuttgart 1925, Calwer Verlag, Stuttgart, 1977.
Sheed, F.J. *To Know Christ Jesus*, Servant Books, Ann Arbor, 1980.
Stalker, James. *Imago Christi. The Example of Jesus Christ*, 19th ed., Hodder and Stoughton, London, 1907.
— *The Life of Jesus Christ*, Academie Books, Grand Rapids, 1983.
Stewart, James S. *The Life and Teaching of Jesus Christ*, Festival Books, Nashville, 1978.
Vermes, Geza. *Jesus and the World of Judaism*, SCM Press, London, 1983.
Ward, Kaari (ed.). *Jesus and His Times,* Reader's Digest, Pleasantville, 1987.
Wendt, Hans Hinrich. *The Teaching of Jesus*, 2 vols., T. & T. Clark, Edinburgh, 1892/93.

3. Discipling

Adsit, Christopher B. *Personal Disciplemaking. A Step-by-Step Guide for Leading a Christian from New Birth to Maturity*, Here's Life, San Bernadino, 1988.
A Kempis, Thomas. *The Imitation of Christ*, transl. by E.M. Blaiklock, Hodder and Stoughton, London, 1979.
Basler, J. Michael. *Discipling One to One. Helping People to Know & Follow Jesus*, InterVarsity, Downers Grove, 1986.
Belben, Howard. *The Mission of Jesus*, Navpress, Colorado Springs, 1985.
Boice, James Montgomery. *Christ's Call to Discipleship*, Moody, Chicago, 1987.
Booker, Richard. *Radical Christian Living*, Victory House, Tulsa, 1985.
Briscoe, Stuart. *Everyday Discipleship for Ordinary People*, STL Books, Bromley, 1989.
Bruce, Alexander Balmain. *The Training of the Twelve*, reproduced from the 4th ed., rev. and improved, (1894), Kregel, Grand Rapids, 1971.
Coleman, Robert E. *The Master Plan of Discipleship*, Revell, Old Tappan, 1987.
— *The Master Plan of Evangelism*, 2nd ed., Revell, Old Tappan, 1964.
— *They Meet the Master. A Study Manual on the Personal Evangelism*

of Jesus, OMF, Manila, 1986.
Eims, Leroy. *Laboring in the Harvest,* Navpress, Colorado Springs, 1985.
— *The Lost Art of Disciple Making,* Zondervan, Grand Rapids, and Navpress, Colorado Springs, 1978.
Hadidian, Allen. *Successful Discipling.* Moody, Chicago, 1979.
Hartman, Doug and Sutherland, Doug. *Guidebook to Discipleship,* Harvest House, Eugene, 1976.
Henrichsen, Walter A. *Disciples Are Made - Not Born,* Victor Books, Wheaton, 1974.
Hull, Bill. *The Disciple Making Pastor,* Revell, Old Tappan, 1988.
— *Jesus Christ, Disciplemaker,* Navpress, Colorado Springs, 1984.
Jernigan, Jeff. "Not According to Plan" *Discipleship Journal,* issue 67, vol. 12, no. 1, 1992, pp. 36-40.
Kincaid, Jorie. *The Power of Modeling,* Navpress, Colorado Springs, 1989.
Kincaid, Ron. *A Celebration of Disciple-Making,* Victor Books, Wheaton, 1990.
Krallmann, Günter. *Following Jesus. A Handbook on Basic Discipleship for Individual and Group Study,* Manna Publications, Delmas, 1986.
Kuhne, Gary W. *The Dynamics of Discipleship Training. Being and Producing Spiritual Leaders,* Zondervan, Grand Rapids, 1978.
Mayhall, Jack. *Discipleship: The Price and the Prize,* Victor Books, Wheaton, 1984.
Moore, Waylon B. *Multiplying Disciples. The New Testament Method for Church Growth,* Navpress, Colorado Springs, 1981.
Phillips, Keith. *The Making of a Disciple,* Kingsway, Eastbourne, 1982.
Powell, Paul W. *The Complete Disciple,* Victor Books, Wheaton, 1982.
Salter, Colin. *Raising the Standard,* Kingsway, Eastbourne, 1987.
Staton, Knofel. *Check Your Discipleship,* New Life Books, Cincinnati, 1982.
Trotman, Dawson E. *Born to Reproduce,* The Navigators, Colorado Springs, s.a.
Vogel, Philip. *Go and Make Apprentices,* Kingsway, Eastbourne, 1986.
Watson, David. *Discipleship,* Hodder and Stoughton, London, 1983.
Wilson, Carl. *With Christ in the School of Disciple Building. A Study of Christ's Method of Building Disciples,* Zondervan, Grand Rapids, 1976.

4. Leadership Development

Anderson, Ray S. *Minding God's Business,* Eerdmans, Grand Rapids, 1986.
Boehme, Ron. *Leadership for the 21st Century. Changing Nations through the Power of Serving,* Frontline Communications, Seattle, 1989.
Borthwick, Paul. *Leading the Way. Leadership Is Not Just for Super Christians,* Navpress, Colorado Springs, 1990.
Chandapilla, P.T. *The Master-Trainer,* Gospel Literature Service, Bombay, 1974.
Chua, Wee Hian. *Learning to Lead. Biblical Leadership Then and Now,* Inter-Varsity, Leicester, 1987.

Clinton, J. Robert. *The Making of a Leader*, Navpress, Colorado Springs, 1988.
Covey, Stephen R. *The 7 Habits of Highly Effective People. Restoring the Character Ethic*, Fireside, New York, 1989.
De Bono, Edward. *Tactics. The Art and Science of Success*, Fontana, London, 1991.
Decker, Phillip J. "Social Learning Theory and Leadership" *The Journal of Management Development*, vol. 5, no. 3, 1986, pp. 46-58.
Deir, Costa S. *The Potential Leader*, Cityhill, Columbia, 1989.
— *The Understanding Leader*, Cityhill, Columbia, 1989.
Duewel, Wesley L. *Ablaze for God*, Francis Asbury, Grand Rapids, 1989.
Eims, Leroy. *Be A Motivational Leader*, Victor Books, Wheaton, 1981.
— *Be the Leader You Were Meant To Be. What the Bible Says About Leadership*, Victor Books, Wheaton, 1975.
Ellis, Joe S. *The Church on Purpose. Keys to Effective Church Leadership*, Standard, Cincinnati, 1982.
Elliston, Edgar J. "Designing Leadership Education" *Missiology: An International Review*, vol. 16, no. 2, 1988, pp. 203-215.
Engstrom, Ted W. *The Making of a Christian Leader*, Pyranee Books, Grand Rapids, 1976.
— with Rohrer, Norman, B. *The Fine Art of Mentoring. Passing on to Others What God Has Given to You*, Wolgemuth & Hyatt, Brentwood, 1989.
Evans, W.A., Han, K.C. and Sculli, D. "A Cross-Cultural Comparison of Managerial Styles" *The Journal of Management Development*, vol. 8, no. 3, 1989, pp. 5-13.
Ford, Leighton. *Jesus: The Transforming Leader*, The Jesus Library, Hodder and Stoughton, London, 1991.
Gangel, Kenneth, O. "Developing New Leaders for the Global Task" *Evangelical Missions Quarterly*, vol. 25, no. 2, 1989, pp. 166-171.
Goodwin II, Bennie E. *The Effective Leader. A Basic Guide to Christian Leadership*, InterVarsity, Downers Grove, 1981.
Greenslade, Philip. *Leadership. A Biblical Pattern for Today*, Marshalls, Basingstoke, 1984.
Griffiths, Michael. *The Example of Jesus*, The Jesus Library, Hodder and Stoughton, London, 1985.
Habecker, Eugene B. *The Other Side of Leadership*, Victor Books, Wheaton, 1987.
Haggai, John. *Lead on! Leadership That Endures in a Changing World*, Word, Milton Keynes, 1987.
Hocking, David L. *Be a Leader People Follow*, Regal Books, Ventura, 1979.
Jordan, Bernard. "The Principle of Mentoring" *Charisma & Christian Life*, vol. 16, no. 10, 1991, p. 48.
King, Philip. *Leadership Explosion*, Hodder and Stoughton, London, 1987.
Krallmann, Günter. *Leading with Jesus. A Handbook on Qualifications for Spiritual Leadership for Individual and Group Study*, Jensco, Hong Kong, 1989.
Le Peau, Andrew T. *Paths of Leadership. Guiding Others toward Growth*

in Christ through Serving, Following, Teaching, Modelling, Envisioning, Scripture Union, London, 1984.

MacArthur, Jr., John F. *The Master's Plan for the Church*, Moody, Chicago, 1991.

McGinnis, Alan Loy. *Bringing out the Best in People. How to Enjoy Helping Others Excel*, Augsburg, Minneapolis, 1985.

McKeen, Carol A. and Burke, Ronald J. "Mentor Relationships in Organisations: Issues, Strategies and Prospects for Women" *The Journal of Management Development*, vol. 8, no. 6, 1989, pp. 33-42.

Manz, Charles C. and Sims, Jr., Henry P. *Superleadership. Leading Others to Lead Themselves*, Berkley Books, New York, 1990.

Mahoney, Ralph. *The Making of a Leader*, World Missionary Assistance Plan, Burbank, 1985.

Marshall, Tom. *Understanding Leadership. Fresh Perspectives on the Essentials of New Testament Leadership*, Emerald Books, Lynnwood, 1991.

Richards, Lawrence O. and Hoeldtke, Clyde. *A Theology of Church Leadership*, Ministry Resources Library, Grand Rapids, 1980.

Rush, Myron. *Managing to Be the Best. A Personal Approach*, Victor Books, Wheaton, 1989.

— *The New Leader*, Victor Books, Wheaton, 1987.

Sanders, J. Oswald. *Paul the Leader*, Kingsway, Eastbourne, 1983.

— *Spiritual Leadership*, Lakeland, London, and STL Books, Bromley, 1981.

Schaller, Lyle E. *Getting Things Done. Concepts and Skills for Leaders*, Abingdon, Nashville, 1986.

Sibthorpe, Charles. *A Man under Authority*, Kingsway, Eastbourne, 1984.

Smith, Fred. "Giving People Permission to Succeed" *Leadership. A Practical Journal for Church Leaders*, vol. 9, no. 3, 1988, pp. 50-56.

— *Learning to Lead. Bringing out the Best in People*. The Leadership Library, vol. 5, Christianity Today, Carol Stream, and Word, Waco, 1986.

Stott, John R.W. "What Makes Leadership Christian?" *Christianity Today*, August 9, 1985, pp. 24-27.

Stumpf, Stephen A. and Mullen, Thomas P. "Strategic Leadership: Concepts, Skills, Style and Process" *The Journal of Management Development*, vol. 10, no. 1, 1991, pp. 42-53.

Wright, Robert G. and Werther, Jr., William B. "Mentors at Work" *The Journal of Management Development*, vol. 10, no. 3, 1991, pp. 25-32.

Youssef, Michael. *The Leadership Style of Jesus*, Victor Books, Wheaton, 1986.

5. Missiology

Adeney, David H. *The Unchanging Commission*, Inter-Varsity Fellowship, London, 1961.

Allen, Roland. *Missionary Methods: St. Paul's or Ours?*, Eerdmans, Grand Rapids, 1962.

— *The Spontaneous Expansion of the Church*, Eerdmans, Grand

Rapids, 1962.
Anderson, Gerald H., Phillips, James M. and Coote, Robert T. (eds.). *Mission in the Nineteen 90s*, Eerdmans, Grand Rapids, and Overseas Ministries Study Center, New Haven, 1991.
Barrett, David B. "Annual Statistical Table on Global Mission: 1992" *International Bulletin of Missionary Research*, vol. 16, no. 1, 1992, pp. 26f.
— and Johnson, Todd M. *Our Globe and How to Reach It. Seeing the World Evangelized by AD 2000 and Beyond*, Global Evangelization Movement: The AD 2000 Series, New Hope, Birmingham, Alabama, 1990.
Borthwick, Paul. *A Mind for Missions. 10 Ways to Build Your World Vision*, Navpress, Colorado Springs, 1987.
Bosch, David J. "The Missionary: Exemplar or Victim?" *Theologica Evangelica*, vol. 17, no. 1, 1984, pp. 9-16.
— *Transforming Mission. Paradigm Shifts in Theology of Mission*, American Society of Missiology Series, no. 16, Orbis Books, Maryknoll, 1991.
— *Witness to the World. The Christian Mission in Theological Perspective*, John Knox Press, Atlanta, 1980.
Bowen, Earl and Bowen, Dorothy. "Contextualizing Teaching Methods in Africa" *Evangelical Missions Quarterly*, vol. 25, no. 3, 1989, pp. 270-275.
Clark, Larry. "But We Like Snake Meat!" *In Other Words*, vol. 10, no. 4, 1984, p. 6.
Deibler, Ellis. "Yeast or Gall?" *In Other Words*, vol. 11, no. 4, 1985, p. 6.
"18 More GCI Graduates Set Out to Change Asia" *Asian Report*, issue 170, vol. 21, no. 1, 1988, pp. 12f.
Eitel, Keith. "The Transcultural Gospel - Crossing Cultural Barriers" *Evangelical Missions Quarterly*, vol. 23, no. 2, 1987, pp. 130-138.
Escobar, Samuel. "The Elements of Style in Crafting New International Mission Leaders" *Evangelical Missions Quarterly*, vol. 28, no. 1, 1992, pp. 6-15.
Fernando, Ajith. "Servanthood: Jesus' Model for Missions. An Exposition of Mark 10:35-45" *Mission Frontiers*, vol. 9, no. 10, 1987, pp. 8-14.
"GCI: A Launching Pad for Asia Mission" *Asian Report*, issue 163, vol. 19, vol. 6, 1986, pp. 12-14.
Gilliland, Dean S. *Pauline Theology & Mission Practice*, Baker, Grand Rapids, 1983.
— (ed.). *The Word Among Us. Contextualizing Theology for Mission Today*, Word, Dallas, 1989.
Glasser, Arthur F. "Training to Go Now! Missionary Training Today & Tomorrow" *Mission Frontiers*, vol. 12, no. 12, 1990, pp. 31-33.
—, Hiebert, Paul G., Wagner, C. Peter and Winter, Ralph D. *Critical Dimensions in World Evangelization*, William Carey Library, Pasadena, 1976.
Glover, Robert Hall. *The Bible Basis of Missions*, Moody, Chicago, 1946.
"*The Great Commission Institute. A Handbook for Leaders*," Asian Outreach International, Hong Kong, s.a., (unpublished manual).

Griffith, Henry. "We Can Teach Better Using African Methods" *Evangelical Missions Quarterly*, vol. 21, no. 3, 1985, pp. 248-252.
Harper, Jean. "Church Planting with GCI Graduates" *Asian Report*, issue 194, vol. 25, no. 2, 1992, pp. 16-18.
— "Fulfilling the Vision" *Asian Report*, issue 189, vol. 24, no. 2, 1991, pp. 17-20.
Hesselgrave, David J. *Communicating Christ Cross-Culturally*, Academie Books, Grand Rapids, 1978.
— *Today's Choices for Tomorrow's Mission. An Evangelical Perspective on Trends and Issues in Missions*, Academie Books, Grand Rapids, 1988.
— and Rommen, Edward. *Contextualization. Meanings, Methods, and Models*, Baker, Grand Rapids, 1989.
Hill, Harriet. "Incarnational Ministry: a Critical Examination" *Evangelical Missions Quarterly*, vol. 26, no. 2, 1990, pp. 196-201.
Jones, E. Stanley. *The Christ of the Indian Road*, Hodder and Stoughton, London, 1925.
Kane, J. Herbert. *Christian Missions in Biblical Perspective*, Baker, Grand Rapids, 1976.
— *Understanding Christian Missions*, 4th ed., Baker, Grand Rapids, 1986.
— *Wanted: World Christians*, Baker, Grand Rapids, 1986.
Kauffman, Paul E. "When the Plowman Overtakes the Reaper" *Asian Report*, issue 191, vol. 24, no. 4, 1991, pp. 3-5.
Konrad, Marla Stewart. "GCI: An Asian Power Force" *Asian Report*, issue 180, vol. 22, no. 5, 1989, pp. 20-22.
— "Lifeboat to Palawan Island" *Asian Report*, issue 185, vol. 23, no. 4, 1990, pp. 15f.
Kraft, Charles H. *Christianity in Culture. A Study in Dynamic Biblical Theologizing in Cross-Cultural Perspective*, Orbis Books, Maryknoll, 1979.
— "What Kind of Encounters Do We Need in Our Christian Witness?" *Evangelical Missions Quarterly*, vol. 27, no. 3, 1991, pp. 258-265.
— and Wisley, Tom N. (eds.). *Readings in Dynamic Indigeneity*, William Carey Library, Pasadena, 1979.
Krallmann, Günter (ed.). "Missionary Strategy and Effectiveness. Thoughts from J. Hudson Taylor," Delmas, s.a., (unpublished manual).
Lane, Denis. *Tuning God's New Instruments. A Handbook for Missions from the Two-Thirds World*, World Evangelical Fellowship and Overseas Missionary Fellowship, Singapore, 1990.
Lingenfelter, Sherwood G. and Mayers, Marvin K. *Ministering Cross-Culturally. An Incarnational Model for Personal Relationships*, Baker, Grand Rapids, 1986.
Loux, Gordon D. "It's Time for a "New World Order" in Missions Leadership" *Evangelical Missions Quarterly*, vol. 27, no. 4, 1991, pp. 402-408.
Luzbetak, Louis J. *The Church and Cultures. New Perspectives in Missiological Anthropology*, American Society of Missiology Series, no. 12, Orbis Books, Maryknoll, 1988.
McClung, Jr., Floyd and Moala, Kalafi with Benge, Geoff. *Nine Worlds to Win. Missions and Evangelism in the 1990's*, Youth With A Mission, Arnhem, 1988.

McElhanon, Kenneth. "Don't Give up on the Incarnational Model" *Evangelical Missions Quarterly*, vol. 27, no. 4, 1991, pp. 390-393.

Mayers, Marvin K. "Training Missionaries for the 21st Century" *Evangelical Missions Quarterly*, vol. 22, no. 3, 1986, pp. 306-312.

Mbiti, John S. *African Religions & Philosophy*, Heinemann, London, 1969.

Meiring, Piet G.J. "'Your Will Be Done: Mission in Christ's Way': Discerning God's Will for Mission in South Africa . . . Tomorrow" *Missionalia*, vol. 18, no. 1, 1990, pp. 248-258.

Murray, Andrew. *Key to the Missionary Problem*, contemporized by Leona F. Choy, Christian Literature Crusade, Fort Washington, 1979.

Mwakanandi, Dolb Simion. *The Role of African Traditional Religion in the Promotion of the Christian Faith in Malawi*, D. Theol Thesis, University of Stellenbosch, 1990.

Newbigin, Lesslie. *Mission in Christ's Way. Bible Studies*, WCC Mission Series, WCC Publications, Geneva, 1987.

Ohm, Thomas. *Machet zu Jüngern alle Völker. Theorie der Mission*, Erich Wewel, Freiburg im Breisgau, 1962.

Pate, Larry D. "The Changing Balance in Global Mission" *International Bulletin of Missionary Research*, vol. 15, no. 2, 1991, pp. 56-61.

"Pilot GCI a Success" *Asian Report*, issue 164, vol. 20, no. 1, 1987, pp. 14-16.

Poston, Larry. "Should the West Stop Sending Missionaries?" *Evangelical Missions Quarterly*, vol. 28, no.1, 1992, pp. 58-62.

Richardson, Don. *Eternity in Their Hearts*, rev. ed., Regal Books, Ventura, 1984.

Romack, Jeffrey P. "Understanding the Relationship of the Individual and Culture in the YWAM Context", Fuller Theological Seminary/School of World Mission, Pasadena, 1990, (unpublished paper).

Rosedale, Roy. "Mobile Training Centers: Key to Growth in Thailand" *Evangelical Missions Quarterly*, vol. 25, no. 4, 1989, pp. 402-406.

Samuel, Vinay K. and Hauser, Albrecht (eds.). *Proclaiming Christ in Christ's Way. Studies in Integral Evangelism. Essays Presented to Walter Arnold on the Occasion of His 60th Birthday*, Regnum Books, Oxford, 1989.

Shenk, Wilbert R. (ed.). *Mission Focus. Current Issues*, Herald Press, Scottdale, 1980.

Smith, Alex G. *Strategy to Multiply Rural Churches. A Central Thailand Case Study*, O.M.F., Bangkok, 1977.

Smith, Oswald J, *The Challenge of Missions*, Lakeland, Basingstoke, and STL Books, Bromley, 1983.

Sookdheo, Patrick (ed.). *New Frontiers in Mission*, Paternoster, Exeter, and Baker, Grand Rapids, 1987.

Stafford, Tim. *Friendship across Cultures*, MARC Europe, s.l., STL Books, Bromley, and Evangelical Missionary Alliance, London, 1986.

"This Is a GCI Baby!" *Asian Report*, issue 166, vol. 20, no. 3, 1987, pp. 12-15.

Thornton, W. Philip "The Cultural Key to Developing Strong Leaders" *Evangelical Missions Quarterly*, vol. 20, no. 3, 1984, pp. 234-241.

Tippett, Alan R. *Introduction to Missiology*, William Carey Library, Pasadena, 1987.

— *People Movements in Southern Polynesia. Studies in the Dynamics of Church-planting and Growth in Tahiti, New Zealand, Tonga, and Samoa,* Moody, Chicago, 1971.
Wagner, C. Peter. *On the Crest of the Wave. Becoming a World Christian,* Regal Books, Ventura, 1983.
— *Spiritual Power and Church Growth,* Creation House, Altamonte Springs, 1986.
— *Strategies for Church Growth. Tools for Effective Mission and Evangelism,* Regal Books, Ventura, 1987.
Wakatama, Pius. *Independence for the Third World Church. An African's Perspective on Missionary Work,* InterVarsity, Downers Grove, 1976.
Wang, Thomas (ed.). *Countdown to AD 2000. The Official Compendium of the Global Consultation on World Evangelization by AD 2000 and Beyond, Singapore, January 5-8, 1989,* The AD 2000 Movement, in cooperation with the William Carey Library, Pasadena, 1989.
Winter, Ralph D. "Crucial Issues in Missions", *Mission Frontiers,* vol. 12, nos. 6-10, 1990, pp. 36-38 (Part I); vol. 12, no. 11, 1990, pp. 19-21 (Part II).
— and Hawthorne, Steven C. (eds.). *Perspectives on the World Christian Movement. A Reader,* William Carey Library, Pasadena, 1981.
Yamamori, Tetsunao and Taber, Charles R. (eds.). *Christopaganism or Indigenous Christianity,* William Carey Library, South Pasadena, 1975.
Yohannan, K.P. *The Coming Revolution in World Missions,* Creation House, Altamonte Springs, 1986.
Zahniser, A.H. Mathias. "The Trinity: Paradigm for Mission in the Spirit" *Missiology,* vol. 17, no. 1, 1989, pp. 69-82.
Zwemer, Samuel M. *Thinking Missions with Christ. Some Basic Aspects of World-Evangelism, Our Message, Our Motive and Our Goal,* Marshall, Morgan & Scott, London, s.a.

6. History of Missions

Anderson, Alpha E. *Pelendo. Der Mann, der aus dem Dschungel kam,* Hermann Schulte, Wetzlar, 1978.
Anderson, Courtney. *To the Golden Shore. The Life of Adoniram Judson,* Zondervan, Grand Rapids, 1972.
Andrews, C.F. *Sadhu Sundar Singh. A Personal Memoir,* Hodder and Stoughton, London, 1934.
Axling, William. *Kagawa,* 6th ed., Student Christian Movement, London, 1937.
Barnes, Cyril. *God's Army,* Lion Publishing, Berkhamsted, 1978.
Barr, Pat. *To China with Love. The Lives and Times of Protestant Missionaries in China 1860-1900,* Victorian (& Modern History) Book Club, Newton Abbot, 1973.
Beach, Harlan P. *Princely Men in the Heavenly Kingdom,* Forward Mission Study Courses, Young People's Missionary Movement, New York, 1907.

Blaikie, William Garden. *The Life of David Livingstone*, 6th ed., John Murray, London, 1910.
Booth, General. *In Darkest England and the Way Out*, International Headquarters of the Salvation Army, London, 1890.
Broomhall, Marshall. *Hudson Taylor. The Man Who Believed God*. Wesleyan Reform Book Room, Sheffield, 1929.
— (ed.). *Hudson Taylor's Legacy. Daily Readings*, Hodder and Stoughton, London, 1974.
Campbell, George H. *Lonely Warrior*, CLAIM, Blantyre, Malawi, 1975.
Carré, E.G. *Praying Hyde. A Challenge to Prayer*, Bridge Publishing, South Plainfield, s.a.
Casalis, Eugene. *The Basutos; or, Twenty-Three Years in South Africa*, James Nisbet, London, 1861.
— *My Life in Basuto Land. A Story of Missionary Enterprise in South Africa*, transl. from French by J. Brierley, Religious Tract Society, London, 1889, facsimile reprint as vol. 38 of the Africana Collectanea Series by C. Struik, Cape Town, 1971.
Chalmers, James and Gill, W. Wyatt. *Work and Adventure in New Guinea 1877 to 1885,* Religious Tract Society, London, 1885.
Cheng, Marcus. *Lamps Aflame*, China Inland Mission, London, 1949.
Collier, Richard. *The General Next to God. The Story of William Booth and the Salvation Army*, Collins, London, 1965.
Davey, Cyril J. *Sadhu Sundar Singh*, STL Books, Bromley, 1980.
Dekker, John with Neely, Lois. *Torches of Joy*, Crossway Books, Westchester, 1985.
Drewery, Mary. *William Carey. A Biography*, Zondervan, Grand Rapids, 1979.
DuBose, Francis M. (ed.). *Classics of Christian Missions*, Broadman Press, Nashville, 1979.
Ellis, James J. *Dan Crawford of Luanza, or 37 Years' Missionary Work in Darkest Africa*, John Ritchie, Kilmarnock, and Hulbert Publishing, London, s.a.
— *John Williams. The Martyr Missionary of Polynesia*, S.W. Partridge, London, s.a.
Elmslie, W.A. *Among the Wild Ngoni. Being Some Chapters in the History of the Livingstonia Mission in British Central Africa*, Oliphant Anderson & Ferrier, Edinburgh, 1899.
Fraser, Agnes R. *Donald Fraser of Livingstonia*, Hodder and Stoughton, London, 1934.
Fugmann, Wilhelm (Hrsg.). *Christian Keyßer. Bürger zweier Welten*, Hänssler, Neuhausen-Stuttgart, 1985.
Gairdner, W.H.T. *D.M. Thornton. A Study in Missionary Ideals and Methods*, Hodder and Stoughton, London, 1909.
Garrett, John. *To Live among the Stars. Christian Origins in Oceania*, World Council of Churches, Geneva, in association with the Institute of Pacific Studies of the University of the South Pacific, Suva, 1982.
Goforth, Rosalind. *Goforth of China*, Dimension Books, Minneapolis, copyright 1937 by Zondervan, Grand Rapids.
Grubb, Norman P. *C.T. Studd, Cricketer & Pioneer,* Lutterworth Press,

London, 1933.
Guinness, M. Geraldine. *The Story of the China Inland Mission*, vol. 2, Morgan and Scott, London, 1894.
Gutch, John. *Beyond the Reefs. The Life of John Williams, Missionary*, Macdonald, London, 1974.
Hayes, Ernest H. *Robert Morrison, China's Pioneer*, Pioneer Series No. 4, 5th ed., Religious Education Press, Wallington, 1942.
Heiler, Friedrich. *Sadhu Sundar Singh. Ein Apostel des Ostens und Westens*, Turm, Bietigheim, 1987.
Hildebrandt, Jonathan. *History of the Church in Africa. A Survey*, Africa Christian Press, Achimota, 1981.
Hoffmann-Herreros, Johann. *Matteo Ricci. Den Chinesen Chinese sein ein Missionar sucht neue Wege*, Topos Taschenbücher Bd. 202, Matthias Grünewald, Mainz, 1990.
Johnston, James. *Robert Laws of Livingstonia*, Pickering & Inglis, London, s.a.
Kane, J. Herbert. *A Concise History of the Christian World Mission. A Panoramic View of Missions from Pentecost to the Present*, Baker, Grand Rapids, 1978.
Kuhn, Isobel. *Ascent to the Tribes. Pioneering in North Thailand*, OMF Books, London, (1956) 1968.
Landgrebe, Wilhelm. *I. Ludwig Nommensen*, 3., bearb. Aufl., Brunnen, Gießen, 1986.
Livingstone, W.P. *Laws of Livingstonia. A Narrative of Missionary Adventure and Achievement*, Hodder and Stoughton, London, s.a.
— *Mary Slessor of Calabar, Pioneer Missionary*, 24th ed., Hodder and Stoughton, London, 1925.
Lovett, Richard. *James Chalmers. His Autobiography and Letters*, 4th ed., Religious Tract Society, London, 1903.
— *Tamate. The Life and Adventures of a Christian Hero*, Religious Tract Society, London, s.a.
— (ed.). *James Gilmour of Mongolia. His Diaries, Letters and Reports*, Religious Tract Society, London, 1892.
Lyall, Leslie T. *Flame for God. John Sung and Revival in the Far East*, Overseas Missionary Fellowship, London, 1972.
— *A Passion for the Impossible. The China Inland Mission 1865-1965*, Hodder and Stoughton, 1965.
Make Jesus King. The Report of the International Student's Missionary Conference, Liverpool, January 1-5, 1896, 2nd ed., Student Volunteer Missionary Union, London, 1896.
Michael, Charles D. *John Gibson Paton, D.D., The Missionary Hero of the New Hebrides*, S.W. Partridge, London, s.a.
Miller, Basil. *Praying Hyde, A Man of Prayer*, 5th ed., Zondervan, Grand Rapids, 1943.
Miller, Kevin A. (ed.). *William & Catherine Booth*, Christian History, Issue 26, vol. 9, no. 2, Christianity Today, Carol Stream, 1990.
Miller, R. Strang. "Greatheart of China. A Brief Life of William Chalmers Burns, Scottish Evangelist and Revival Leader, and Early Missionary to China", in: *Five Pioneer Missionaries*, Banner of Truth,

Edinburgh, 1965.
Moffat, John S. *The Lives of Robert & Mary Moffat*, 9th and popular ed., T. Fisher Unwin, London, s.a.
Morse, Eugene. *Exodus to a Hidden Valley*, Collins, London, 1975.
Oehler, Wilhelm. *Geschichte der Deutschen Evangelischen Mission. Erster Band: Frühzeit und Blüte der deutschen evangelischen Mission 1706-1885*, Wilhelm Fehrholz, Baden-Baden, 1949.
Olson, Bruce. *For This Cross I'll Kill You*, Lakeland, Basingstoke, 1983.
Oussoren, A.H. *William Carey, Especially His Missionary Principles*, A.W. Sijthoff's Uitgeversmaatschappij N.V., Leiden, 1945.
Owen, Bob with Howard, David M. *The Victor. The Victor Landero Story*, Revell, Old Tappan, 1979.
Padwick, Constance E. *Henry Martyn*, Moody, Chicago, 1980.
Parker, Mrs Arthur. *Sadhu Sundar Singh. Called of God*, 6th rev. ed., Student Christian Movement, London, 1927.
Paton, James (ed.). *John G. Paton, Missionary to the New Hebrides. An Autobiography*, 2 vols., Hodder and Stoughton, London, 1889/90.
Phiri, D.D. *From Nguni to Ngoni. A History of the Ngoni Exodus from Zululand and Swaziland to Malawi, Tanzania and Zambia*, Popular Publications, Limbe, and Likuni Publishing House, Lilongwe, 1982.
Rattenbury, Harold B. *David Hill, Friend of China. A Modern Portrait*, Epworth Press, London, 1949.
The Salvation Army Year Book 1992, International Headquarters of the Salvation Army, London, 1991.
Sandall, Robert. *The History of the Salvation Army*, 3 vols., Thomas Nelson and Sons, London, 1947-1955.
Selfridge, John. *The Church's First Thirty Years in Nyasaland (Now Malawi), 1861-1891. A Thesis*, Nkhoma Press, Nkhoma, 1976.
Sharpe, Eric J. "The Legacy of Sadhu Sundar Singh" *International Bulletin of Missionary Research*, vol. 14, no. 4, 1990, pp. 161-167.
Smith, George. *The Life of William Carey, Shoemaker & Missionary*, J.M. Dent, London, and E.P. Dutton, New York, 1909.
— *Short History of Christian Missions from Abraham and Paul to Carey, Livingstone, and Duff*, 8th ed., T. & T. Clark, Edinburgh, s.a.
Stiles, Alice R. *Samuel Logan Brengle, Teacher of Holiness*, 2nd ed., Challenge Books, London, 1980.
Taylor, Dr and Taylor, Mrs Howard. *Hudson Taylor in Early Years. The Growth of a Soul*, China Inland Mission, London, 1911.
— *Hudson Taylor and the China Inland Mission. The Growth of a Work of God*, China Inland Mission, London, 1918.
Taylor, Gwendoline. *William Booth, Prophet and General*, rev. ed., Challenge Books, London, (1985) 1988.
Taylor, J. Hudson. *Hudson Taylor's 'Retrospect'*, 18th ed., OMF Books, London, 1974.
Taylor, Mrs Howard. *Behind the Ranges. Fraser of Lisuland Southwest China*, OMF Books, London, 1970.
— *Pastor Hsi, Confucian Scholar and Christian*, Overseas Missionary Fellowship, London, (1900) 1949.
— *William Borden. A Life and Fortune Dedicated to the Cause of the*

Gospel, Moody, Chicago, 1980.
Thompson, Phyllis. *D.E. Hoste, "A Prince with God". Hudson Taylor's Successor as General Director of China Inland Mission 1900-1935*, China Inland Mission, London, 1947.
Tucker, Ruth A. *From Jerusalem to Irian Jaya. A Biographical History of Christian Missions*, Zondervan, Grand Rapids, 1983.
Vernon, R. *James Calvert; or, From Dark to Dawn in Fiji*, S.W. Partridge, London, s.a.
Warneck, Gustav, *Outline of a History of Protestant Missions from the Reformation to the Present Time*, 3rd English ed., transl. from the 8th German ed., ed. by George Robson, Oliphant Anderson & Ferrier, Edinburgh, 1906.
Wells, James. *Stewart of Lovedale. The Life of James Stewart*, Hodder and Stoughton, London, 1908.
Williams, Harry. *Booth-Tucker. William Booth's First Gentleman*, Hodder and Stoughton, London, 1980.

7. Miscellaneous

Anderson, Neil T. *The Bondage Breaker*, Harvest House, Eugene, 1990.
Barclay, William. *Ambassador for Christ. The Life and Teaching of Paul.* Saint Andrew Press, Edinburgh, 1973.
— *The Daily Study Bible. The Gospel of Matthew Volume 1*, 2nd ed., Saint Andrew Press, Edinburgh, 1958.
— *The Daily Study Bible. The Gospel of Matthew Volume 2*, rev. ed., Saint Andrew Press, Edinburgh, 1975.
— *The Mind of St Paul*, Fontana Books, London, 1965.
— *The Promise of the Spirit*, Epworth Press, London, 1960.
Betz, Otto. *Der Paraklet. Fürsprecher im häretischen Spätjudentum, im Johannes-Evangelium und in neu gefundenen gnostischen Schriften*, Arbeiten zur Geschichte des Spätjudentums und Urchristentums 2, E.J. Brill, Leiden, 1963.
Boice, James Montgomery. *Witness and Revelation in the Gospel of John*, Paternoster, Exeter, 1970.
Bonar, Andrew A. *Memoir and Remains of Robert Murray M'Cheyne*, repr. from the enlarged 1892 ed., Banner of Truth, Edinburgh, 1966.
Brengle, Samuel Logan. *Helps to Holiness*, Salvationist Publishing and Supplies, London, 1896.
Campolo, Tony and Campolo, Bart. *Things We Wish We Had Said. Reflections of a Father and His Grown Son*, Word, Milton Keynes, 1989.
Choy, Leona. *Andrew Murray. Apostle of Abiding Love*, Christian Literature Crusade, Fort Washington, 1978.
Coleman, Robert E. *The Heartbeat of Evangelism*, Navpress, Colorado Springs, 1985.
Cornwall, Judson. *Let Us Be Holy*, Logos International, Plainfield, 1978.

Drummond, Henry. *Natural Law in the Spiritual World*, 38th ed., Hodder and Stoughton, 1901.
Engstrom, Ted, W. *The Pursuit of Excellence*, Zondervan, Grand Rapids, 1982.
Finney, Charles G. *Revivals of Religion*, Revell, Old Tappan, s.a.
Getz, Gene, A. *Sharpening the Focus of the Church*, Moody, Chicago, 1974.
Guder, Darrell L. *Be My Witnesses*, Eerdmans, Grand Rapids, 1985.
Inrig, Gary. *A Call to Excellence*, Victor Books, Wheaton, 1985.
Jones, E. Stanley. *Growing Spiritually*, Abingdon-Cokesbury, New York, 1953.
Keller, Phillip. *A Shepherd Looks at the Good Shepherd and His Sheep*, Pickering & Inglis, London, 1979.
McGinnis, Alan Loy. *The Friendship Factor. How to Get Closer to the People You Care for*, Augsberg, Minneapolis, 1979.
Murray, Andrew. *In Search of Spiritual Excellence*, Whitaker House, Springdale, 1984.
— *With Christ in the School of Prayer*, Spire Books, Old Tappan, 1965.
Packer, J.I. *Keep in Step with the Spirit*, Power Books, Old Tappan, 1984.
Porsch, Felix. *Pneuma und Wort. Ein exegetischer Beitrag zur Pneumatologie des Johannesevangeliums*, Frankfurter Theologische Studien Bd. 16, Josef Knecht, Frankfurt am Main, 1974.
Richards, Lawrence O. *Creative Bible Teaching*, Moody, Chicago, 1970.
— *A Theology of Christian Education*, Zondervan, Grand Rapids, 1975.
Ryle, J.C. *Holiness. Its Nature, Hindrances, Difficulties, and Roots*, James Clarke, Cambridge, repr. 1956.
Sanders, J.Oswald. *Men from God's School*, Lakeland, London, 1974.
— *The Pursuit of the Holy. Conquest and Fulfillment of Attainable Levels in Christian Living*, Zondervan, Grand Rapids, 1972.
Scroggie, W. Graham. *Eight Things That Matter. Searching Messages to Young Believers in Christ*, New Mildway, London, s.a.
Stott, John R.W. *Christian Mission in the Modern World*, Falcon, London, 1975.
Swindoll, Charles R. *Improving Your Serve. The Art of Unselfish Living*, Bantam Books, Toronto, 1986.
Taylor, John V. *The Go-Between God. The Holy Spirit and the Christian Mission*, SCM Press, London, 1972.
Tippit, Sammy. *The Prayer Factor*, Moody, Chicago, 1988.
Torrey, R.A. *How to Obtain Fullness of Power in Christian Life and Service*, Sword of the Lord Publishers, Murfreesboro, (copyright 1897 by Revell, Old Tappan).
Tozer, A.W. *The Knowledge of the Holy. The Attributes of God: Their Meaning in the Christian Life*, Harper & Row, New York, 1961.
Trites, Allison A. *The New Testament Concept of Witness*, Society for New Testament Studies, Monograph Series 31, Cambridge University Press, Cambridge, 1977.
Wong, Ming-Dao. *A Stone Made Smooth*, 2nd ed., Mayflower Christian Books, Southampton, 1984.

Index of Persons

Adeney, D.H. 152, 174
Allen, R. 193
Anderson, A.E. 227f.(n. 84)
Anderson, G.H. 226(n. 42)
Anderson, N.T. 137
Anderson, R.S. 220(n. 27)
Andrews, C.F. 224(n. 96), 225(n. 28)
Aristotle 31
Axling, W. 107

Barclay, W. 26, 61, 85, 109, 114, 216(n. 19), 220(n. 18)
Barney, G.L. 226(n. 51)
Barrett, C.K. 219(n. 59)
Barth, K. 158
Beach, H.P. 215(+)
Benniss, W. 123
Betz, H.D. 218(n. 28)
Bietenhard, H. 109, 222(n. 23)
Blaikie, W.G. 106, 223(n. 49), 224(n. 80)
Boehme, R. 224(n. 4)
Boice, J.M. 80, 219(n. 59)
Bonar, A.A. 224(n. 87, n. 95)
Booth, B. 182, 227(n. 70)
Booth, C. 182, 227(n. 70)
Booth, E. 227(n. 70)
Booth, W. 181-183, 227(n. 70), 229(n. 119)
Booth-Tucker, F. 184
Borden, W. 204
Borthwick, P. 222(n. 42), 229(n. 116)

Bosch, D.J. 85, 103, 220(n. 29)
Brengle, S.L. 140, 162, 229(n. 119)
Briscoe, S. 85, 220(n. 13)
Broomhall, M. 208, 221(*, n. 1), 230(n. 127, n. 128, n. 130)
Brown, C. 216(n. 16)
Bruce, A.B. 69, 91, 217(n. 12), 218(n. 37), 219(n. 45, n. 53)
Bruce, F.F. 73

Calvert, J. 203, 228(n. 96)
Campbell, G.H. 225(n. 19, n. 20)
Campolo, B. 221(n. 6)
Campolo, T. 105
Carey, W. 154, 192
Carré, E.G. 224(n. 92)
Casalis, E. 226(n. 55), 228(n. 92)
Chalmers, J. 107, 163, 195f., 229(n. 121)
Chandapilla, P.T. 14
Charlesworth, J.H. 67, 220(n. 18)
Choy, L.F. 224(n. 88), 229(n. 110)
Christie, W.M. 217(n. 9)
Chua, W.H. 129
Clark, D. 222(n. 20)
Clark, L. 174
Clinton, J.R. 136, 164, 218(n. 15), 222(n. 38)
Cobaydra 153
Coe, S. 166
Coenen, L. 78, 219(n. 1, n. 6)
Coleman, R.E. 49, 53f, 70, 131, 201f., 215f.(n. 11), 219(n. 61,

n. 1), 229(n. 113)
Collier, R. 227(n. 69, n. 70, n. 72, n. 73, n. 74)
Crawford, D. 203

Danby, H. 216(n. 25)
Davey, C.J. 225(n. 29, n. 33, n. 34)
Deane, A.C. 217(n. 2)
De Bono, E. 227(n. 78)
Decker, P.J. 158
Deibler, E. 174
Deir, C.S. 142, 157
Dekker, J. 154, 171f., 227(n. 81)
Denney, J. 40, 72, 216(n. 32)
Dodd, C.H. 27
DuBose, F.M. 225(n. 27)
Duewel, W.L. 60, 108, 139, 157, 205
Dye, T.W. 151

Edersheim, A. 216(n. 22)
Eims, L. 62, 116
Eliezer b. Hyrcanus 32, 34
Ellis, J.J. 222(n. 33), 229(n. 107)
Ellis, J.S. 149
Elliston, E.J. 118
Elmslie, W.A. 225(n. 21)
Engstrom, T.W. 141, 223(n. 52)
Epstein, I. 216(n. 25)
Escobar, S. 225(n. 39)

Finkel, A. 64
Finney, C.G. 204
Flusser, D. 67, 217(n. 3), 220(n. 18)
Ford, L. 117, 134, 150, 223(n. 53), 226(n. 44)

Fraser, A.R. 223(n. 67), 225(n. 12)
Fraser, D. 130, 154
Friedeman, M. 33, 185, 216(n. 30), 217(n. 2), 223(n. 59)
Friedrich, G. 216(n. 24)
Fugmann, W. 227f.(n. 84)

Gamaliel the Elder 31, 46, 97
Gandhi, M. 157, 159
Gangel, K.O. 135
Gerhardsson, B. 32, 216(n. 26, n. 28)
Gilbert, G.H. 218(n. 30)
Gilliland, D.S. 177, 193
Gilmour, J. 107, 122
Glasser, A.F. 167
Glover, R.H. 121, 221(n. 13)
Goethe, J.W. 132
Goodwin II, B.E. 223(n. 71)
Graham, B. 114
Green, G.S. 224(n. 76)
Griffith-Jones, E. 59, 217(n. 4)
Griffiths, M. 77
Grubb, N. 229(n. 108)
Guder, D.L. 77
Günther, W. 104
Gützlaff, K. 206
Guinness, M.G. 224(n. 83)

Haggai, J. 139
Harper, J. 228f.(n. 101), 229(n. 102)
Hartis, G. 166
Hastings, J. 216(n. 32)
Hauser, A. 226(n. 61)
Hawthorne, S.C. 226(n. 57, n. 62, n. 63), 227(n. 80)
Hayes, E.H. 229(n. 122)

Headlam, A.C. 216(n. 13), 217(n. 2)
Heiler, F. 225(n. 28)
Hengel, M. 218(n. 28), 220(n. 25)
Herod the Great 215(n. 2)
Hesselgrave, D.J. 175, 226(n. 51)
Hill, D. 144
Hillel 31, 34, 46, 64
Hoeldtke, C. 122
Hoffmann, E.G. 221(n. 9)
Hoffmann-Herreros, J. 229(n. 122)
Horne, H.H. 217(n. 4)
Hoste, D.E. 152, 207
Howard, D. 226(n. 56)
Hull, B. 117, 191, 217(n. 12, 218(n. 19), 227(n. 78)
Hyde, J. 142

Inrig, G. 224(n. 93)

Jeremias, J. 218(n. 30, n. 31), 219(n. 47)
Jernigan, J. 223(n. 56)
Johanan b. Zakkai 31f., 34, 46, 86, 223(n. 58)
Jones, E.S. 60, 154, 157, 177
Jose b. Johanan 82
Josephus 24, 48

Kagawa, T. 107
Kane, J.H. 101, 186, 203, 227(n. 84)
Kauffman, P.E. 228(n. 86)
Keller, P. 128
Kilpatrick, T.B. 76
King, M.G. 122
Kittel, G. 57, 216(n. 24)
Klausner, J. 46, 216(n. 23), 217(n. 3, n. 11)
Konrad, M.S. 228f. (n. 101)
Koyi, W. 155-157
Kraft, C.H. 135, 187, 224(n. 5), 227(n. 83)

Lamsa, G.M. 219(n. 64)
Landero, V. 172
Landgrebe, W. 227f.(n. 84)
Lawes, W.G. 196, 229(n. 121)
Laws, R. 138, 155f., 225(n. 38)
Lingenfelter, S.G. 147
Link, H.-G. 104
Livingstone, D. 106, 122, 138
Livingstone, W.P. 224(n. 81), 225(n. 16, n. 17, n. 18, n. 38), 228(n. 92)
Lohse, E. 219(n. 49), 220(n. 12, n. 18)
Lovett, R. 195, 221(n. 11, n. 14), 223(n. 50), 225(n. 38), 228(n. 98, n. 99, n. 100), 229(n. 121)
Luzbetak, L.J. 226(n. 48)
Lyall, L.T. 230(n. 123)

McCarthy, J. 209
M'Cheyne, R.M. 142, 144, 224(n. 87)
MacDonald, W. 151
McGinnis, A.L. 221(n. 16), 223(n. 71)
McKnight, S. 224(n. 76)
Maher, M. 113
Maier, J. 220(n. 18)
Manson, T.W. 55, 217(n. 2), 218(n. 30), 219(n. 56)
Manz, C.C. 125, 130
Marshall, I.H. 224(n. 76)

Martyn, H. 114
Mayers, M.K. 147
Mbiti, J.S. 226(n. 54)
Miller, K.E. 227(n. 68)
Moffat, J.S. 222(n. 40), 228(n. 92)
Moffat, R. 117f.
Moore, W.B. 219(n. 50), 222(n. 35)
Morrison, R. 206
Morse, E. 227(n. 82)
Morton, A.W. 215(n. 9)
Moss, R.W. 219(n. 58)
Müller, D. 218(n. 17)
Mundle, W. 222(n. 36)
Murdoch, N.H. 227(n. 68)
Murray, A. 140, 145, 203, 205
Mwakanandi, D.S. 167

Neely, L. 225(n. 14)
Neusner, J. 220(n. 25)
Nevius, J.L. 11

Oehler, W. 229(n. 122)
Olson, B. 153
Oussoren, A.H. 228(n. 92)
Owen, B. 226(n. 56)

Packer, J.I. 26
Padilla, C.R. 164, 169
Padwick, C.E. 222(n. 32)
Parker, Mrs A. 161, 225(n. 28, n. 32, n. 35, n. 36)
Paton, J. 222(n. 34), 227f.(n. 84)
Paton, J.G. 114
Phillips, K. 137, 179
Pileggi, D. 220(n. 18)
Plato 31
Price, J.M. 219(n. 50)
Rabbi Joshua 32

Railton, G.S. 184
Rarotongans 194-196
Rattenbury, H.B. 224(n. 97)
Rengstorf, K.H. 56f, 216(n. 24), 218(n. 17, n. 28)
Ricci, M. 206
Richards, L.O. 121, 184
Richardson, D. 90
Riesner, R. 216(n. 17), 217(n. 2), 218(n. 25, n. 28), 219(n. 47), 222(n. 19)
Robertson, A.T. 215f.(n. 11)
Rohrer, N.B. 223(n. 52)
Ronai, A. 217(n. 3)
Rosedale, R. 229(n. 103)
Ross, D.M. 217(n. 2)
Ruatoka 196
Rush, M. 91, 130, 191

Samuel, V.K. 175
Sanders, J.O. 88, 93, 202
Sapsezian, A. 166
Schlatter, A. 46, 61, 216(n. 21), 217(n. 3, n. 7), 220(n. 29)
Schofield, H. 138
Schubert, K. 220(n. 18)
Scroggie, W.G. 86
Shammai 31, 64
Sharpe, E.J. 225(n. 36)
Shogren, G.S. 136
Sims, Jr., H.P. 125, 130
Singh, Sádhu S. 144, 160-162, 168
Singh, Sirdar S. 160
Smith, F. 222(n. 27)
Smith, G. 198, 225(n. 10), 228(n. 91)
Smith, O.J. 221(n. 10)
Socrates 31

Stalker, J. 94, 126, 128(n. 43)
Stewart, J. 122, 156
Stewart, J.S. 52, 217(n. 38)
Stiles, A.R. 226(n. 43)
Stott, J.R.W. 118f., 222(n. 45)
Strong, J. 220(n. 34)
Studd, C.T. 107, 203, 207
Swindoll, C.R. 220(n. 17)

Tasker, J.G. 217(n. 11)
Tasker, R.V.G. 84
Taylor, Dr H. 221(n. 8, n. 15), 222(n. 31), 224(n. 82), 225(n. 13, n. 26), 228(n. 92), 230(n. 124, n. 126, n. 129, n. 131, n. 132, n. 133, n. 134, n. 135)
Taylor, J.H. 17, 99, 101, 106f., 114, 138, 152, 154, 158, 206-210
Taylor, J.V. 91
Taylor, Mrs H. 221(n. 8, n. 15), 222(n. 31), 224(n. 82), 225(n. 13, n. 26), 228(n. 92), 229(n. 114), 230(n. 124, n. 126, n. 129, n. 131, n. 132, n. 133, n. 134, n. 135)
Tenney, M.C. 215(n. 9)
Thayer, J.H. 219(n. 60), 220(n. 28)
Tippett, A.R. 166, 226(n. 45), 227(n. 83, n. 84)
Trotman, D. 191
Tozer, A.W. 139
Tucker, R.A. 227(n. 84)

Van Pelt, J.R. 79
Vermes, G. 19, 217(n. 8)
Vernon, R. 228(n. 96), 229(n. 109)
Vine, W.E. 218(n. 26)
Von Siebenthal, H. 221(n. 9)

Wagner, C.P. 13, 227(n. 76)
Wahle, H. 217(n. 3)
Wakatama, P. 152
Ward, K. 215(n. 2), 219(n. 49), 220(n. 14, n. 18)
Watson, D. 53
Wells, J. 223(n. 51, n. 68)
Wendt, H.H. 217(n. 2)
Wesley, J. 204
Williams, H. 227(n. 74)
Williams, J. 114, 194
Winter, R.D. 226(n. 57, n. 62, n. 63), 227(n. 80)
Wisley, T.N. 224(n. 5)
Wong, M.-D. 124

Zahniser, A.H.M. 135
Zinzendorf, Count 107

Select Subject Index

Abba 56
abiding in Christ 73, 142-144, 176, 229(n. 120)
accountability 69, 80, 112, 129, 137, 176
affiliation 148-152, 155, 166, 176, 190
agape 104-106, 153
akoloutheo 57, 61
akolouthesis 57
allos 71
anointing 37-39, 176, 202
apostle 67, 92
apprenticing 25-28, 31, 172
association 13, 28, 33, 40f., 53, 59, 66, 76, 80, 92f., 97, 103, 125, 134, 140, 143, 145, 150, 188, 199
authenticity 32, 80, 171f., 206
authority 95, 118f., 136, 159, 176, 187, 200

baptizontes 90
bar-mitzvah 35

Capernaum 87
case studies 125f.
Cephas 93
character 23, 25, 28, 33, 53, 60, 63, 75-78, 112, 116, 119, 123, 127, 134, 141, 152, 159, 162-166, 184, 188, 191
Christlikeness 14, 66, 85, 92, 96, 119-122, 124, 136, 139, 141-144, 153, 157, 159, 161, 163, 177f., 187f., 190, 206, 208
consociation 53-61, 67, 69, 72, 113, 120, 143
consociational discipling 58, 65, 78, 83, 91f., 97, 101, 116, 127, 148
contagion 60, 158
contextualization 166-178, 197
cross-cultural acceptance 154
culture 82, 147-153, 159, 166-178, 190, 192f., 196, 203
cultural arrogance 151
cultural dissonance 174

delegation 69, 95, 136, 179
de-westernizing effort 169
didaskale 108
didaskalos 108f.
didaskontes 90
'director syndrome' 152
dominance 112, 152, 192
double encounter effect 134
dynamic equivalence 173-176, 178

eklego 51
ephebi 109
epistates 109
Essenes 30f., 220(n. 18)
ethnocentrism 151, 177
excellence 73, 128, 140f.
exchanged life 143, 206, 209

exemplification 69, 128, 153, 157-166, 176, 185, 190f., 196, 206f.

faith 81, 92, 95, 125, 127, 143, 161, 205-209
faithfulness 28, 80, 112-114, 117, 119, 121, 125, 164
Fatherhood of God 56, 218(n. 30), 219(n. 56)
following Jesus 50, 61f., 65, 104, 109, 115, 121, 130, 161f., 176f., 205
formal correspondence 173f.
formal education 25, 171
fruit 84

Galileans 30, 48, 51, 92
Galilee 24, 30, 48, 87
global perspective 15, 85-91, 189
God of strategy 43, 134, 217(n. 1)
Great Commission 15, 50, 88-91, 106, 111, 119, 127, 137, 147, 163, 167, 175, 192, 197, 199, 202

hetairos 55
holiness 83, 120, 130, 139f., 142f., 159, 176, 200, 208
Holy Spirit 15f., 37, 40, 70-74, 79f., 84, 89, 91-93, 96f., 111, 131, 141, 159, 175, 177f., 183, 187-190, 192-194, 199-206, 208f.
humility 22, 63-65, 84, 112, 117, 119, 121, 125, 127, 131, 133, 137, 153, 161, 168, 172, 176, 185, 207

imitation 27, 33f., 61-66, 78, 83, 89, 115f., 120-123, 159, 166, 177, 200
Immanuel 40, 135
impartation 140, 157, 176, 198-202, 206
implementation 61, 68f., 124, 140, 145, 172, 175, 178-181, 185f.
Incarnation 91, 134-137, 139f., 172, 175
indigenous teaching modes 171f.
informal training 124, 171, 222(n. 38)
integration 176, 178-181, 184, 195, 197
integrity 65, 137, 164-166, 176, 185

Jesus Christ
alternative life-style 80-83, 121
anointed 37-41, 123
authority 45, 81, 90, 110f., 129, 136
carpenter 25-29, 113, 173, 216(n. 18)
Jesus 40, 215(n. 4)
leader 49-52, 108-110, 128
Lordship 43, 109f., 114, 120, 141
Master 108f., 114, 129
mentor 14f., 60, 69, 78, 116, 122-130, 162, 173, 175, 177-179, 188, 190, 198f.
model 14-16, 53, 56, 60-66, 68, 72, 78, 80, 83, 85, 87, 89, 101-105, 115-121, 124, 129-135, 138-140, 144f., 159, 163f.,

175-178, 187-190, 199
prayer 20, 23, 81, 123, 141
servant 118-121, 123, 222f.(n. 46)
strategy 15f., 28, 41, 43, 48, 52, 67, 70, 87, 90, 97, 116, 125, 198
teacher 44-46, 82, 173, 198, 213(n. 2, n. 4), 215(n. 56)
theology of leadership 56, 119, 218(n. 29)
upbringing 19-22
Joshua 215(n. 4)

kathegetes 108
kyrios 109

leadership style 170, 176
light of the world 84f., 88, 138
local leadership idiom 171
love 22, 65, 83, 102-108, 117, 133, 142, 153, 161, 176, 180

managerial fallacy 163
managing 226(n. 40)
manthano 179
martys 75
mathetes 57, 179
matheteusate 90
memorization 25, 32f., 124, 172
mentoring 14, 16, 80, 104, 107, 122-125, 129-133, 136, 144, 147, 149, 166, 169-171, 188-191, 202f.
Messiah 40
misdirected dependence 152
mnemotechnic devices 25, 216(n. 14)

modelling 116, 121, 125, 158, 162, 172, 177, 190, 193, 206
multiplication 34, 67, 91, 96, 116, 127, 142, 176, 188-192, 194, 198

Nazareth 24, 87

obedience 22f., 106, 110-112, 117, 119, 123, 125, 127, 129, 147, 176, 180, 185, 204
observational learning 27, 49, 60, 158
oral instruction 25, 32, 124, 172

parables 124-126, 219(n. 58)
parakletos 71
paternalism 153, 192
people-orientation 54, 60, 164
personality 59, 66, 76, 116, 122, 127, 141, 164, 168, 198
Peter 93
Pharisees 29-31, 64f., 82
philos 55
pleres 37
poreuthentes 90
power 81, 89, 91f., 95f., 119, 124, 130, 187f., 197, 199, 201, 203-206, 208f.
power encounter 187
prayer 74, 94f., 116, 122, 160f., 169, 176, 190, 199-202, 204-209
praÿs 63
pride 63, 119, 131, 152, 207
priorities 91, 94, 112, 117f., 120, 127, 139, 205

rabbi 108f., 212(n. 20)
rabbinic ordination 215(n. 49)
rabbinic tutoring 31-36, 45-47, 56f., 61, 64, 77, 128
rabboni 221(n. 18)
relationship 22f., 50-63, 73, 84, 104, 112, 117, 122, 124, 136, 143, 148-151, 168, 171, 190
reproduction 65, 91, 116, 125, 142, 188, 190f., 206

Sadducees 29
Sanhedrin 29, 59, 80
salt of the earth 84, 138
sanctification 143, 202
scribes 29f., 35, 64
servanthood 83, 118-121, 129, 141, 153-155, 169, 172, 176, 179, 181, 185, 194, 206f.
Shema 21f., 103, 211(n. 7, n. 8)
shepherding 128f., 137, 219(n. 62)
stewardship 112, 129
strategy 101, 127, 149, 163, 171, 191, 197f., 208
submission 114, 137
supracultural principles 15f., 148, 175-178, 190
synagogue service 21, 211(n. 9)
synecho 105

talmîd 31-34, 78, 86
tapeinos 63
task orientation 149f., 164, 170
team setting 58, 185
Tefillah 215(n. 8)
tekton 26
Torah 21f., 25, 30, 32, 82, 104, 139, 211(n. 3)

truth 79, 126, 133, 136, 167, 169, 172f., 179, 181, 184., 193, 199, 201

unity 83f., 143
use of time 117

Way movement 96, 138, 189, 200
with-ness 13, 23, 33, 41, 43, 78, 173
  God's with-ness 38, 135, 148, 187, 198
  Jesus' physical with-ness 15, 52-54, 61f., 66, 93, 116, 123, 125, 198
  Jesus' permanent with-ness 72, 90, 119, 136, 175, 188, 200, 210
witness 15, 74-80, 86, 88f., 92-94, 110, 121, 133, 141, 144f., 147, 156, 160-164, 166, 171, 173-176, 184-188, 195, 198f., 200, 202, 204f., 209
  alternative witness 80, 83-85, 142
  authentic witness 66, 77-80, 116, 120, 127, 142, 159, 190
  Christlike witness 96, 136, 188
  incarnational witness 136f.
worldwide movement 15, 49, 58, 67f., 72f., 91, 96, 125, 142, 205

Yeshua 20, 215(n. 4)
Yehoshua 215(n. 4)
yoke 113

Zealots 30

Other titles available from Gabriel Publishing...

Gabriel
Publishing

Contact us for details on any of these books -
PO Box 1047, Waynesboro, GA 30830
Tel: (706) 554-1594   Fax: (706) 554-7444
e-mail: gabriel@omlit.om.org
1-8-MORE-BOOKS

God's Great Ambition
Dan & Dave Davidson & George Verwer
ISBN: 1-884543-69-3

This unique collection of quotes and Scriptures has been designed to motivate thousands of people into action in world missions. George Verwer and the Davidsons are well-known for their ministries of mission mobilization as speakers and writers. Prepare to be blasted out of your comfort zone by this spiritual dynamite!

Principles of Effective Prayer
Wentworth Pike
ISBN: 1-884543-65-0

What is prayer? Why pray? Created as a devotional study for individuals or a textbook for groups, *Principles of Effective Prayer* answers these questions and many others. Developed as a class taught at Prairie Bible Institute (Canada), this book will lead you into a life and ministry of effective, God-glorifying prayer!

The Cross and The Crescent
Understanding the Muslim Heart and Mind
Phil Parshall
ISBN: 1-884543-68-5

Living as a missionary among Muslims, Phil Parshall understands the Muslim heart and mind. In this very personal book, he looks at what Muslims believe and how their beliefs affect - and don't affect - their behavior. He compares and contrasts Muslim and Christian views on the nature of God, sacred Scriptures, worship, sin and holiness, Jesus and Muhammed, human suffering, and the afterlife.

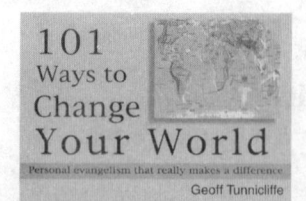

101 Ways to Change Your World
Geoff Tunnicliffe
ISBN: 1-884543-49-9

Geoff Tunnicliffe has compiled an invaluable collection of ways to change the world in his newly revised *101 Ways to Change Your World*. In addition to 101 practical ways to put faith into action, Tunnicliffe has also included statistics and resources for individuals desiring to make a difference in God's World.

Street Boy
Fletch Brown
ISBN: 1-884543-64-2

Jaime Jorka, a street boy in the Philippines, lays a challenge before the missionary whose wallet he has stolen - and discovers for himself what Jesus can do. This true-to-life story reveals the plight of street children worldwide and shows that they too can be won to Christ. "The lot of the street children of the world is a guilty secret that needs to be exposed and addressed. This book does it admirably." - Stuart Briscoe

**Operation World
21st Century Edition**
Patrick Johnstone & Jason Mandryk
ISBN: 1-85078-357-8

The definitive prayer handbook for the church is now available in its 21st Century Edition containing 80% new material! Packed with informative and inspiring fuel for prayer about every country in the world, *Operation World* is essential reading for anyone who wants to make a difference! Over 2,000,000 in print! Recipient of 2002 ECPA Gold Book Award.

Operation World Prayer Calendar
ISBN: 1-884543-59-6

This spiral desk calendar contains clear graphics and useful geographic, cultural, economic, and political statistics on 122 countries of the world, the *Operation World Prayer Calendar* is a great tool to help you pray intelligently for the world. Pray for each country for three days and see how God works!

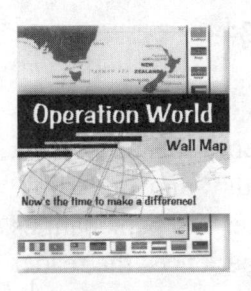

Operation World Wall Map
22" x 36"
ISBN: 1-884543-60-X (Laminated)
ISBN: 1-884543-61-8 (Folded)

This beautiful, full-color wall map is a great way to locate the countries each day that you are praying for and build a global picture. Not only an excellent resource for schools, churches, and offices, but a valuable tool for the home.

The Challenge of Missions
Oswald J. Smith
ISBN: 1-884543-02-2

Almost 2000 years have passed and the desire of Jesus that all should hear his good news is as strong as ever. In this remarkable book Oswald J. Smith maintains that the church which takes this command seriously will experience the blessing of God. *The Challenge of Missions*, which has sold more than 100,000 copies since its first publication, remains compelling reading in this period of exciting growth of the Church worldwide.

Dr. Thomas Hale's Tales of Nepal

Living Stones of the Himalayas
ISBN: 1-884543-35-9

Don't Let the Goats Eat the Loquat Trees
ISBN: 1-884543-36-7

On the Far Side of Liglig Mountain
ISBN: 1-884543-34-0

These fascinating accounts of the true-life stories of doctors Tom and Cynthia Hale share everyday and incredible experiences of life with the beguiling character and personalities of the Nepalese people. In sharing these experiences the reader is truly transported to a most enchanting land.